T5-BQB-833

Struggles for Justice
in Canada and Mexico

Struggles for Justice in Canada and Mexico

Themes and Theories
about Social Mobilization

LINDA SNYDER

WILFRID LAURIER
UNIVERSITY PRESS

LAURIER
Inspiring Lives.

This book has been published with the help of a grant from the Canadian Federation for the Humanities and Social Sciences, through the Awards to Scholarly Publications Program, using funds provided by the Social Sciences and Humanities Research Council of Canada. Wilfrid Laurier University Press acknowledges the support of the Canada Council for the Arts for our publishing program. We acknowledge the financial support of the Government of Canada through the Canada Book Fund for its publishing activities. This work was supported by the Research Support Fund.

Library and Archives Canada Cataloguing in Publication

Snyder, Linda, [date], author
  Struggles for justice in Canada and Mexico : themes and theories about social mobilization / Linda Snyder.

Includes bibliographical references and index.
Issued in print and electronic formats.
ISBN 978-1-77112-278-8 (paperback).—ISBN 978-1-77112-269-6 (pdf).—
ISBN 978-1-77112-270-2 (epub)

    1. Social movements—Canada—Case studies. 2. Social movements—Mexico—Case studies.
3. Community organization—Canada—Case studies. 4. Community organization—Mexico—
Case studies. 5. Social justice—Canada—Case studies. 6. Social justice—Mexico—Case studies.
7. Canada—Social conditions—Case studies. 8. Mexico—Social conditions—Case studies. I. Title.

HN107.S58 2016   303.48'40971   C2016-903698-7
                                               C2016-903699-5

Cover art: *Communal Fire* (acrylic on canvas), by Wendy L. Fletcher.
Cover design by hwtstudio.com. Text design by Lime Design, Inc.

© 2017 Wilfrid Laurier University Press
Waterloo, Ontario, Canada
www.wlupress.wlu.ca

This book is printed on FSC® certified paper and is certified Ecologo. It contains post-consumer fibre, is processed chlorine free, and is manufactured using biogas energy.

Printed in Canada

Every reasonable effort has been made to acquire permission for copyright material used in this text, and to acknowledge all such indebtedness accurately. Any errors and omissions called to the publisher's attention will be corrected in future printings.

No part of this publication may be reproduced, stored in a retrieval system, or transmitted, in any form or by any means, without the prior written consent of the publisher or a licence from the Canadian Copyright Licensing Agency (Access Copyright). For an Access Copyright licence, visit http://www.accesscopyright.ca or call toll free to 1-800-893-5777.

To Kaden, Beckett, Ava, & Jordan

—

May they, in the social struggles of their times, be part of effective

social movement communities working for greater justice.

Contents

1 | The Context of the Struggles

2 | The Stories of Struggle for Change

3 | Themes and Theories in the Struggles for Justice

List of Acronyms

APPO   Asamblea Popular de los Pueblos de Oaxaca;
Popular Assembly of the Peoples of Oaxaca

CASART   Casa de las Artesanías; the House of Crafts

CBC   Canadian Broadcasting Corporation

CEAA   Canadian Environmental Assessment Agency

CEBs   Comunidades Eclesiales de Base; Christian Base Communities

CED   Community Economic Development

CEDAW   Convention on the Elimination of all forms of Discrimination against Women

CEPCO   Coordinadora Estatal de Productores de Café de Oaxaca;
State Coalition of Coffee Producers of Oaxaca

CNOC   Coordinadora Nacional de Organizaciones Cafetaleras;
National Coalition of Coffee Organizations

CODIMUJ   Coordinadora Diocesana de Mujeres;
Women's Council of the Diocese (of San Cristóbal)

COMPA   Convergencia de Movimientos de los Pueblos de las Américas;
Convergence of People's Movements in the Americas

CONEVAL   Consejo Nacional de Evaluación de la Política de Desarrollo Social;
National Council for Evaluation of Social Development Policy

CSO   Civil Society Organization

ECLAC   Economic Commission for Latin America and the Caribbean (United Nations)

EZLN   Ejército Zapatista de Liberación Nacional; Zapatista National Liberation Army

FONV   Friends of the Nemaiah Valley

GDP   Gross Domestic Income

GNI   Gross National Income

GSO   Grassroots Support Organization

HDI   Human Development Index

IMF   International Monetary Fund

INMECAFE Instituto Mexicano del Café; Mexican Coffee Institute

MP   Member of Parliament

MUSA   Mujeres de la Unión de la Selva; Women of the Jungle Federation

NAFTA   North American Free Trade Agreement

NGO   Non-Governmental Organization

OECD   Organisation for Economic Co-operation and Development

PAN   Partido Acción Nacional; National Action Party

PRI   Partido Revolucionario Institucional; Institutional Revolutionary Party

PRD   Partido de la Revolución Democrática; Democratic Revolutionary Party

PROCAMPO Programa de Apoyos Directos al Campo;
          Program of Direct Supports to the Countryside

RAVEN   Respecting Aboriginal Values and Environmental Needs

REMA   Red Mexicana de Afectados por la Minería;
          Mexican Network of People Affected by Mining

RMALC   Red Mexicana de Acción Frente al Libre Comercio;
          Mexican Network for Action against Free Trade

TADECO   Taller de Desarrollo Comunitario; Community Development Workshop

UCIRI   Unión de Comunidades Indígenas de la Región del Istmo;
          Federation of Indigenous Communities in the Isthmus Region

UN   United Nations

UNEAMICH Unión Estatal de Artesanos de Michoacán;
          State Federation of Michoacán Artisans

UNDP   United Nations Development Programme

WEE   Women's Economic Equality

WTO   World Trade Organization

Acknowledgements

THE PUBLICATION OF THIS BOOK was made possible because of the contributions of many people. As in the stories of the struggles for justice, much can be attained when many join hands in work toward a common purpose.

My deepest gratitude is to the people involved in the struggles who shared their stories with me. They took time away from their important work to describe the challenges they were confronting and how they brought about change, so that others could learn from their experience.

I am very appreciative of the good folks at Renison University College – University of Waterloo and, in particular, the School of Social Work and the Social Development Studies program, for providing me with sabbatical time and non-teaching terms to carry out the case studies and to connect the emergent themes with the relevant literature. I am also indebted to the kind people at the Universidad Veracruzana, Facultad de Trabajo Social, Minatitlán, in Mexico, for welcoming me as a visiting professor and introducing me to the social movement communities they were supporting. Thus began the snowball-like accumulation of inspiring stories in Veracruz, Chiapas, and Oaxaca. Similarly, I am grateful to the people of CETLALIC who introduced me to people involved in social movement activities in Morelos, who in turn knew of other important community endeavours in Guerrero and Michoacán. Canadian colleagues in Nova Scotia and British Columbia were also very helpful in connecting me with social justice movements in their areas.

Academic colleagues have been invaluable throughout this project. For example, Dr. Gail Cuthbert Brandt and Dr. Debra Chapman commented on my drafts of the histories of Canada and Mexico, respectively, and referred me to superb texts. Colleagues who attended presentations of preliminary findings raised interesting questions and pointed out worthwhile avenues of inquiry. Academic reviewers who read earlier drafts of the manuscript offered valuable suggestions and challenged me to incorporate additional perspectives.

In the final phase of turning this work into a publishable book, I am thankful for a grant approved by the Federation for the Humanities and Social Sciences through the SSHRC-funded Awards to Scholarly Publications Program. And I am tremendously appreciative of the people at WLU Press: Lisa Quinn, for believing the potential was there and overseeing the peer review process; Siobhan McMenemy, for pulling the pieces together for editorial production; Rob Kohlmeier, for managing the final edits with timely responses to my questions; Mike Bechthold, for the prompt production work; and Clare Hitchens, for making the book known in the academic and public realms. My gratitude goes also to Valerie Ahwee, for the detailed copy editing and for the consistent formatting of translations. I am also immensely grateful to the current principal of Renison University College, Dr. Wendy Fletcher, for her gift of an original work of art, *Communal Fire*, created for the cover of the book.

A big thank-you to my friends and family for their support and encouragement over the bumps in the road along this journey. My greatest debt is to my husband, Paul, who accompanied me on many field trips and took care of the multitude of practical arrangements; served as a wise sounding board as ideas developed; and, on the many days when I lost track of time at the keyboard, called me when supper was ready. May we live long enough for me to reciprocate his enormous generosity. ∎

Introduction

PEOPLE COMING TOGETHER to address issues critical to the well-being of the community are at the core of achievements in human and social development. Mobilizations of sufficient numbers to correct the balance of power have been necessary to bring about positive change for the common good. Struggles and projects related to such matters as poverty, health problems, inadequate housing, gender oppression, and disregard for environmental and human rights are the sites in which processes of social mobilization play out. Our current environment of aggressive capitalism, which favours the economic freedom of the powerful over the needs of people and the planet, has heightened the need for collective action. Examples of collective action from both Canada and Mexico illustrate important aspects of organizing to promote justice.

Social mobilization work has involved practitioners with a thirst for justice from many fields of practice: social work, social development, health, human rights, environmental protection, and faith-based justice movements, among others. Similarly, knowledge-building in relation to social mobilization is of interest to many of the social sciences, including social work, sociology, political science, social psychology, education, organizational behaviour, theology, philosophy, and other disciplines. Knowledge from these multiple disciplines provides useful information for the practitioners engaged in social change processes. Social work with a particular focus on community organizing has been my academic discipline and area of practice, but I hasten to add that many of the organizers in my practice experience and in the cases studied in this research project were not social workers. It is my hope that these case studies and the themes related to social mobilization that they illustrate will be valuable to others in the multiple disciplines and fields of practice engaged in this justice work.

An Interdisciplinary Approach

BOTH "SOCIAL MOBILIZATION" and "community organizing" describe the actions of bringing people together to address their collective concerns. "Social mobilization" is the term used more commonly in the academic disciplines of sociology and political science, whereas "community organizing" is used more commonly in the practice professions of social work, health promotion, and international development. Piven and Cloward (1977), who contributed the pioneering analysis of poor people's movements, used "mobilization" to refer to marshalling large numbers of people to engage in short-term disruption and to make immediate demands for, as one example, welfare services. They used "organizing" to refer to building ongoing organizations of the oppressed for continued activity such as advocacy or service provision. However, Jack Rothman (2001),[1] in his classic conceptualization of "three models of community organization practice" in social work, considers mobilization to be social action; development of ongoing organizations of the oppressed to be locality development; and the activities related to service development and advocacy to be social planning and policy practice; and all three of these to be various forms of "community organizing." More recently, Rothman prefers the term "community intervention" and most academics studying social movements emphasize the importance of social movement building and the involvement of many forms of organizations and entities.

Social movements are considered, herein, to be collective actions in which people, as members of civil society (rather than in the workplace or political institutions), have become active in changing social arrangements in order

---

1. The sixth edition provides the clearest articulation; however, Rothman first published the concept in the mid-1970s.

to attend to vital human needs and promote essential social values. This is consistent with definitions put forward by Goodwin and Jasper (2009), Kane (2001), and Moyer (2001) from a Western perspective and by Ballón (1990) writing from Latin America. It is broader than Tilly's (2002) definition of social movements, for example, which doesn't include popular collective action and that requires such public displays as "marching, petitioning, propagandizing, sloganeering, and brandishing of symbols" (p. 90). My broader delineation is also compatible with Oxhorn's (1995) "low threshold" definition of "what is political" in civil society organizing in Latin America, which he maintains includes activities that "might represent an alternative model for the alleviation of societal problems that is contrary to the one being imposed by those in control of the state, such as through collective group solutions to problems of hunger or unemployment rather than relying on individualistic, market-oriented approaches" (p. 306).

Collective action is conceptualized in the same way as Eschle and Maiguashca (2010) to include conventional and disruptive protest as well as "advocacy, service provision, knowledge production, population education, and movement building" (p. 184). Social movement organizations, from my perspectives, include the groups, collectives, communities, community associations, and other civil society organizations engaged in this activity. This is consistent with Staggenborg's (2013) position that "the concept of *social movement community* is useful in conceptualizing the diffuse nature of social movements and their changing structures" since mobilization and organizing are not done only by organizations: "other important mobilizing structures include social networks, cultural groups, movement habitats within institutions, and more established organizations that become movement allies at times" (p. 125).

The analysis of social mobilization in these Mexican and Canadian case examples draws considerably on existing knowledge about social mobilization and community organizing. Choudry, Hanley, and Shragge (2012) point out that much of the sociology literature on social movements is "overly theorized and abstract" (p. 4) and that a large portion of the social work literature on community organizing is "undertheorized and descriptive" (p. 5) and often lacking "critical social analysis of the nature of capitalism" (p. 5). Hence an interdisciplinary approach provides the opportunity to elicit the most useful knowledge from sociology and social work as well as other disciplines, so that the strengths of each can compensate for shortcomings in others.

Sociology theory about social movements has evolved considerably from the theories of the 1960s equating collective behaviour with irrational mobs or fads. Resource mobilization theory argues that social movement organizations respond rationally when necessary resources, such as people, money, energy, and external support, are available (McCarthy & Zald, 1973, 1977). Political process approaches, introduced by Tilly (1978), recognize that power structures generate incentives to act as well as provide spaces or restrict opportunities for collective action (McAdam, Tarrow, & Tilly, 2001). Social constructionism adds recognition of the importance to social movements of people's understanding or interpretation of their realities, borrowing Goffman's notion of "frames" to articulate how activists conceptualize and make claims regarding issues (Snow, Rochford, Worden, & Benford, 1986). Also from the social constructionist paradigm has come an appreciation of new social movements based on collective identities such as gender, ethnicity, and sexual orientation in addition to the "old" social movements based on class (Leonard, 1997). Most recently, syntheses have acknowledged the truths in many of these approaches, which, as Buechler (2011) notes, "means that social movement scholars not only have a rich toolkit but also that this diversity of approaches and the novel combinations of concepts it encourages enjoys scholarly legitimacy" (p. 227). A movement-relevant approach, suggested by Bevington and Dixon (2005), is one such synthesis that also attempts to address the earlier criticisms by building theory through "critically engaging with the dialogues and questions that concern the movements themselves" (p. 197). There is also considerable promise in recent contributions that recognize the role that human agency plays (Morris, 2004) while simultaneously acknowledging the structural and contextual factors (Kutz-Flamenbaum, (2012). Nepstad and Bob's (2006) comparative study of leadership in two Mexican social movements is an example of this type of useful work.

Community practice was an integral part of social work in Canada and other English-speaking countries since its origins in the settlement movement, but it has not always been given the same professional recognition as more apolitical practice with individuals, families, and groups (Lundy, 2004). Some of the earliest theoretical contributions were Rothman's delineation of three models of community organizing, mentioned earlier, and Warren's (1975) typology of change strategies: collaborative, campaign, and contest. In Mexico and other Latin American countries, the community perspective has traditionally been predominant in social work (Mendoza Rangel, 2005) and, in the 1960s, the profession in Latin America undertook a reformulation to increase the relevancy of theory and practice to the injustices in their context (Zúñiga Zárate & Garza Treviño, 2007). Now previously well-developed welfare states like Canada have experienced the dismantling of their social programs, and more critical approaches to social work and community organizing have emerged to confront these new realities (Campbell & Baikie, 2012). Structural social work attends to "the ways in which the rich and powerful in society define and constrain the poor and the less powerful" (Moreau, 1979, p. 78) and insists that, in addition to dealing with the immediate survival needs of the exploited, the underlying societal structures must be transformed (Mullaly, 1997). Feminist and anti-oppressive practices recognize the structural oppression of particular social identities (race, gender, class, sexual orientation, ability, age, ethnicity, religion, etc.) and challenge the dominant powers' constructions of privilege, often in concert with "new social movements" (Dominelli, 2002). Empowerment practice proposes crucial components in the work to overcome oppression, including collectivization of the experience of oppression and means of addressing it as well as increasing the person's or community's belief in their own efficacy as agents of change (Gutiérrez, Parsons, & Cox, 2003).

Convergences between theory on social movements and theory on critical approaches to social work are apparent in the above description. In addition, social psychology has relevant theories on motivation related to participation in social movements (Pinard, 2011). Theology of liberation with its convictions regarding bringing about justice on earth has a strong presence in the thinking of many social movement participants in Latin America and elsewhere (Boff & Boff, 1986). Paulo Freire's (1968/1984) classic *Pedagogy of the Oppressed* provides valuable wisdom on effective educational processes that are part of community organizing and social mobilizing. Hence, theory will be drawn from these multiple disciplines and a few others to promote a well-rounded understanding of social mobilization.

The Case Study Method

THE CASE STUDIES IN THIS BOOK illustrate processes of social mobilization in collective endeavours, specifically: the types of social change activities in which participants are engaged; the motivating influences for the projects; the collective nature of the work; organizational structures developed; sources of support and networks; organizing principles and strategies; challenges to social mobilization; and the mobilization outcomes. The examples in Mexico and Canada, as common lesser powers in the North American Free Trade Agreement (NAFTA) but with distinct political, economic, social, and cultural contexts, reveal some of the similarities and some of the contextually different aspects of social mobilization. The data were collected between 2004 and 2010 in Mexico and Canada from communities engaged in collective endeavours because their well-being was threatened by poverty or injustice. These included urban, rural, mainstream, and Indigenous communities in each country.

In Mexico, case examples were located in the southern states where greater class, ethnic, and gender oppression are experienced. In addition, the state of Morelos was included since it has been a centre of social activism, liberation theology practice, and critical intellectual discourse[2] as well as being a receiving area for migration from poorer Mexican states and conflicted Latin American countries. In the winter of 2004, I collected data within Veracruz, Chiapas, and Oaxaca. This included such examples as a marginalized neighbourhood in a small city in southern Veracruz; the women's committee of the San Cristóbal diocese in Chiapas; the women's centre in Oaxaca; as well as regional and state-level coffee co-operatives in Chiapas and Oaxaca respectively. During the winter of 2009, I engaged in data collection in the Mexican states of Morelos, Guerrero, and Michoacán. There my focus included health services using traditional medicines and women's advocacy in Morelos, struggles for human and environmental rights because of mining in Guerrero, and a federation of artisan guilds in Michoacán.

In Canada, cases were located in the eastern province of Nova Scotia with its rich history of co-operatives and in the western province of British Columbia (BC), where First Nations communities, similar to those in Mexico, face challenges due to activities of mining corporations. In the summer of 2006, I explored case examples in Nova Scotia, including income generation and advocacy programs for women and a coffee-roasting/distribution

---

2. Morelos was the birthplace of Emiliano Zapata, a leader of the Mexican revolution; it was the seat of Don Sergio Méndez Arceo's service as bishop from 1952 to 1982 promoting liberation theology and Christian Base Communities; and it was where Ivan Illich established the Centro Intercultural de Documentación (CIDOC).

co-operative. During the summer of 2010 in British Columbia, I studied a First Nations community's struggle for environmental rights and a women's resource centre. Follow-up on both the Mexican and Canadian communities' struggles against mining corporations continued into 2012.

All case studies included interviews, most had documentation that was reviewed, in some instances focus groups were held, and in a few situations observation was possible. In addition, participant observation occurred in the two cases of struggles against mining. In the Guerrero, Mexico, example, the people were involved in a fight to protect their environment and their health from the actions of a Canadian mining company and the activists were reaching out to me as a Canadian for support in dealing with the problem. I felt compelled to participate in advocacy for Canadian legislation to increase corporate social responsibility. In the British Columbia example where the First Nation people in the Nemaiah Valley were also engaged in a struggle against a Canadian mining company, participant observation occurred because it was necessary to stay with a First Nation family in the valley in the absence of restaurants or overnight accommodation less than two and three hours, respectively, from the community. In the Canadian example also, but to a much lesser extent, I participated in some advocacy for a federal government decision to protect the environment and respect the rights of the Indigenous peoples. Both of these were very rich opportunities for data gathering.

As with most researchers operating within a post-positivist framework, I don't believe any academics can conduct their research from a neutral perspective. Rather, I acknowledge my interests and questions are influenced by my own beliefs in the worth and dignity of all human beings and the importance of building a society that meets the needs of all human beings in a just and respectful manner while providing for the sustainability of the earth and other living beings for future generations. Of the four political-philosophical paradigms outlined by Bob Mullaly (2007), an important Canadian social work theorist and early proponent of structural social work, my own values and practice philosophy align most closely with those of the social democracy paradigm. I also concur with aspects of the socialist perspective when violent revolution is ruled out as a means of achieving the egalitarian ideals and when democratic accountability sustains it.

The Structure of the Book

PART 1 OF THIS BOOK provides the context of the struggles—the current realities globally, as well as in Canada and Mexico, that underlie many of the issues that the various communities are facing and that influence what strategies are relevant and possible in their situations. Part 2 recounts the stories of struggle for change and presents them in clusters of examples with similar objectives. Part 3 describes the themes and theories in the struggles for justice that emerged in the case studies of mobilization for positive change and locates them within the existing literature. It also puts forward some overall conceptualizations for going about the work in a principled and congruent manner. The conclusion summarizes the key theories and important questions for the multiple disciplines and practice professions that, along with social work, are active in social mobilization activities to promote justice and well-being in local and larger communities. ∎

1 | The Context of the Struggles

THE GLOBAL CONTEXT and the national situations in both Canada and Mexico constitute the backdrop of the struggles that are the focus of this study. The neo-liberal economic framework, emphasizing the freedom of the market and the neo-conservative ideology from which it springs, are especially relevant in the current era. Almost universally, the workings of neo-liberalism are evident: decreased taxation and consequent cuts to government social spending, the opening of borders to foreign products and industries, flexibilization of the labour market, and deregulation of environmental protections. For individual countries like Canada and Mexico, the distinct histories, politics, economies, social situations, and cultures are also important aspects of the contexts, along with the specific neo-liberal policies and their impacts. The particular circumstances of the poor, women, and Indigenous peoples reveal some of the greatest challenges. This contextual information provides important background for understanding the realities in each setting that shaped the priorities, the constraints, and the possibilities of the communities in their mobilizations for social justice.

(ONE)

GLOBAL

T HROUGHOUT THE WORLD, the holders of power and wealth are promoting neo-conservative political-philosophical ideologies that uphold inequality, hierarchy, and traditional values such as patriarchy. Governments aligned with national elites and enmeshed in the global economy are intensifying unfettered free-market economic practices. This neo-liberalism constitutes the economic component of neo-conservative ideology (Mullaly, 2007). Key elements of globalized neo-liberalism are the mobility of jobs, free trade agreements, growing economic inequality, and environmental destruction. Challenges to neo-liberalism have taken the form of protest and resistance. The impact of these economic practices and neo-conservative belief systems is most pronounced among particular populations for whom oppression is an international phenomenon. The poor, women, and Indigenous peoples are among those who suffer most in this context of inequality, patriarchy, and racism, and who are often the ones involved in social movement activities to contest it.

Aggressive Capitalism

NEO-LIBERAL ECONOMIC THEORY, with "liberal" connoting liberty/ freedom, proposes that governments not interfere with the workings of the market and is a rebirth of many of the principles of classic liberal (laissez-faire) economics outlined by Adam Smith (1776/1978). This contrasts with

Keynesian economics introduced in the 1930s, which advocated an important role for government, particularly in recessions, to stimulate the economy by creating jobs in public works and providing financial assistance to people in need (Keynes, 1936/2007). Since the 1980s and increasingly aggressively since the mid-1990s, governments have been lowering taxes, gutting social programs, opening their borders to free trade (thus ending protection of domestic producers), privatizing former public utilities, and loosening regulations. As the market is granted greater importance, natural resources are overexploited without concern for the environment or future generations and the welfare and rights of masses of people are ignored. We have seen this neo-liberal economic model in the structural adjustment programs that low-income countries were required to implement in order to renegotiate loans in the 1980s, in the stripping of social programs in previously advanced welfare states since the 1990s, and in the austerity measures imposed on European and other countries subsequent to the global economic crisis and bank bailouts of the 2000s (McNally, 2011).

Concurrent with the rise of neo-liberalism in the present period is the prominence of globalization, made possible with the advancement of electronic information/communication technology and low-cost international transportation. Although globalization has many positive aspects, the ability of corporations to relocate jobs to places with lower labour costs and less regulated environments has created many serious problems. Unemployment has increased in countries where workers have fought for fair wages and benefits while environmental threats and safety hazards have accrued to people in countries with less regulation (Petras & Veltmeyer, 2001). The garment factory collapse on April 24, 2013, in Bangladesh that killed 1,127 is a tragic example.

Free trade is the neo-liberal form of international trade that is bolstered by sanctions against partner countries if they interfere with the profit-making ability of corporations from the country of the other partner. Thus, tariffs to protect domestic producers from cheaper foods or manufactured goods exported by the partner country must be reduced. Environmental rules to protect a nation's land or people from the actions of a corporation from a partner country operating in one's own country also can result in lawsuits. In 1817, David Ricardo (1817/1948), in elaborating on the ideas of Adam Smith, suggested that nations would benefit from international trade if each would concentrate production in its area of comparative advantage. The lived experience, however, has demonstrated that exploitative trade arrangements, which were at their peak in colonial times, have advantaged wealthier and more powerful countries over lower income countries (Frank, 1975; Oxfam Canada, 2015). The World Trade Organization (WTO), created in 1995 as the third of the international financial institutions (along with the World Bank and the International Monetary Fund, founded in 1944), establishes the rules of international trade at its ministerial conferences, which are generally held every two years. In an important turn of events at the WTO meeting in September 2003, a coalition of low- and middle-income countries demanded that trade agreements respect their interests as well and a walk-out by a group of African countries brought the session to a close (Dyer, 2003). Nevertheless, free trade agreements continue to be enthusiastically pursued to obtain cheap inputs and provide more export markets for the produce and products of the growth-oriented corporations (Engler, 2013). Frequently now bilateral agreements are sought, outside the purview of the WTO, in order to establish even greater economic liberalization. In addition, there are often geopolitical aspirations in forming trade partnerships that constitute a militarization of globalization (Choudry, 2007). The emphasis of the NAFTA partners on building a North American security framework exemplifies this (Gabriel, 2014).

Concern for the environment does not receive priority in neo-liberal economic frameworks. Several international bodies have called for a global commitment to more sustainable practices—from the World Commission on Environment and Development (1987), through the establishment of the Kyoto Protocol in 1997 (United Nations Framework Convention on Climate Change, 2013) targeting reductions in greenhouse gases emissions, to the declaration of 2005-14 as the United Nations Decade of Education for Sustainable Development. But, as Perkins (1996) said regarding neo-liberal objectives, "the environment suffers twice from trade liberalization: natural assets are depleted faster, and environmental controls are more difficult to implement" (p. 236). The devastation caused by mining is a prime example of profits being prioritized over the environment and people. Wastes from mining processes, known as tailings, contain dangerous toxins such as arsenic, lead, and mercury, as well as processing chemicals like cyanide, which can threaten "drinking water, food supply and health of communities as well as aquatic life and ecosystems" (Earthworks & Mining Watch, 2012, p. 2). A vivid illustration is provided near Andalgalá, Argentina, where a Swiss-Canadian mining company's use of cyanide in the extraction of gold and silver has contaminated the water and soil; resultant increases in cancer (800 percent) and respiratory illnesses in children (300 percent) have led many people to move off the lands of their ancestors, leaving their villages as ghost towns (Marinelli & Jaimovitch, 2011).

Neo-liberal economic policies are also implicated in the growing divide between the rich and the poor. Oxfam International (2014) reports that almost half of the world's wealth goes to the richest 1 percent with the other half going to the remaining 99 percent. The Organisation for Economic Co-operation and Development (OECD) provides valuable economic comparison data and analysis regarding its thirty-four member countries (most European and English-speaking nations, as well as some "emerging economies," including Mexico, Chile, and Turkey). They found growing inequality within countries in their study:

> The Gini coefficient, a standard measure of income inequality that ranges from 0 (when everybody has identical incomes) to 1 (when all income goes to only one person), stood at an average of 0.29 in OECD countries in the mid-1980s. By the late 2000s, however, it had increased by almost 10% to 0.316. (OECD, 2011a, p. 22)

The OECD study determined that, in particular since the mid-1990s, the income shares of top earners (the decile or 10 percent with the highest incomes) surged while marginal tax rates for this same group decreased substantially. Low-income earners' share fell while the quality of jobs deteriorated (e.g., more jobs were part-time), training opportunities were not inclusive (tax incentives benefited high-income earners more), and transfers (e.g., benefits for unemployed workers) were less adequate than previously in redistributing income.

The growing divide between the rich and the poor is also evident in the proportion of the country's total income received by the richest 1 percent of earners. Table 1.1 displays the changing shares of income every thirty years since 1920 in Canada, the United States, and Sweden using data available from the World Top Income Database (Alvaredo, Atkinson, Piketty, & Saez, 2013).

Table 1.1

Income Share (as a percent of the nation's total income) of the Top 1 Percent

Year	Canada	United States	Sweden
1920	14	14	13
1950	11	11	8
1980	8	8	4
2010	12	17	7

One can see that incomes were moving toward greater equality during the years when Keynesian economics were in operation until the 1980s, when neo-liberal economic policies came to the fore. The jump between 1980 and 2010 for Canada and especially for the United States, where the income share of the richest 1 percent more than doubled from 8 percent to 17 percent of the nation's total income, is shocking. Even Sweden, which can be characterized as a social democratic welfare state in comparison with Canada and the United States as liberal welfare states (Esping-Andersen, 1990), has struggled to maintain equality in a globalized market.

Responses to Neo-liberalism

THE GLOBALIZATION OF NEO-LIBERALISM has not gone unchallenged. Much more will be said about activist responses in the description of case examples and the discussion of social mobilization. However, it is important to note the protest and resistance activities as elements, too, of the global context. The "Battle of Seattle" at the 1999 meeting of the World Trade Organization was the first protest against globalized neo-liberalism that drew large numbers of representatives of union, environmentalist, human rights, and student groups from many parts of the United States and from other countries (Vidal, 1999). Interestingly, the same technological advances that have enabled the globalization of neo-liberal economics have made possible the rapid convergence of multitudes of protesters as well. Another internationalized site of protest has been the World Social Forum initiated in Port Alegre, Brazil, in 2001 as a civil society foil to the annual meetings of economic and political leaders at the World Economic Forum in Davos, Switzerland (Houtart & Polet, 2001). At the third meeting of the World Social Forum, John Hammond (2003) notes:

> One hundred thousand people came together from 156 countries and a broad array of social movements united in their opposition of neoliberal capitalist globalization…. Against Margaret Thatcher's oft-repeated injunction that "there is no alternative" to transnational capitalism, the forum's slogan insists that "another world is possible." (p. 3)

The 2013 World Social Forum was held in Tunisia, where a declaration of the Social Movements Assembly (2013) articulated a broadening of their commitment to fight against all forms of oppression, including capitalism, patriarchy, and racism. State repression in some of these protests has demonstrated that governments operating within a neo-liberal framework will intervene, often with instances of police brutality, in order to ensure the required stability, as identified by Gamble (1994), for the free operation of the market.

Another response to globalized neo-liberal economics has been through resistance—finding alternate ways to live apart from its lashing tides. Fair trade is one form of resistance offering an alternative to the free market for both producers and consumers. It began in the 1940s, as international development organizations like Oxfam International and Mennonite Central Committee brought handcrafted articles from low-income countries to the high-income countries to access a market that would pay fair prices to the producers (Fair Trade Advocacy Office, 2006). More recently, producers themselves have organized co-operatives and sought partners willing to market their products at fair prices. By the late 1980s, fair trade became more formalized as certification labels were developed; in 1997, Fairtrade Labelling Organizations International (FLO) was formed to unite the various organizations under one umbrella, which sets standards, then inspects and certifies producers and audits traders (Fairtrade International, 2011). A next step is being explored through the Intercontinental Network for Promotion of Social Solidarity Economy toward formation of partnerships across low-income countries so that, for example, cocoa producers can connect with sugar growers and manufacture the chocolate products themselves—the goal being to create a solidarity economy in lieu of the capitalist model of accumulation (Silva, 2008).

Oppressed Populations

IN ADDITION TO the neo-liberal economic paradigm, which exacerbates the gulf between the wealthy and the rest of us in our global context, there are social structures and ideologies that perpetuate significant injustices. Class structures, patriarchy, and racism stemming from imperialist ethnocentric belief systems, which are consistent with the pervasive neo-conservative ideology, underlie the privilege and power that accrue to some and the oppression that persists for many others. Oppressions experienced by the poor, women, and Indigenous peoples, in the current neo-liberal context, are especially relevant to the social movement communities studied.

The World's Poor

The poor face barriers to meeting their basic needs and obstacles to attaining good health and employment skills that make it difficult to overcome their poverty. The first of the eight Millennium Development Goals adopted by the United Nations (UN) is to eradicate extreme poverty and hunger. Target 1.A to "halve, between 1990 and 2015, the proportion of people whose income is less than $1.25 a day" has already been met (United Nations, 2013, para. 1). However, the same report indicates, 1.2 billion of the world's 7 billion people continue to live in extreme poverty and about 870 million are undernourished.

In examining poverty and oppression based on class, it is important to note that low socio-economic class intersects with many other population categories that experience oppression and exclusion—gender and race being two of those. This is because low socio-economic class is both a population category experiencing oppression and an outcome of oppression; for example, Indigenous women, who as a group experience marginalization, have a high rate of poverty. Thus, the United Nations Development Programme (UNDP, 2013) in noting the significant progress in human development indicators, particularly in Brazil, China, and India, adds that inequality must be addressed to ensure that economic growth benefits all populations: "No one should be doomed to a short life or a miserable one because he or she happens to be from the 'wrong' class or country, the 'wrong' ethnic group or race or the 'wrong" sex" (p. 29).

The World's Women

Gender injustice remains a significant global problem despite momentous progress in the past century in equality and empowerment for women (Drolet & Heinonen, 2012). The first wave of feminism, at the beginning of the twentieth century, secured women's right to vote and the second wave, which began in the late 1960s, focused on equality in the workplace, more flexible gender roles, and women's rights. The current third wave of feminism emerged in the 1990s in response to the earlier dominance of white middle-class perspectives and attends to the intersection of race, class, and place with experiences of gender oppression and patriarchy. The United Nations held four world conferences on women: 1975 in Mexico City, 1980 in Copenhagen, 1985 in Nairobi, and 1995 in Beijing, and hosts reviews on implementation of the Beijing Platform for Action. The UN General Assembly adopted the Convention on the Elimination of all forms of Discrimination against Women (CEDAW) in 1979 and made the promotion of gender equality and empowerment of women one of the Millennium Development Goals. These United Nations actions have been useful reference points for women's advocacy in many countries of the world.

Nevertheless, there is much to be accomplished across the globe to ensure women's freedom from violence, their economic equality, and political participation. Women are at risk of violence as a result of female infanticide and selective abortion to the degree that a "missing women" phenomenon is evident in the population statistics of such countries as China and India (Green, 2008). Women also experience violence from attacks, including sexual assault, perpetrated by soldiers, fellow citizens, and intimate partners while only a fraction of incidents are redressed in courts of law (UN Women, 2012). Income inequality endures as evidenced by a more recent study of OECD member countries: "Women still earn less than men do, do more unpaid work such as housework and child care and are more likely to end their lives in poverty" (OECD, 2013a, para. 2). Political empowerment for women has changed dramatically since 1911 when women could vote in only two of the world's countries. However, women's representation in national legislatures has reached only 30 percent in twenty-eight countries and this participation is important in the advancement of women rights (UN Women, 2012).

The World's Indigenous Peoples

Indigenous peoples, in many parts of the world, have been subjected to displacement from their lands and the imposition of foreign cultures. Much of this has taken place in the past five hundred years beginning with the conquests carried out by several European empires. This Eurocentric practice was justified by the "Doctrine of Discovery," the idea that Christians, through papal decrees and the instructions of monarchs (entrenched in a legal legacy that persists to today), had the prerogative to seize the lands of non-Christian people and to subjugate and proselytize the occupants (World Council of Churches, 2012). Ronald Wright (2005) provides some Indigenous perspective on this discovery of the "new world" from an Iroquois chief, who said, "You cannot discover an inhabited land. Otherwise I could cross the Atlantic and 'discover' England" (p. 5).

The particular histories of Indigenous peoples vary from place to place, but the experience of exclusion from productive resources and decision-making powers has been common and the consequent poverty and social malaise is widespread. The World Bank estimates that one-third of Indigenous peoples are poor and, if numbers from China are removed due to its now low national and Indigenous poverty rates, Indigenous poverty would approximate 50 percent (Hall & Patrinos, 2012).

In recognition of historical injustice and current disenfranchisement, two United Nations instruments have been adopted to address the rights and needs of Indigenous peoples—the substance of pertinent articles from each are noted below. The International Labour Organization, a specialized agency of the United Nations, adopted The Indigenous and Tribal Peoples Convention (No. 169) in 1989, which states that ratifying governments must respect the full citizenship rights of Indigenous peoples, consult with them regarding measures that may affect them, and ensure that they have opportunities to participate in planning with "the right to decide their own priorities for the process of development as it affects their lives, beliefs, institutions and spiritual well-being and the lands they occupy or otherwise use." In 2007, the United Nations proclaimed the Declaration on the Rights of Indigenous Peoples affirming their full rights under international human rights law, their right to self-determination, and their right to "autonomy or self-government in matters relating to their internal and local affairs." Venne (2013), however, recounts from the perspective of Indigenous nations not recognized as sovereign nations by the member states of the United Nations how the initial draft of the declaration crafted by Indigenous nations and peoples was revised without their input. Furthermore, since individual states can decide to ratify these instruments or not, their limitations must be acknowledged (Hartley, Joffee, & Preston 2010a). At an incremental level, they have gained recognition and influenced some policies and legal decisions at national and international levels. For example, as Bajak (2009) noted, Latin America's Indigenous peoples have won a good number of major battles over access to resources on their land by referencing the UN documents in the Inter-American Court of Human Rights. Similarly, the Bolivian government incorporated the declaration into the new constitution proclaimed in 2007 (Hartley, Joffee, & Preston, 2010b).

In summary, the pervasiveness of aggressive capitalism based on neo-liberal economic theory and the predominance of ideologies subjugating peoples on the basis of identities such as race, gender, and class are central aspects of the current global context in which struggles for social justice emerge. How such theories and ideologies are manifest in specific countries, however, has much to do with their distinct histories, political and economic arrangements, and socio-cultural realities. ∎

TWO

CANADA

CANADA'S SOCIO-HISTORICAL BACKGROUND, the impact of neo-liberalism on the country as well as responses to it, and the realities of particular oppressed populations are critical elements of the context in which its social movement communities are located.

The Socio-historical Background

CANADA HAS A POPULATION OF 35 MILLION PEOPLE (Canada, Statistics Canada, 2013a). The majority of Canadians are located within a few hundred kilometres of the southern border shared with the United States. Many Indigenous peoples, however, are located in more marginal areas often as a result of displacement.

A very brief summary of Canada's history is provided here drawing on information from Conrad (2012) and the Canadiana (2004) digital library. Indigenous peoples have inhabited Canada's vast reaches for over twenty thousand years, and the Vikings visited its eastern coast in the eleventh century. Nearly five hundred years later, explorers representing European empires arrived with John Cabot claiming what is generally believed to be present-day Newfoundland for England (1497) and Jacques Cartier laying claim to the east coast of Canada and the St. Lawrence River valley for the French (1534). As the Report of the Royal Commission on Aboriginal Peoples (1996) describes, both England and France formed economic and military alliances with

Indigenous peoples and made nation-to-nation treaties agreeing to share the land. A settler model of colonial expansion was practised in Canada, in which the European powers shed their poor by offering them land in Canada. The resultant influx contributed to the eventual incursions on Indigenous territories. Subsequent policies of the colonial governments reflected ethnocentric and racist ideologies and sought to assimilate Indigenous peoples by suppressing their forms of government and stifling their cultural identity.

Britain secured control of the colonies that would comprise British North America through battles with France in the eighteenth century and with the United States in the early nineteenth century. Rebellions (1837–1838) in the two central colonies of Upper and Lower Canada sought to end the power of the ruling elites and to bring about the formation of governments more directly responsible to the local populations. In 1840, the British government united the two Canadas into one colony, but that arrangement came to an end in 1867 with the "confederation" of the Province of Canada (which consequently became the provinces of Quebec and Ontario), Nova Scotia, and New Brunswick. The new nation remained subject to colonial laws enacted by the British Parliament until the passage of the Statute of Westminster in 1931. By 1949, with Newfoundland's entry into Confederation, a total of ten provinces and two northern territories had become part of Canada; and, in 1993, legislation was passed for one of the territories to be divided into two, creating a re-delineated Northwest Territories and the new territory of Nunavut.

Immigration became quite diverse over time with the arrival of such groups as the Chinese labourers who worked on the Canadian Pacific Railway in the 1880s, the central and eastern Europeans who settled the prairies toward the end of the nineteenth century, and thousands of people who were displaced by the First and Second World Wars. By the 1960s, many Canadians prided themselves on the country's multiculturalism in comparison with the "melting pot" phenomenon in the United States; however, sociologist John Porter (1965), in *The Vertical Mosaic*, made it clear that hierarchical power structures based on class, ethnicity, and other characteristics continued to shore up an "establishment" elite while disadvantaging many others. Sunera Thobani (2007), similarly, has documented how colonial relations have maintained white European Canadians in a fuller, more privileged form of citizenship than that accorded to Indigenous Canadians and immigrants who are people of colour.

Britain gave up its final limited legislative power in the *Canada Act, 1982,* which enacted the *Constitution Act, 1982,* with the *Canadian Charter of Rights and Freedoms.* Canada, thus, is a democratic constitutional monarchy, sharing the same monarch as other members of the British Commonwealth, with the queen (or king) being represented by the governor general. Although the monarch is the head of state, the leader of the elected party is the head of the government and carries the title of prime minister (Canada, 2013). Rather uniquely, along with Australia and New Zealand, Canada became a sovereign nation without a war of independence (Bouchard, 2008).

Canada's social welfare system had some of its beginnings in aspects of the Elizabethan Poor Laws where local government, with provincial backing, was given responsibility to provide for the poor—with the "deserving poor" accommodated in poorhouses and the "undeserving" sent to workhouses (Graham, Swift, & Delaney, 2003). Upon Confederation, responsibility for social programs was assigned to the provinces and territories while the federal government retained responsibility for all services for First Nations. At the end of the nineteenth century, a sense of collective responsibility was becoming evident in the development of charitable movements and child welfare legislation. A patchwork of social programs developed after the First World War as government pensions were demanded for mothers raising children on their own and for elderly people. During the Depression, relief was required for the multitude of unemployed workers, and Keynesian economic thinking fostered recognition of economic rather than individual causation of poverty. Between the Second World War and 1970, a more comprehensive social safety net was woven with universal programs like Old Age Security and Family Allowance and insurance programs like Unemployment Insurance and the Canada Pension Plan (McBride & Shields, 1993). The Canada Assistance Plan established national standards for social assistance and provided cost-sharing to the provinces for their costs. It was a liberal welfare state as noted earlier (Esping-Andersen, 1990), but it was a source of pride to Canadians distinguishable from the less generous programs in the neighbouring United States, where rugged individualism has prevailed.

The United Nations provides useful social indicators that allow for comparison across countries. For example, it is interesting to note that 80 percent of Canadians live in urban settings; infant mortality is relatively low with approximately five deaths per one thousand live births; and it has an aging population with only about 16 percent under fifteen years while 21 percent are sixty years and over (United Nations Data, 2013a). The United Nations Development Programme's Human Development Index (HDI) is a composite indicator reflecting life expectancy at birth, mean years and expected years of schooling, as well as Gross National Income (GNI) per capita. Canada was rated consistently among the top eight on the HDI ranking of 130 or more countries between 1990 (when the index was developed) and 2012 (UNDP, 1990–2014). This is no reason for celebration, however, since Canada held first place on this index from 1994 to 2000 and is now further than ever from the top position with its eleventh-place rank in 2013 (UNDP, 2013).

Economic Neo-liberalism in Canada

INCREASED NEO-LIBERALISM, as in many other parts of the world, is at the root of much of this decline in Canada's promotion of well-being at home and internationally. In the twentieth century, Canada was respected for much of its international work given the contributions of leaders like John Humphrey in human rights and Stephen Lewis in fighting HIV/AIDS. However, its pro-capitalist stance has been evident from the Cold War era to the present as exemplified in its recognition of governments that usurped power from democratically elected socialist governments such as Chile in 1973 and Honduras in 2009 (Engler, 2009, 2012). Canada's adoption of more aggressive neo-liberal capitalism in the twenty-first century, evidenced in actions such as withdrawing from the Kyoto Protocol and thereby prioritizing its own economic growth over the global environment, diminishes its esteem in the international realm (Stevens, 2012). Further manifestations of Canada's neo-liberal prioritization of the market are evident in its employment expectations, free trade interests, environmental priorities, lowered taxes, decreased social spending with consequent dismantling of social programs, and increased inequality.

Full employment, quantified as less than 3-percent unemployment, was proclaimed a vital and achievable national goal by the governor of the Bank of Canada at the end of the Second World War (McQuaig, 1995). Neo-liberal economics, however, introduced the concept that the market should be left to find the "natural" rate of unemployment that keeps inflation in check—the Non-Accelerating Inflation Rate of Unemployment (NAIRU). Now the achievement of 7-percent unemployment is given a clear passing grade by the Conference

Board of Canada (2013). A flexible labour market is fostered, one that is unencumbered by strong union protections and high wages. Loblaw Companies, owned by the wealthy Weston family, have been able to convert many of their grocery stores to new Great Food and Real Canadian SuperStore formats with less restrictive union contracts (Flavelle, 2010). The minimum wage in Canada ranges from $9.95 in Alberta to $11.00 in Nunavut (Canada, Employment & Social Development, 2014). Many well-paying jobs in Canada's manufacturing sector have been lost to countries with lower labour and environmental protection costs and, as the controversial replacement of forty-five Canadian workers at the Royal Bank of Canada has shown, information technology jobs also can be easily outsourced (Donkin, 2013). Regrettably, much of new job creation is precarious work in self-employment, contract, or part-time positions often with low wages, limited benefits, and lack of security (Canadian Labour Congress, 2013a).

Free trade agreements, another feature of neo-liberalism, have been promoted by the Canadian government since the Canada–United States Free Trade Agreement of 1988, which expanded to include Mexico in the North American Free Trade Agreement (NAFTA) of 1994. NAFTA's Chapter 11, dealing with investment, reveals how corporate profit-making in free trade agreements has primacy over the collective will of citizens. Through Chapter 11, corporations and investors in the United States, for example, are able to sue the Canadian government for policies it makes that infringe on the investors' potential profits. Many of the policies that have been challenged relate to environmental protection such as the Quebec ban on the use of 2,4-D as a lawn weed killer (Corcoran, 2011). According to the Council of Canadians (2013a), about twenty investor lawsuits have been filed against the government of Canada; over $160 million in fines have been paid already; and suits for $4-5 billion are yet to be resolved. That the final and binding decisions over free trade agreement disputes are made by paid members of private tribunals (World Trade Organization, 2013) is further evidence of their undemocratic nature.

Canada's interests in the resources of foreign countries have not been innocent as will be illustrated in the next chapter by the example of support from the Canadian embassy in Mexico for the Canadian-owned Blackfire mining corporation's activities in Chiapas. Canada, like other economic powers, is now pursuing bilateral trade agreements with more aggressive liberalization than allowed in the multilateral agreements overseen by the WTO (Choudry, 2007).

Protection of the environment is also subordinated to the economy in the neo-liberal framework independent of the impetus of free trade with foreign countries. In December 2012, the federal government removed protection from all of Canada's innumerable water bodies except for the three oceans, ninety-seven lakes, and portions of sixty-two rivers in amendments to the *Navigable Waters Protection Act* when it passed the Omnibus Budget Bill C-45 (Postmedia News, 2012). The government claimed that the changes were essential to the health of the economy. But, as the Council of Canadians (2012) points out, this legislative change will "make it easier for companies to proceed with projects that would harm waterways such as the tar sands, mines, dams, pipelines, logging, and interprovincial power lines" (para. 3).

Lowering of income taxes is another hallmark of neo-liberalism's market focus. Canada has cut the top marginal rate for federal personal income tax from 43 percent in 1981 to 29 percent in the 2000s (OECD, 2011b). Even more severely, the federal corporate income tax rate has been nearly halved since 2000 when the rate was 28 percent in comparison with the 2012 rate of 15 percent (Macdonald, 2011). Lowered revenue, then, is accompanied by the lowering of social expenditures and the dismantling of social programs.

Canada's public social expenditures as a percentage of its Gross Domestic Product (GDP) rose throughout the 1980s and reached a high of 21.3 percent in 1992 (OECD, 2000). By 2012, however, Canada's public social expenditures had dropped to 18.1 percent of GDP, well below the OECD average of 21.8 percent and ranking twenty-seventh out of thirty-three OECD member countries for which data were available (OECD, 2013b). Gary Teeple (1995) in *Globalization and the Decline of Social Reform* was one of the first to identify the assault of neo-liberalism on the welfare state. One common means of eroding social programs, as Teeple noted, has been the restriction of access to benefits. The insurance program for unemployed workers in Canada provided coverage in the early 1970s to around 96 percent of the unemployed (McBride & Shields, 1993). More recently, as the Canadian Labour Congress (2013b) notes, only 38 percent of unemployed workers are receiving Employment Insurance. In some of the more restrictive eligibility criteria, Teeple detects a regression to Poor Law principles that delineate an "undeserving poor" as exemplified in workhouse-like workfare programs. By the mid- to late 1990s, many provinces introduced requirements that single parents, along with other employable recipients of social assistance, must accept jobs regardless of the level of earnings and must do unpaid service in the interim (Snyder, 2006). Actual benefit rates were left to deflate as is evident in Ontario's 2013 social assistance rate of $606 per month for single individuals (Ontario, Ministry of Community & Social Services, 2013), which holds 50 percent less spending power than the rate of twenty years ago (Ontario Coalition against Poverty, 2013). Cuts to service delivery systems, even for vulnerable children, are also occurring as illustrated in the need to close group homes and lay off staff at an Ontario Children's Aid Society in order to meet a 5-percent budget shortfall (Barrick, 2012). As government-supported programs are slashed, responsibilities for meeting people's needs are downloaded to voluntary community-based programs and to families, especially women (Kelly & Caputo, 2011). Food banks, for example, now assist nearly 900,000 Canadians per month (Food Banks Canada, 2013). In the transformation from a liberal welfare state to a neo-liberal Canada, residents are at risk in times of need of reverting from citizens with rights to the previous-century status of objects of charity.

Inequality has increased in Canada during the neo-liberal era and this is evident in both the Gini coefficient measures and the proportion of income received by sections of the population. Canada's Gini coefficient of 0.32 in the late 2000s was very close to the median of 0.31 for the thirty-four OECD member countries, an increase for Canada of 0.04 since the mid-1980s (OECD, 2011a, 2013c). This change in Canada was more intense from the mid-1990s forward, according to an earlier OECD (2008) report, which noted that Canada's levels of inequality didn't change between the mid-1980s and the mid-1990s when it did in seventeen of the other member nations; however, from the mid-1990s to the mid-2000s, "Canada was one of only three OECD member countries who experienced significant increases in income inequality" (p. 286). This has meant a slip in Canada's ranking "from the 14th most equal to 22nd, from above-average to below-average equality" (Yalnizyan, 2013, p. 2).

The income accruing to the various sections of the Canadian population also demonstrates this inequality. In 2011, the top-earning quintile (20 percent) of the Canadian population held 44 percent of the nation's income (up from 41 percent in 1995) and the lowest-earning quintile held only 4.8 percent (down from 5.4 percent in 1995) (Canada, Statistics Canada, 2013b). And, as referenced in the earlier chart with data from Alvaredo et al. (2013), Canada's top 1 percent received 12.2 percent of national income in 2010. Data from the 2011 National Household Survey provide the 2010 income levels of the highest income earners in Canada: the individuals in the top 10 percent had incomes of more than $80,400; the top 5 percent had incomes exceeding $102,300; and the top 1 percent had incomes above $191,100, which is almost seven times the median income of $27,800 (Canada, Statistics Canada, 2013c). The OECD (2011b) data note that the average income of the top 10 percent in Canada is now ten times higher than the average of the bottom 10 percent, an increase from the ratio of eight to one in the early 1990s. The emergence of the ultra-rich is a relatively new phenomenon in Canada. Yalnizyan's (2013) analysis of individual tax data showed that 32 percent of the gains from economic growth in Canada in each of the two decades between 1987 and 2007 went to the top 1 percent of income earners. In contrast, in the decades between 1928 and 1987 the percent of the income gains to the top 1 percent ranged between only 6 and 11 percent. Brennan (2012) connects this concentration of income among the richest 1 percent to the concentration of corporate power in Canada. This is consistent with Porter's identification of Canadian class and power structures in the 1960s and Grabb's research on corporate concentration from the 1990s to the present (Grabb, 1999; Grabb & Hwang, 2009). The salaries paid to top corporate executives are indicative of this excessive income to the privileged few. The average compensation (salary, bonus, stock options, etc.) of the one hundred highest-paid chief executive officers (CEOs) in Canada in 2012 was $8 million—their remuneration undiminished in the aftermath of the 2009 global recession (Mackenzie, 2014). Also in 2012, Barrick Gold's incoming co-chairman was paid a signing bonus of US $11.9 million, making his total compensation for the year $17 million (Jordan, Berman, & Erman, 2013). When neo-liberal leaders urge austerity in social spending due to scarce resources, we have to ask, "Scarce for whom?"

Such inequality has negative impacts for all residents. The Canadian Institute of Wellbeing (2012) has found little growth in measures of vitality in relation to the environment, leisure and culture, time use, and population health since 1994 and even less since 2008 despite simultaneous growth in GDP.

Responses to Neo-liberalism in Canada

THERE IS A STRONG TRADITION of social movements in Canada. Some of the early militant mobilizations include the settler rebellions of 1837 and 1838 for responsible government described above, as well as the Riel rebellions that took place shortly after Confederation to protect Indigenous land (Frideres, 2011). The co-operative movement, promoting collective activities to circumvent exploitation by middlemen, was also an early example of social mobilization in Canada with the first co-operative store established in Stellarton, Nova Scotia, in 1861 (Lotz, 1997). Priests Jimmy Tompkins and Moses Coady (Lotz & Welton, 1997), along with others connected to the extension program at St. Francis Xavier University in Antigonish, Nova Scotia, brought about major changes during the 1920s and 1930s in the fishery and other economic ventures in which ordinary people came together to sell and buy their products jointly. In Quebec, social movements have also been strong and particularly reflective of its distinct culture and realities. Unique practices, such as social animation, and international influences less present in other parts of Canada, like that of the progressive wing of the Catholic Church, have made solid contributions to the development of social policies and programs in Quebec (Panet-Raymond & Mayer, 1997). The Quebec sovereignty movement, as well, composed of organizations, political parties, and activists, has won Quebecers many social and jurisdictional rights beyond those of the other provinces (Dufour & Traisnel, 2014). Indigenous social movements have continued from the Riel rebellions, through the Plains Cree contestation of the Crown's purchase of the Northwest Territories from the Hudson Bay Company in the 1870s; the establishment of the League of Indians in Canada after the First World War in response to the government's imposition of band councils to replace traditional governments; the formation of the National Indian Brotherhood under the leadership of Harold Cardinal, which responded to the federal government's assimilationist plan in the 1969 White Paper with their Red Paper; the defeat of the Meech Lake Accord in June 1990 with Elijah Harper (a member of the Manitoba Legislative Assembly) representing Indigenous interests; the Mohawk uprising in summer 1990 over the town of Oka's proposal to expand a golf course on land traditionally used by the Mohawks as a burial ground; the influence of the Assembly of First Nations under the leadership of George Erasmus, who co-chaired the Royal Commission on Aboriginal Peoples, which published its report in 1996; to the Idle No More movement of today (Ladner, 2014).

More directly related to the current neo-liberal economic doctrine, there have been challenges from social movement organizations, including advocacy groups and activists. The Council of Canadians and the Canadian Centre for Policy Alternatives, whose research was cited above, are examples of organizations that carry out their analysis and publication work in order to increase public awareness about the impacts of neo-liberalism and to contest the messaging of governments and business elites. Some other groups function as hubs for networks of resistance. Common Frontiers, for example, served as a forum for coordinating national opposition to free trade agreements in concert with international counterparts such as the Hemispheric Social Alliance to counter the proposal for a Free Trade Area of the Americas and the Mexican Network for Action against Free Trade (Red Mexicana de Acción Frente al Libre Comercio) (RMALC).

Protests in Canada are confronted with disturbing levels of repression. The Toronto meeting in June 2010 of the G20, comprised of finance leaders from the world's largest economies, was protested by over ten thousand demonstrators, many of whom were vocal about the injustice of banks' private investment losses being covered by public funds, which, in turn, required the public to accept austerity measures (Malleson & Wachsmuth, 2011). After a radical contingent broke away from the larger march, police attacked both radical and peaceful protesters, beating some of them brutally (Hasham, 2013). As Naomi Klein (2011) notes, "over eleven hundred people were arrested—the largest mass arrest in Canadian history" (p. xiii), many confined without basic human services, many with highly exaggerated charges, and many given bail conditions that prohibited engagement in political organizing.

Oppressed Populations

A BROAD, THOUGH BRIEF, SKETCH of the Canadian context, as was attempted in the description of the global context, requires a depiction of the realities of the most oppressed populations in addition to the outline of the ramifications of the pervasive neo-liberal economic model. Again, the situation of the poor, women, and Indigenous peoples are featured.

The Poor in Canada

Poverty in Canada is now commonly measured using the Low Income Measure (LIM) in both national and international analysis, although it must be noted that the government maintains this is a measure of low income and not a measure of poverty. It is a relative measure and uses 50 percent of median household income, adjusted for household size, as the demarcation point (Canada,

Statistics Canada, 2012). The 2011 National Household Survey results based on 2010 data provide insight into who is poor in Canada, using the After-Tax Low Income Measure (LIM-AT) of approximately $14,000 given a median income of $27,800 before adjustments (Canada, Statistics Canada, 2013d). Among the overall population, 14.9 percent were poor, with the rate for men at 13.9 percent and for women at 15.8 percent. Two-parent families with children have a poverty rate of 10.0 percent; however, for female-headed lone-parent families the rate is 33.8 percent and when they have children less than eighteen years of age, the rate rises to 43.4 percent. Youth fifteen to twenty-four years of age have a poverty rate of 17.3 percent and seniors over sixty-four years of age have a rate of 13.4 percent. Immigrants have a poverty rate of 18.3 percent, although those who have been in Canada for less than five years have a rate of 34.2 percent. Indigenous peoples (reporting a single ethnic identity) have an overall poverty rate of 25.3 percent.

Changes over time in who comprises the poor in Canada have been analyzed by Yalnizyan (2013). Using the same Low Income Measure, she points out that poverty has grown over the past two or more decades. Poverty for working-age adults increased from around 10 percent in the late 1970s to 12.7 percent in 2010 and after significant improvements for seniors between the 1970s and the 1990s their poverty rates rose from less than 5 percent in the late 1990s to 12.3 percent in 2010. Poverty for children, Yalnizyan notes, is now at 14.5 percent "higher than it was in 1989 when all Parliamentarians unanimously voted to eliminate child poverty by the year 2000" (p. 3).

It is obvious from the above that the population of the poor in Canada intersects considerably with being female and with being Indigenous; the particular injustices faced by these two groups are discussed further below. One commonality of all the poor, however, is the much increased likelihood of poor health and the decreased quality of life that accompanies it. Raphael (2011) has brought knowledge about the social indicators of health to our attention. Most significantly, he notes, "chronic diseases such as coronary heart disease and type 2 diabetes are strongly related to living in poverty, as is the incidence of respiratory disease, lung cancer, and some other cancers" (p. 226).

Women in Canada

A sense of the reality of women in Canada is conveyed in the UNDP's Gender Inequality Index (GII), which was introduced in 2010. Canada ranks eighteenth on the UNDP (2013) GII, which includes measures of maternal mortality (twelve deaths per 100,000 live births), adolescent fertility (11.3 births per one thousand women aged fifteen to nineteen), seats in Parliament (federal and provincial: 28 percent are women), population with some secondary education (100 percent of women and men), and labour force participation (women 61.9 percent; men 71.4 percent). Women's higher level of poverty, noted in the above material about the poor in Canada, is primarily due to women's lower earnings, which, on average, are about 80 percent of men's earnings when comparing full-time workers and only 70 percent of men's earnings when comparing workers who are twenty-five to forty-four years old with at least one dependent child (OECD, 2012). It is women who often need to forfeit working hours when quality child care is unavailable, and it is women who are more likely to be in precarious part-time, temporary, and multiple jobs (40 percent of women in comparison with 30 percent of men), according to the Canadian Research Institute for the Advancement of Women (2010). These differences are reflected in the median after-tax annual incomes of families with children under eighteen years, with couples receiving $80,000, male lone parents receiving $45,000, and female lone parents receiving only $35,000 (Canada, Statistics Canada, 2013e).

Tremendous inequity exists in gender representation at the top levels of organizations and politics. Men outnumber women two to one in the composition of Canada's legislators, senior officials, and managers (McInturff, 2013). In the 2011 federal election, only 25 percent of the members of Parliament (MPs) elected were women, and within the governing Conservative Party of Canada only 17 percent were women (Canada, Elections Canada, 2011).

Women's oppression is most palpable in their experience of violence. As noted in Statistics Canada's 2011 report on women and the criminal justice system, about half of the victims of violent crimes are women, but they represent a minority of the perpetrators. Physical assault was reported in their survey to have been experienced in 2009 by about 7 percent of women, sexual assault by about 3.5 percent, and robbery by about 1 percent. Physical assaults, as well as homicide and attempted murder, were most commonly perpetrated by current or former spouses, sexual assaults by acquaintances, and robberies by strangers.

Despite the ongoing injustice that women face, the Canadian government has moved away from programs designed to promote gender equality. The Canadian Feminist Alliance for International Action and the Canadian Labour Congress (2010) reviewed Canada's performance in this regard during the fifteen years following the Fourth World Conference on Women held in Beijing in 1995. They note Canada's remarkable achievements in past decades citing, in particular, women's increased participation in post-secondary education. More recently, however, a sharp decrease in federal government support for women's rights is evident in decisions such as ending agreements negotiated with the provinces to address child-care needs and severely constraining the scope of the Status of Women program. The mandate of the Status of Women now explicitly excludes funding for advocacy and it has reoriented its focus from rights to services. In the 2004–9 period, the report concludes, "women's achievements in all twelve areas of critical concern outlined in the Beijing Platform for Action have slowed or been turned back" (para. 2). McInturff (2013) adds further reason for alarm about the demise of government funding for gender-sensitive policy analysis since Canada lacks the numerous private philanthropic organizations of the United States and charitable law in Canada prohibits significant contributions to advocacy.

Canada's Indigenous Peoples

Canada's Indigenous peoples are recognized in the repatriated Canadian Constitution of 1982 as "Aboriginal," a term that includes three groups previously defined as "Indian," "Métis," and "Inuit" (Kesler, 2009). The *Indian Act (1876)* and it amendments have defined who is an Indian, their status, and various rights, including living on "reserves." The term "First Nations" has commonly replaced the designation "Indian," in keeping with the sentiment an elected councillor of the Algonquin Nation expressed: "that Columbus arrived here and thought he was in India, doesn't make me an Indian" (Bernard, 2003). The term "Métis" has referred to people of mixed Indigenous and European ancestry, and the term "Inuit" refers to a distinct Indigenous cultural group in northern Canada. According to Statistics Canada (2013f), there were 1.4 million Indigenous peoples in Canada in 2011, now 4.3 percent of the overall population, with an approximate composition of 62 percent First Nations, 33 percent Métis, and 5 percent Inuit. The total number represents an increase of 20 percent since 2006, which is substantially greater than the 5-percent increase in the non-Indigenous population. The survey results also indicate a young population with children and youth under twenty-five years representing 46 percent of the Indigenous population, whereas children and youth make up only 29 percent of the non-Indigenous population.

The colonialist practices of dispossession and assimilation reach into the present day. A tragic example of the latter was the practice, between the late nineteenth century and the late twentieth century, of removing Indigenous children from their families and communities to educate them in residential schools. The federal government in its official apology (Harper, 2008) acknowledges that it, along with major churches, took over 150,000 children into residential schools where they were poorly fed, clothed, and housed and their languages and cultural practices were prohibited; some children died, many were abused, and all were deprived of the nurturance of their own parents. McKenzie and Morrissette (2003) note parallels in the 1960s and 1970s practice of child welfare authorities who paid little heed to the traditional ways that Indigenous communities handled child-care issues and placed most Indigenous children in need of protection in majority-culture foster and adoptive homes. Although these practices related to children have stopped, the "intergenerational effects of oppression" persist in many Indigenous communities (Pugh & Cheers, 2010, p. 61) and many issues related to land and governance remain unresolved.

Poverty among Canada's Indigenous peoples is high with an overall rate of 25.3 percent, as noted earlier, and rates of 30.4 percent for First Nations, 20.0 percent for Métis, and 21.5 percent for Inuk/Inuit (Canada, Statistics Canada, 2013d). No doubt the low income is connected to unemployment levels, which are at 15 percent for Indigenous peoples in comparison with 7.5 percent for the non-Indigenous population (Canada, Statistics Canada, 2013g). One can imagine economic disadvantages accruing from land displacement as well as from the past trauma of culture/family disruption evident, as Pugh and Cheers (2010) noted, in "the relatively high rates of distress, intra-family violence, alcohol and drug problems, accidental injury, [and] self-harm" (p. 61). Health challenges of Indigenous peoples also exceed those of the general population, in particular the incidence of heart disease, type 2 diabetes, and new HIV/AIDS infections for all three groups and tuberculosis infection for First Nations and Inuit (Canada, Health Canada, 2012; First Nations, Métis, and Inuit GBA, 2009). Indigenous children's well-being suffers as well, as MacDonald and Wilson (2013) note, "they trail the rest of Canada's children on practically every measure of well-being: family income, educational attainment, crowding and homelessness, poor water quality, infant mortality, health and suicide" (p. 10). Although child welfare authorities now attempt to keep children in need of protection within their kinship and cultural circles,

Indigenous children are still over ten times more likely to be in foster care than non-Indigenous children (Canada, Statistics Canada, 2013f). For Indigenous women, an additional adversity is the risk of violence. Indigenous women reported twice the amount of spousal abuse as non-Indigenous women in the 2009 government survey with 15 percent identifying spousal violence in the past five years and 34 percent identifying spousal emotional or financial abuse in their lifetime (Canada, Statistics Canada, 2011). Research carried out by the Native Women's Association of Canada (NWAC, 2010) found that Indigenous women are at least three times more likely to be murdered than non-Indigenous women, and that they are more likely than non-Indigenous women to be killed by strangers. Their study documented 582 Indigenous women murdered or missing with nearly half of the murder cases still unsolved. By March 2014, the number had risen to over eight hundred and the response of the government's Special Committee on Violence against Indigenous Women was considered to be inadequate (NWAC, 2014).

Legislative change to address Indigenous rights is complex and slow. The *Indian Act* is commonly acknowledged as outdated, but government proposals for replacement legislation, in the 1969 White Paper and the 2002 First Nations Governance Act, were strongly rejected by First Nations peoples as assimilationist and a denial of their treaty rights (Institute for Research on Public Policy, 2003). Discrimination against women in the *Indian Act* was removed, in accordance with the Charter of Rights and Freedoms, in the 1985 amendments (which ensure that registered women who marry non-Indians do not lose their status) (NWAC, 2007), and, in 2013, a law was enacted clarifying matrimonial rights related to family homes on reserves (Canada, Indigenous and Northern Affairs, 2013). According to Conrad (2012), greater progress has been made in northern Canada, where Nunavut, officially in 1999, became a territory governed by its majority Inuit population.

Intrusions on Indigenous lands by resource industries have had many negative impacts on the environment and the people. Unsustainable forestry practices have, through excessive logging, reduced the habitat for the wildlife that hunting and trapping communities rely on and, through pulp and paper operations using mercury, contaminated waterways and fish that sickened people, as in Grassy Narrows (Crowe, 2014). Oil spills such as the blowouts that occur in oil sands extraction have damaged land, water, and wildlife in Indigenous territories. The Cold Lake First Nation, three hundred kilometres north of Edmonton, Alberta, for example, experienced a blowout from

Canadian Natural Resources Limited oil extraction processes in 2013 that contaminated over forty hectares of their ancestral land with a million of litres of oil as well as a similar spill in 2009 (Nation Talk, 2013). Poisonous mining wastes make water and fish unsafe for consumption, again with massive impact on Indigenous communities in the area. The Mount Polley Mine tailings pond breach near Quesnel Lake in British Columbia in August 2014, according to Mining Watch Canada (2014), "is the largest tailings spill in Canadian history but certainly not the first" and is strongly believed by the Union of BC Indian Chiefs to have been preventable with stronger government oversight (Dhillon, 2014). The landmark Supreme Court ruling in June 2014 on the Chilcotin (Tsilhqot'in) Nation's twenty-four-year court case for title and control over their ancestral lands is an important victory for Indigenous peoples that should shore up their position in future disputes with resource development proponents (Blaze Carlson, 2014).

Struggles over land and rights, even in recent decades, have resulted in violence and repression. During the conflict at Oka, Quebec, in 1990 over expanding a golf course on land claimed by the Kanesatake Mohawk nation, provincial police attacked the Mohawk barricade and during the ensuing gunfight, a police officer was shot (Wright, 2005). At Ipperwash Provincial Park, Ontario, in 1995, Chippewas of the Kettle and Stony Point First Nation attempted to reclaim land that was appropriated during the Second World War and in a confrontation with police, an unarmed Chippewa man was killed (Ontario, Attorney General, 2007). More subtle repression was evident in the federal government's monitoring of Cindy Blackstock after the organization she manages filed a complaint with the Canadian Human Rights Tribunal about underfunding of children's services in First Nations communities (Amnesty International Canada, 2013).

The international community has also noted Canada's shortcomings in relation to its poor, women, and Indigenous peoples. The Universal Periodic Review process of the United Nations Office of the High Commissioner for Human Rights (UN OHCHR, 2013a) was established in 2006 such that every four to five years, a Working Group composed of the representatives of the forty-seven states elected to the Human Rights Council examines the human rights record of each member state. Canada's second review was completed in 2013 with 162 recommendations made by the UN Working Group at the April meeting (UN OHCHR, 2013b) and Canada responding in September by accepting (at least in principle) about three-quarters of the recommendations

(UN OHCHR, 2013c). Canada has no plans to ratify any of the international agreements it hasn't already signed. For example, it has not ratified the International Labour Organization (ILO) Convention 169 concerning Indigenous and Tribal Peoples in Independent Countries. However, it did accept the recommendation to "continue efforts toward the establishment and implementation of an effective regulatory framework for holding companies registered in Canada accountable for the human rights impact of their operations" (UN OHCHR, 2013c, item128.151). Canada endorsed the UN Declaration on the Rights of Indigenous Peoples in 2010, but it rejected a recommendation to adopt a national plan pursuant to this since it considers the declaration to be "an aspirational, non-binding instrument" (UN OHCHR, 2013c, para. 19). Canada did approve recommendations to advance equality for women, to ensure effective implementation of CEDAW, and to strengthen measures to eradicate violence against women especially minority and Indigenous women; however, it rejected recommendations to develop a national plan addressing violence against Indigenous women. Canada accepted recommendations regarding poverty alleviation, but it rejected those that included development of national plans or strategies regarding poverty and food security.

Clearly, Canadians face challenges in the market-focused world of neoliberalism, especially those left behind in the widening gap between the rich and the poor, women who confront gender inequality, and Indigenous peoples whose claims for land and rights have not been met. These are the Canadian groups whose struggles are featured in the case examples of Part II. ∎

THREE

MEXICO

A MORE DETAILED CONTEXTUALIZATION of Mexico is provided than of Canada because Mexico's history includes a war of independence and a revolution and its present includes narco-violence and militarization. The general topics, however, are the same: socio-historical background, impact of neo-liberalism as well as responses to it, and realities of particular oppressed populations.

The Socio-historical Background

THE POPULATION OF MEXICO in 2010 was 112 million. About one-fifth of the population live in Mexico City, which is also the capital and federal district, and in the surrounding state of Mexico (Mexico, Instituto Nacional de Estadística y Geografía, 2013). Important socio-historical information includes Mexico's history, its economic and social policy, the socio-cultural context, and the current narco-violence and militarization of the country.

History of Mexico

Mexico's original people, including the Olmecs, had established sophisticated civilizations as early as 1200 BCE (Hamnett, 1999). By 1500 CE, the Aztec/ Mexica empire numbered around 20 million in comparison with Spain's population of 8 million, and the Mayan civilization included city-states in the present-day Mexican Yucatan peninsula and state of Chiapas as well as in Central America (Wright, 2005). When Hernán Cortés arrived at the Gulf coast in 1519, he found allies in the Tlaxcaltecas—a conquered people within the Aztec empire—who led him to the ruler, Moctezuma II, in Tenochtitlán, now Mexico City (Escalante Gonzalbo, 2004). Within two years Moctezuma was killed, smallpox took his brother and millions of Indigenous peoples, Cuauhtémoc (the last Mexica emperor) was captured, and the territories of the Aztec empire fell under Spanish control (Wright 2005).

The Spanish crown captured the wealth of the Aztecs/Mexicas as well as the silver mines. The vast lands were parcelled out in state-size pieces to conquerors like Cortés, who became the marquis of the Oaxaca valley and the *altépetl* or *señoríos* (pre-Hispanic county-size political entities) were granted to Spanish colonists as *encomiendas* with the right to tax or require labour of Indigenous occupants (Bouchard, 2008; García Martínez, 2004). It was a form of exploitation colonialism that contrasts with the settler model of colonialism that took place in Canada (Ashcroft, Griffith, & Tiffin, 2000). Bartolomé de las Casas, who was the bishop of Chiapas for a brief period, wrote to the king of Spain about the rampant abuse of the Indigenous peoples and advocated for the end of the *encomienda* system (Hamnett, 1999). Paradoxically the hacienda system that replaced it continued the growth of Spanish-owned property while the Indigenous land holdings became smaller and smaller (Lockhart, 1969).

There was a mixing of cultures during the three centuries of direct European rule that began perhaps with the mestizo child of Cortés and his Indigenous mistress *Malintzin* (also commonly known as *La Malinche*) (Wright, 2005). Within a decade of the Spanish Conquest, a brown-skinned, Náhuatl-speaking Virgin Mary was said to have appeared to an Indigenous man at the shrine of the Mexica goddess Tonantzin and through a process of religious syncretism the most popular religious icon of Mexico, the Virgin of Guadalupe, was created. Wright identifies the culmination of this fusion in the 1790s, with the unearthing of the buried statue of Tonantzin in Mexico City and the declaration by a Dominican friar that Tonantzin was the Virgin Mary, as the birth of "a new people, both Aztec and Spanish…Mexicanos" (p. 159).

The *grito* (shout) for independence from Spain came in 1810 from Miguel Hidalgo, a populist priest in Dolores, Guanajuato (Wright, 2005). He, along with Morelos, Torres, Allende, and other leaders of a broad resistance movement, was able to rouse the anger of the Creoles (people born in Mexico of

Spanish parents) and the Indigenous peoples against the imperialism of the European Spanish (Zoraida Vázquez, 2004). Although most of the early leaders of the insurgency were executed before independence was achieved, Colonel Iturbide, a conservative Creole, was successful in overtaking Mexico City and setting himself up as the Emperor of Mexico in 1822 (Wright). Subsequently Guatemala (which included most of present-day Central America) separated from newly independent Mexico, and the United States expanded into territory that had belonged to New Spain (Hamnett, 1999). Benito Juárez, of fully Zapotec Indigenous origins, rose from the position of governor of Oaxaca to president of Mexico in the mid-1800s; however, the French under Napoleon III interrupted his presidency (1862–1867) and installed Maximilian of Austria as the monarch. A long dictatorship followed under Porfirio Díaz (1884–1911) during which mining, railways, industry, and plantation agriculture developed, but Indigenous peoples were steadfastly displaced from their communal lands in the process and left impoverished as labourers on the plantations and migrant workers in the mines.

The Mexican revolution began in 1910 with Francisco Madero denouncing the tyranny of Díaz and raising rebel armies (Hamnett, 1999; Wright, 2005). Pancho Villa responded in the north and Emiliano Zapata in the central-south area—both rallying the dispossessed Indigenous and peasant farm workers to fight so the land would be owned again by those who worked it. Madero was executed early in the struggle; however, Carranza and Obregón joined as insurgent leaders who helped to secure the victory of the revolution but subsequently turned on Villa and Zapata and killed them. Nevertheless, the 1917 Constitution, in Article 27, did provide for "government expropriation of under-utilized land in favour of smallholdings or reconstituted community properties...[and specified that] subsoil deposits belonged to the national patrimony and not to the private interests in the process of exploiting them" (Hamnett, 1999, p. 222). The National Revolutionary Party (PRN) was founded in 1929 and, though renamed the Party of the Mexican Revolution (PRM) in 1938 and eventually the Institutional Revolutionary Party (PRI) in 1946, it remained in power, uninterrupted, until 2000.

The redistribution and return of land was not seriously undertaken until Lázaro Cárdenas became president (1934–1940), but by the time the process ended in 1992, about thirty thousand collectively owned *ejidos* and twenty-four hundred agrarian communal land parcels had been constituted covering over half of Mexico's land surface (Mackinley & Otero, 2004). Also during

Cárdenas's presidency, a system of state corporatism was instituted whereby organizations of labourers, *campesinos* (farmers), Indigenous peoples, and popular movements were formally incorporated into the state's operations and the ruling PRI. An example is found in Chapman's (2012) description of how the Cárdenas government founded the Confederation of Mexican Workers (CTM), appointed a long-term leader, and required all unions to affiliate and negotiate through it; subsequently, the CTM orchestrated a mass show of support for the government's nationalization plans after which the government expropriated the oil industry. In this way, the government was able to use corporatization to build its base of popular support, giving "the illusion of working with the people through *their* organizations" (Chapman, 2012, p. 50) while controlling potential opposition at the same time. Union leadership bereft of accountability to a membership was susceptible to corruption; the charges against Elba Esther Gordillo, head of the national teachers union, for embezzling US $154 million are illustrative (Tuckman, 2013). At the local level, the PRI established patron-client relations (clientelism)—rewarding very poor communities with small gifts of food for their political compliance—a practice that created a cultural pattern of non-participation in political life without external incentives (Zúñiga Zárate & Garza Treviño, 2007).

After Cárdenas, the Mexican state became increasingly authoritarian (Otero, 2004). In the Cold War period, the National Security Directorate (DFS) was created and used for many decades to suppress social movements and protests, often invoking the discourse of fighting drugs as the rationale for disappearances (Watt & Zepeda, 2012). The massacre of hundreds of students protesting peacefully in Mexico City's Tlatelolco square just before the 1968 Olympic Games revealed the level of brutality the state would carry out (Hamnett, 1999). Electoral processes were gradually reformed during the 1960s and 1970s in response to concerns about corruption; however, the presidential election of 1988 created outrage when the PRI candidate was declared the winner after the "computers crashed" with the opposition candidate in the lead. The seventy-one years of uninterrupted rule by the PRI ended in 2000 with the election of the right-wing National Action Party (PAN), which won again in 2006 in a highly contested race with the left-of-centre Democratic Revolutionary Party (PRD) and lost in 2012 to the PRI, although accusations of vote-buying by the PRI were made (Associated Press, 2012).

Mexico's Economy and Social Policy

The Mexican economy has suffered from the legacy of colonialism, which exploited resources for the benefit of Spain and the Creole aristocracy and ignored the needs of the masses. In the middle of the twentieth century, a Keynesian-inspired, state-led development model was employed that included "import substitution industrialization" to protect fledgling domestic industries by imposing tariffs on cheaper imports from more mechanized countries (Nutini & Issac, 2009). However, the continued impoverishment of the majority hampered the formation of a strong domestic market (Cockcroft, 2010). As the population grew in the countryside and further splitting of agricultural allotments became untenable, the rural poor migrated to the cities and joined the ranks of the urban poor facing a saturated labour market (Nutini & Issac). Migration continued north to temporary labour programs in the United States and Canada as well as to *maquiladoras*, foreign-owned assembly plants in "free trade zones" established by the Mexican government in the 1960s to attract foreign corporations to low-cost Mexican labour and a tariff- and tax-free environment located close to the US border (Kamel & Hoffman, 1999). National financial crises in 1982, 1994, and since have continued to block access to economic well-being for the Mexican majority.

Currently one in every five or six people in Mexico's labour force have left the country to find employment, a phenomenon reflected in Mexico's largest sources of foreign exchange, which in 2009 were from (in order, without illicit drug revenue) oil, remittances from family members outside the country, and tourism (Cockcroft, 2010; Durand, 2010). An OECD study by Dougherty and Escobar (2013) found that the informal sector, composed of self-employed people and employees not enrolled in health insurance, comprises 62 percent of employment, not counting the primary sector (agriculture, fishing, etc.). The highest levels of informal employment were found in the least developed states (Chiapas, Guerrero, Michoacán, and Oaxaca) with rates at or above 80 percent; in the two other states where social movement communities were studied for this research, Veracruz and Morelos, the rate is about 72 percent. Despite this evidence that the formal economy is not serving the majority of its people, Mexico has the second-largest economy in Latin America (World Bank, 2013a) and President Enrique Peña Nieto (2012) proudly quotes Goldman Sachs's prediction that "by 2020, Mexico's economy will be among the ten largest in the world" (para. 2).

The evolution of social policy in Mexico has been chronicled for English readers by Tetreault (2013a). In the period after the Second World War, the state-led developmental model fostered the creation of basic social security and health programs for employees in the formal labour market (IMSS) and public sector (ISSSTE) as well as support such as marketing assistance for agricultural producers with viable acreage. In the 1970s, with the abundance of international petro-dollars available for lending, Mexico increased public spending on health, education, housing, social security, and food subsidies with the result that income poverty dropped from 73 percent in the mid-1960s to 42 percent toward the end of the 1970s. But with escalating interest rates in the 1980s Mexico, like many other low-income countries, had to implement structural adjustment programs (SAPs) in order to renegotiate its loans through the International Monetary Fund (IMF). The arrival of SAPs signals the advent of neo-liberalism in Mexico—other manifestations of which will be described below. The SAPs resulted in reductions in social spending (which decreased from 9.2 percent to 6.1 percent of GDP by the end of 1988) and this, along with high levels of inflation, resulted in decreases of 40 percent in the real value of workers' wages and a return to a 60-percent poverty level. President Salinas, following cries of election fraud, sought legitimacy by establishing an anti-poverty program called PRONASOL which channeled funds to local "solidarity committees." This program, along with improvements to health and education, increased social spending from 6.1 percent to 9.1 percent of GDP between 1988 and 1994. At the beginning of Ernesto Zedillo's presidency in 1995, the value of the peso plummeted and, in the next year, poverty climbed beyond 60 percent; he imposed austerity measures replacing PRONASOL with Progresa, a conditional cash transfer program targeting the rural poor, which, nevertheless, excluded nearly 60 percent of the extremely poor. When Vicente Fox, representing the PAN, took over the presidency in 2000, Progresa was renamed Oportunidades and extended to the cities. Fox also tied social spending to increases in the GDP and added a new public insurance program, Seguro Popular, to provide basic medical attention for about 20 percent of the population not covered through their employment by the state or private (formal) sector; however, 10 percent of the population remain uninsured and that includes about 70 percent of the Indigenous population. Felipe Calderón Hinojosa, holding the second PAN presidency from 2006 to 2012, continued to promote the existing programs under a new umbrella, Vivir

Mejor (Live Better), which also proclaimed improved access to formal employment but budgeted very little for job creation.

The Oportunidades program, by 2009, provided an average of US $50 per month to about one-quarter of the population, improving poor children's likelihood of better health and school attendance, but there has been no evidence of a greater probability of employment in the labour market (Tetreault, 2013a). As Luccisano (2006) noted, Oportunidades has increased the social responsibilities of overworked mothers as they attempt to meet the programs' requirements that they attend monthly workshops, ensure all family members have regular medical checkups, and make sure their children are in school; meanwhile, the government has not addressed the need for improvements in the quality and accessibility of health services or education.

The Socio-cultural Context

Information about Mexico's socio-cultural context is also important for understanding the people's struggles for social justice. There is a long tradition of working collectively in Mexico that contrasts with Canada's more individualistic nature. In addition to the custom of holding land jointly, neighbours and villagers have long worked together on projects for mutual benefit in a form of communal service known as *tequio* (Cohen, 2004). The word, meaning "gift of labour," is derived from the Náhuatl language, although the practice extends beyond Náhuatl-speaking communities. The organizing of craft cooperatives by Vasco de Quiroga, the first bishop of Michoacán in the 1500s, fit very well with the collective practices of the Indigenous peoples (Verástique, 2000). Quiroga's work is considered to be "a seminal founding example of social work as community organization" (Mendoza Rangel, 2005, p. 12) in Mexico and is also an illustration of how the practice of social mobilization has not been limited to the profession of social work.

Religious thought in Mexico is primarily conservative with some progressive elements. Despite the protective pastoral actions of Bartolomé de las Casas and Vasco de Quiroga, it is important to remember that it was the conservative Catholicism of the Counter-Reformation that accompanied the Spanish colonialists to Mexico (Paz, 1985). This is relevant to the decision of the revolutionary leaders, in the writing of the 1917 Constitution, to severely constrain the activities of the clergy, prohibiting them from speaking publicly about politics (Cockcroft, 2010). In 1992, however, Salinas removed the constitutional constraints and encouraged the Catholic Church's support for the government and its more right-wing and neo-conservative approach. This has included opposition to claims for women's reproductive rights and to same-sex marriage. Progressive Catholic thought was most striking during the twentieth century in the development of liberation theology consistent with the message that came out of Vatican II in the 1960s. Theologians like Leonardo and Clodovis Boff (1986) of Brazil prompted Catholics throughout Latin America to bring the poor together to understand their oppression and to act collectively to transform society. Liberation theology fostered the emergence in the mid-1960s of Comunidades Eclesiales de Base (Christian Base/ Grassroots Communities) (CEBs) throughout poor neighbourhoods that met regularly to read Bible passages, reflect on their daily realities in light of the readings, and ask themselves what Christ would want in this current situation. The activities they undertook were varied, as Hoogvelt (2001) explains:

> Many remained devotional groups without any overt political, let alone revolutionary, aspirations. Others blended with, or inspired, urban dwellers' groups and neighbourhood associations with more modest social goals: housing, public transportation and other urban services, land, clean water, electricity, health and education. (p. 253)

By the 1980s, the Catholic hierarchy rejected the central tenets of liberation theology and bishops, like Sergio Méndez Arceo in the state of Morelos, where over eight hundred CEBs flourished, were replaced by much more conservative bishops (Cockcroft 2010).

Paulo Freire's (1968/1984) *praxis* method of education through a continuous cycle of action and reflection also had great influence throughout Latin America. His experience, teaching the poor in Brazil how to read, led him to develop a group approach focusing on the central issues in the people's lives and facilitating a process of conscientization leading to action to overcome their oppression. Freire's methods were used in the CEBs in Latin America and in the consciousness-raising groups of the second wave of the women's movement in many parts of the world, including Mexico. Many men's upholding of an exaggerated sense of masculinity and male privilege, known as *machismo*, along with conservative Catholic teachings, has entrenched Mexican women in a strongly patriarchal tradition that is being challenged through women's increased political consciousness.

Narco-Violence and Militarization

Another significant element of Mexico's current socio-cultural reality is the violence related to narcotics and organized crime as well as the associated militarization that has intensified since 2000. Between 2006 and 2012 there were ten thousand drug-related killings on average each year (Grillo, 2012; Human Rights Watch, 2013). This astounding number does not include the people who have disappeared since 2006, whose number, according to a 2012 government document, was estimated at twenty-five thousand (Human Rights Watch, 2013). In addition to the lost lives, many people have been forced to relocate: one study found that over 220,000 people in Ciudad Juárez, the city across from El Paso, Texas, had left their homes in a three-year period, half of whom crossed into the United States (Internal Displacement Monitoring Centre, 2011).

There are several interrelated factors that have contributed to the evolution of this staggering level of violence in Mexico. One important element is the changed structure of the Mexican drug trade since its early smuggling of domestic marijuana and opium/heroin into the United States when it became illegal there in 1914 (Bucardo, Brouwer, & Strathdee, 2005). In the 1980s, Mexico became the key route for traffic in cocaine from Colombia, and Mexico's criminal organizations have gradually taken over transportation directly from the Colombian sources (Insight Crime, 2012). Although there were two main cartels in the 1980s—the Guadalajara Cartel and the Gulf Cartel—Miguel Angel Félix Gallardo, the leader of the Guadalajara Cartel, after his imprisonment in 1989, divided his territory into the Tijuana, Juárez, and Sinaloa cartels; the Gulf Cartel, in the late 1990s received members of Mexico's "special forces," who became the notoriously brutal Zetas cartel, which itself became independent and, in turn, spawned a Michoacán subgroup known as La Familia (Insight Crime, 2012). The numerous cartels fight over territory, leaving many dead in their wake, and continue to fragment, federate, and morph into changed structures. The fractious nature of the cartels means that when government forces arrest one of the "drug lords," violence is unleashed in a struggle over the power vacuum (Burton, 2007).

Another factor contributing to the growth of the drug trade is the impact of the harsher neo-liberal Mexican economy since 1990. Drug-trade dollars became more attractive with the peso crisis of 1995 and the loss of factory jobs to the cheaper Asian labour market (Grillo, 2011). Cheaper grain imports from the United States resulted in some farm families switching to production of marijuana or opium poppies and other families sending members to the north as migrant workers. Ciudad Juárez has experienced these changes intensely as migrants arrive to compete for the diminishing maquiladora jobs and rival cartels battle for control of the border location. Here, where Bowden (2010) notes that half of the high-school-aged kids are neither in school nor employed and some districts have the killing rate of a war zone, youth are paid US $85 for each assassination that they carry out (Grillo, 2011).

A third factor in the escalating violence is the change in government response. During the decades of PRI monopoly rule, the government allowed the drug cartels some latitude, "taking down a token few gangsters and taxing the rest" (Grillo, 2011, p. 10). In contrast, the PAN, declared war on the cartels and, during Calderón's presidency (2006–2012), called in the military (Bricker, 2011). Subsequently, the cartels have intensified the killing of security forces, members of other cartels, and civilians—targeted and otherwise (Tremonti, 2013). The United States has augmented the Mexican government's response through its Merida Initiative, which approved US $1.6 billion in equipment and training between 2008 and 2010 (Grillo, 2011; Bricker, 2011). It is worth noting here that annual income from illicit drugs sold in the United States is estimated at US $30 billion, ranking second after oil in Mexico's largest sources of foreign income (Grillo, 2011).

A final element in the spiralling violence is the diversification in the criminal activities of the cartels. No longer are the cartels focusing only on drug dealing; they have expanded into kidnapping, extortion, and human trafficking (Grillo, 2011; Hampson, 2013). Insight Crime (2012) claims that Mexico has one of the highest kidnapping rates in the world, which, by extrapolation from their figures, approximates four thousand per year. Extortion is clearly apparent in Monterrey, where the Zetas tax bars and discos across the city, except for the richest district, where the disco owners pay another cartel to keep the Zetas out (Grillo, 2011). Mexico's Comisión Nacional de los Derechos Humanos (National Human Rights Commission) (2013) acknowledges that human trafficking in Mexico now victimizes thousands of people every year and news reports indicate that migrants from Central America (Shahani, 2013) and young women are particularly at risk (BBC, 2011).

Corruption within the Mexican government systems and rampant human rights violations by the government's law enforcement and military forces have created a difficult context for many, including social movement activists. There have been links between criminal activities and high-ranking officials from the outset (Watt & Zepeda, 2012), but only a few examples from recent decades are presented here. Félix Gallardo, the founder of the Guadalajara cartel in 1980s, had a close relationship with the Sinaloa state governor, and when Félix Gallardo was arrested by federal officials, the state and Culiacan municipal police chiefs were jailed and dozens of their officers deserted (Rohter, 1989); Arturo Guzmán Decena was a federal forces commander with US training and it was he who supplied the aforementioned special forces officers to the Gulf cartel in the late 1990s and formed the Zetas (Grillo, 2011); Miguel Ortiz Miranda worked for the Michoacán state police as well as for the La Familia cartel, and he used state police support for an attack by La Familia on the federal police in 2009 (Grillo, 2011). There are more stories than can be recounted here of heads of federal drug or organized crime units and frontline officers by the thousands suspected of accepting bribes (Grayson, 2010; Ha, 2009; Tuckman, 2010).

Human rights violations against civilians, aside from the violence of organized crime, are a grave and mounting concern in this environment of militarization and corruption. Bricker (2011) reported a 26-percent increase in human rights abuse complaints against the government since the beginning of Calderón's presidency in 2006 and an increase in complaints against the military from 182 in 2006 to 1,415 in 2010. Mexico's human rights organizations are particularly critical of the impunity granted to active-duty soldiers and they have called on the government to reform the Code of Military Justice so that civilian courts try cases when soldiers are accused of crimes against civilians (Bricker, 2011). The jurisdictional problem is exemplified in the cases of two Indigenous women who were raped by soldiers in Guerrero in 2002—cases that were thrown out by the federal courts; in the end, the victims were represented by the Tlachinollan human rights organization at the Inter-American Court of Human Rights and won (Price, 2012). Regarding forced disappearances, Human Rights Watch (2013) has found evidence of state involvement in 60 percent of the cases they documented and they observed a clear pattern:

> Members of security forces arbitrarily detain individuals without arrest orders or probable cause. In many cases, these detentions occur in victims' homes, in front of family members; in others, they take place at security checkpoints, at workplaces, or in public venues, such as bars. Soldiers and

police who carry out these detentions almost always wear uniforms and drive official vehicles. When victims' relatives inquire about detainees' whereabouts at the headquarters of security forces and public prosecutors' offices, they are told that the detentions never took place.... The common *modus operandi* in these cases suggests that these crimes may have been planned and coordinated, or at the very least could not have taken place without the knowledge of high-ranking [military] officials. (para. 2 and 3)

Social activists have been targets of killings in which state authorities have knowingly allowed the murder or have been implicated in it. Two examples illustrate the risks to activists in the Red Mexicana de Afectados por la Minería (Mexican Network of People Affected by Mining) (REMA). Bety Cariño, a member of the national coordination team for REMA, was killed along with another human rights observer in April 2010 as they accompanied a humanitarian caravan taking supplies to an Indigenous community in Oaxaca that was occupied by a government-created paramilitary group (Centro de Estudios de la Región Cuicateca, 2010; Cockcroft, 2010; Enlazando Alternativas, n.d.). In the second example, there is a disturbing Canadian connection. Mariano Abarca was the leader of the REMA group opposed to the Canadian-owned Blackfire mine in his home community of Chicomuselo, Chiapas, who was assassinated by a gunman connected with the mining company in November 2009 (Nestor, 2009; Sher, 2013). A study conducted by Mining Watch Canada (2013) revealed that Blackfire paid Cdn. $20,000 plus other gifts to the mayor of Chicomuselo for benefits to the company, and that the Canadian Embassy in Mexico provided support to Blackfire throughout its explorations and operations in Chiapas, including after the state environment secretariat closed the mine in December 2009, when "the Embassy continued to defend the company to Mexican state officials and provided it with information on how to sue the state of Chiapas under the North American Free Trade Agreement (NAFTA) for closing the mine" (p. 4). Popular mobilization is clearly difficult in a militarized context; Mexico's resistance groups and social movements have experienced many defeats because of it in recent years (Cockcroft, 2010).

Social Indicators

Social indicators, again mostly from the United Nations, allow for interesting cross-country comparisons. Similar to Canada, nearly 80 percent of the Mexican population live in urban areas (United Nations Data, 2013b). However, quite uniquely, as much as 10 percent of the Mexican population live outside the country, most frequently in the United States, and over half of those are there illegally (World Bank, 2011a; Terrazas, 2010). The infant mortality rate is approximately fourteen deaths per one thousand live births (in comparison with only five in Canada); Mexico has a younger population than Canada with about 28 percent under fifteen years while only 9.5 percent are sixty years and over (United Nations Data, 2013b). Mexico ranked sixty-first out of 186 countries on the United Nations Development Programme (2013) Human Development Index, which places it among other countries like Romania and Peru, which are considered to have "high human development" in comparison with Canada's "very high" categorization. Table 3.1 shows the two countries' data on the three components of the index.

Mexico's ranking, like Canada's, has dropped in relation to other countries in the past two decades, although, the HDI composite values have gradually and consistently increased in both countries (UNDP, 1990–2014).

Table 3.1

Comparison of Human Development Index Data

Country	Rank	HDI Composite Value	Life Expectancy at Birth	Mean/ Expected Years of Schooling	GNI per Capita in 2005 US$
Mexico	61	0.775	77.1 yrs.	8.5/13.7	$12,947
Canada	11	0.911	81.1 yrs.	12.3/15.1	$35,369

Source: UNDP (2013), p. 144.

Neo-liberalism in Mexico

NEO-LIBERALISM HIT MEXICO harder and earlier than Canada. In many ways the application of neo-liberal policies in Mexico and other low-income countries acts as a form of neo-colonialism in which the weaker players are again exploited by the stronger ones who structure the economic relations in their own favour (Snyder, 2012). As mentioned above, Mexico was required to accept the conditions of the IMF structural adjustment programs in the early 1980s in order to renegotiate its loans; further reforms were required before the implementation of NAFTA and again with the 1995 peso crisis in order to receive a US $50 billion bailout (Tetreault, 2013a). Yet, as will become clear in the details below, the rich countries, despite espousing free-market principles, continue to protect their own products, and the rich within each country manage to profit from the new arrangements while the austerity measures hurt the poor the most.

Consistent with neo-liberal principles, Mexico has kept its taxation rates low. However, according to Brandt and Paillacar's (2011) assessment based on 2008 data, Mexico's tax revenue is lower than other OECD member countries and efforts to increase it would be beneficial. Mexico's tax revenue from all sources, including goods and services, personal income, and corporate profits, was around 22 percent of GDP in comparison with Canada's 32 percent. Mexico's top marginal income tax rate at 30 percent also was the lowest among OECD countries. Although there is a flat corporate tax of 30 percent, Tetreault (2013a) notes that the four hundred largest corporations in Mexico pay, on average, only 1.7 percent of their earnings in tax. Even at current tax rates, Brandt and Paillacar suggest that revenues could increase by about 30 percent if the base of taxpayers could be broadened and payment compliance could be improved. These would be significant challenges, however, given that a large portion of the labour market is employed outside of the formal economy, corporations operating in the maquiladora sector are tax-exempt, and many citizens are skeptical about the fairness and prudence of government financial decisions.

The dismantling of social programs in Mexico's transition from state-led developmentalism to neo-liberalism began with the structural adjustment programs of the early 1980s. Cuts to social spending included removing the subsidies that ensured affordable prices for basic foods such as tortillas and milk (Durand, 2010). Subsidies and supports to the agricultural sector were eliminated as well (Otero, 2004). For example, the government's Instituto

Mexicano del Café (Mexican Coffee Institute) (INMECAFE), which had been created to manage the marketing of coffee on behalf of the producers, was terminated in 1989 (Martínez Torres, 2004). The programs, like PROCAMPO (Program of Direct Supports to the Countryside), created in the 1990s to help the agricultural sector adjust to the neo-liberal approach, have favoured agribusiness having criteria that exclude small farms and an application process that is inaccessible to farmers with limited education or Spanish-language skills (Tetreault, 2013b). Although the Oportunidades program described earlier was extended in the 2000s, it is typical of neo-liberal social assistance programs: targeted, conditional on behaviours intended to develop human capital, and bereft of job creation efforts (Tetreault, 2013a). By 2012, Mexico's social expenditures constituted 7.4 percent of GDP (OECD, 2013b)—less than half of the average for the twenty-one countries of Latin America and the Caribbean (United Nations Economic Commission for Latin America and the Caribbean [ECLAC], 2012).

Free trade has been a highly significant aspect of neo-liberalism for Mexico. The North American Free Trade Agreement is described by Watt and Zepeda (2012) as the peak of the counter-revolution wherein the accomplishments of the Mexican revolution begun in 1910 were upended and power was restored to wealthy private interests. On January 1, 1994, the day that the agreement came into effect, an uprising of historic proportions occurred in the southernmost state of Chiapas (Hayden, 2002). A large movement of Mayan people from across the state, calling themselves "Zapatistas" in accord with Emiliano Zapata's fight for land and liberty, had formed a people's army, the Ejército Zapatista de Liberación Nacional (Zapatista National Liberation Army) (EZLN), and in an early-morning surprise insurrection took control of six municipalities in Chiapas. Their spokesperson, Subcomandante Marcos (1994), decried the illegitimacy of the current government and described NAFTA as "a death sentence for the Indigenous ethnicities of Mexico" (p. 216). Dozens died in the twelve days of conflict with the Mexican army before the government agreed to begin peace negotiations. Prior to NAFTA, Indigenous and mestizo families on small (less than five hectares) and medium (around ten hectares) farms produced corn, beans, and basic grain crops for their own needs and to satisfy three-quarters of the national market; larger mechanized farms in northern Mexico provided the balance (Acuña Rodarte, 2003). NAFTA required the elimination of Mexican price guarantees and supports for its producers as well as the phase-out of tariffs on imported grains;

meanwhile, the United States government's support for its own agricultural producers increased a stunning 350 percent from 1994 to 2000 (Acuña Rodarte). Thus grains, subsidized by the US government at levels up to 40 percent of net farm income, were sold in Mexico at prices that were less than the Mexican cost of production (Watt & Zepeda, 2012). As a result Mexico lost its relative self-sufficiency in food production and, in the first decade of NAFTA, 1.8 million *campesinos* (farmers) had to abandon their families in search of work in the North (Cockcroft, 2010). Consumers suffered as well since without the former controls, the price of tortillas doubled to the benefit of the Maseca corporation, which monopolized production, and Wal-Mart, which became the largest retailer (Bacon, 2008). NAFTA resulted in hardships for workers in the manufacturing sector as well. Former national content law required foreign automakers within Mexico to purchase a portion of their parts from Mexican producers; without this requirement, the manufacturers now use parts from their own foreign subsidiaries, putting thousands of Mexican parts makers out of work (Bacon, 2008). Even when lower wages attracted new manufacturing, further exploitation of labourers occurred; for example, when Ford transferred its Fiesta production to Mexico, it imposed a two-tier wage structure, paying the new workers only half of the existing employee's wage of MXN $45 pesos (about Cdn. $4) per hour (Durand, 2010). Despite protests, political leaders have been unwilling to renegotiate NAFTA (Bartra, 2004) and Mexico has since signed free trade agreements with many other countries, including most of those in Central America, plus Colombia, Peru, Chile, Israel, Japan, and the European Union (Villarreal, 2012).

Privatization was a central element of Mexico's neo-liberal reforms. In 1992, the Salinas government amended Article 27 of the Constitution, ending the process of land redistribution and, in the same year, they passed the Agrarian Law, making collectively held lands available for sale or rent on the private market (Nutini & Issac, 2009). The privatization process required the agreement of the majority of each parcel's landholders and provided financial incentives, creating a situation in which people from financially strapped communities were vulnerable to conflict and pressure (Tetreault, 2013b). For the Indigenous peoples, as Cockcroft (2010) noted, "land is not a commodity to be bought and sold but an integral part of their worldview of respect for nature" (p. 91). The prospect of the privatization of their traditional lands was, along with the "dumping" of US subsidized grain, a fundamental issue in the Zapatistas' uprising and outcry of "enough." In addition to land, public utilities and enterprises were privatized. Over nine hundred state-owned enterprises were sold between 1982 and 1994, which benefited Mexico's small economic elite (Watt & Zepeda, 2012)—for example, Carlos Slim, who bought Telmex alternates with Bill Gates for the position of richest person in the world (Forbes, 2013; Bloomberg Billionaires, 2014).

Some aspects of labour force changes in Mexico's neo-liberal environment are apparent in the above description. Early efforts to increase the flexibility of the workforce occurred during Salinas's presidency with untruthful defamation of union leaders and harsh crackdowns on striking workers, including the use of the military at the Cananea mine walkout in 1989 (Watt & Zepeda, 2012). Unemployment rates published by the Mexican government do not include people who are "occupied" in unpaid activities; however, it is known that in 1996 with the impact of the peso crisis and NAFTA, 1 million jobs in the formal economy were lost and informal employment rose rapidly thereafter (Watt & Zepeda, 2012). Wages have been kept low with a minimum wage of MXN $61 pesos (Cdn. $4.90) per day and MXN $65 pesos (Cdn. $5.20) per day in high-cost areas like Acapulco (Mexico, Comisión Nacional de los Salarios Mínimos, 2014). In this economy, where it is exceedingly difficult to earn a living in agriculture or the labour market, workers, like jobs and capital, have become mobile, some moving to the north of Mexico and many to the United States. As Cockcroft (2010) notes, "Mexico has transferred unprecedented amounts of capital to the United States—not only in terms of its natural resources and 'value added' by labor at the points of production, but also in the literal transfer of almost a fifth of its labor force" (p. 136). Sacrifice is entailed for the workers and the families left behind, and there is danger for those who go to places like Ciudad Juarez and for the half of migrants to the United States who enter illegally (Terrazas, 2010; Tetreault, 2013b).

Mexico's foray into free-market capitalism has incurred environmental costs that remain "externalities" (using Daly and Cobb's 1989 terminology) from the accounting perspectives of the foreign corporations generating them. The maquiladoras operating in free trade zones since the mid-1960s left such costs to municipalities bereft of tax dollars to provide clean water, sewage treatment, and livable neighbourhoods for their workforce. Kelly (1992) provided a vivid description of Matamoros, across the border from Brownsville, Texas, which had orange and purple slime oozing from discharge pipes and flowing down open canals to a coastal lagoon and into the Gulf of Mexico. Children played along the edges of the murky water, and adults scavenged the dump to bring home empty chemical barrels to collect water for their homes. Contamination from mining in Mexico intensified with the further liberalization that accompanied NAFTA. Laws related to mining and foreign investment were amended in 1993 and 1996 respectively, allowing foreign ownership of mineral rights through concessions granted by the government without community input and after very limited environmental impact assessments (Estrada Ochoa, 2006). This opening of mining opportunities has resulted in a rapid increase in exploration and exploitation. Canadian interests have been at the forefront, holding 624 of the 803 (78 percent) mining projects active during 2012 that were operated by foreign-owned corporations (Mexico, Secretaría de Economía, 2012). Harm to the environment, such as cyanide contamination of the water with subsequent human health problems, has been central to conflicts with the mining companies that have arisen in as many as two hundred Mexican communities where the mining projects operate (United Nations Permanent Forum on Indigenous Issues, 2013).

Inequality is very high in Mexico as is typical of countries in Latin America (ECLAC, 2012). At the end of the first decade of the twenty-first century, the richest 20 percent of the population held about 53 percent of the country's income, while the poorest 20 percent held only 5 percent (World Bank, 2013b and 2013c). Mexico's inequality had been declining in the decades leading up to the 1980s and the advent of neo-liberal reforms (Polaski, 2003). However, its Gini coefficient increased from 0.45 in 1984 to its peak at 0.52 in 1994; it then declined slightly to 0.47 in 2004 and has remained there as of 2010, the most recent year for which OECD (2013c) data were available. This was the second highest level of inequality among the thirty-four OECD member countries in the late 2000s whose average Gini coefficient was 0.31 (OECD, 2011c). Polaski also notes that Mexico's southern states, which traditionally were poorer than the northern states, had been closing the gap in the mid-twentieth century; however, this convergence halted in the 1980s and the geographical inequality has been widening since the 1990s. One must conclude that the full recipe of the neo-liberal economic model, including lower taxation and social expenditures, free trade, privatization, and a more flexible labour force, has not contributed to increased prosperity for the people of Mexico; rather, there is increased immiseration borne out in inequality, environmental devastation, and difficulty in making a living and keeping families together in healthy communities.

Responses to Neo-liberalism in Mexico

THE PEOPLE OF MEXICO, who often comment that for them this struggle against oppression has been going on for more than five hundred years, have found means of resistance and forms of activism in the face of globalized neo-liberalism that provide them with hope for a better future. Academics like Prevost, Vanden, and Olivia (2012), who have studied social movements in Latin America, also note that many of the "new" social movements are a continuation of the long history of struggles in the continent against inequality and domination by colonialism, neo-colonialism, and internal elites. Many of the current resistance movements in Mexico were strongly influenced by the teachings of liberation theology and the Freirian practices of conscientization referenced in the socio-cultural context described earlier. The formation of co-operatives for producing collectively and selling artisanal products and agricultural produce often through the fair trade market, also introduced earlier, is one such mode of resistance. Coffee co-operatives, for example, were formed in the southern states, including Oaxaca (Aranda Bezaury, 2003) and Chiapas (Martínez Torres, 2004) after the government role through INMECAFE ceased in 1989. Las Abejas (the Bees), a group from the Chenalhó region in the Chiapas Diocese of San Cristóbal de las Casas with its much-loved bishop Samuel Ruiz, implemented the praxis of reflection and non-violent action in the pursuit of human dignity, employing civil disobedience by cutting trees without a permit in order to grow corn and protesting wrongful arrests over a land dispute in the early 1990s (Kovic 2003a). La Vía Campesina (The Peasant Farmer Way) is an international farmer-led organization, formed in 1993 from the agroecology movements in countries like Mexico, that advocates an end to national and international neo-liberal policies that jeopardize sustainable agriculture, replacing them with policies to ensure people's food self-sufficiency at local and national levels (Tetreault, 2013c).

More militant activism, epitomized by the Zapatista uprising on January 1, 1994, emerged in response to the intensification of neo-liberal policies and the loss of credibility of the political institutions (Watt & Zepeda, 2012). Civil society protests of the government's military offensive against the Zapatistas forced a ceasefire on January 12 to begin peaceful negotiations; however, the Zapatistas, in their response to Salinas's initial offer to pardon rebels who accepted the ceasefire, made no apology for taking arms:

For what must we ask pardon? For what will they "pardon us"? For not dying of hunger? For not accepting our misery in silence?...For having shown the country and the whole world that human dignity still exists and is in the hearts of the most impoverished inhabitants? For what must we ask pardon, and who can grant it?

(Subcomandante Marcos on January 18, 1994, as cited in Gilbreth & Otero, 2001, p. 19)

The Zapatistas engaged in a thorough participatory process, holding large assemblies in jungle amphitheatres they called Aguascalientes, after the city where Emiliano Zapata and his followers held their constitutional assembly (Gilbreth & Otero, 2001). The process culminated in a National Indigenous Forum to determine their input to the San Andrés Accords on Indigenous Rights and Culture, which they signed with the government in February 1996. However, after lack of progress on implementation of the accords, negotiations were suspended in September 1996. When the government approved an Indigenous Law concerning Indigenous rights and culture in 2001, omitting the autonomy provisions of the San Andrés Accords, the Indigenous peoples felt betrayed and began a strategy of separating from the state. This strategy has been identified as an approximation of Amin's (1990) notion of "delinking" in Chapman's (2012) analysis of state–society relations in Mexico, and her description of its implementation is paraphrased briefly below. In the summer of 2003, the Zapatistas dismantled the Aguascalientes and established *caracoles* as autonomous regions to bring together the Zapatistas and the non-Zapatistas in the Indigenous communities for dialogue, cultural activities, and political decision making. Each caracol elects its own Junta de Buen Gobierno (Council of Good Government), which oversees the collection of taxes, economic strategy, education, health services, physical infrastructure, security, and coordination of civil society support. In this manner, the Indigenous peoples are able to operate independent of the state with the exception of serious medical or judicial matters. The Zapatistas most recent project, La Otra Campaña (The Other Campaign), began in 2005 holding consultations across Mexico with other communities and organizations struggling against neo-liberalism in hopes of encouraging more widespread delinking from the state, including from its electoral processes. The current focus of La Otra

Campaña is more local and with organizations that have declared their support for the Zapatista movement (Comisión Sexta del EZLN, 2013).

Several other social movements, aside from the Zapatista endeavours, illustrate the activism in Mexico in response to neo-liberalism and the recent handling of drug-related crime. The Barzón movement emerged during the 1994 financial crisis in which the government devalued the peso. Farmers with agricultural loans were joined by hundreds of thousands of other Mexicans with crippling debt repayment costs, all of whom blamed the recklessness of the elite for the crisis and together staged street protests and made demands for new bank legislation (Williams, 2001). In the state of Guerrero, communities and farmers living near the Papagayo River formed a council, CECOP, in 2003 to organize their opposition against the proposed La Parota Dam, which would have displaced approximately twenty-five thousand people and impacted another seventy-five thousand others downstream (Amnesty International, August 2007). CECOP, with support from environmental and human rights organizations, protested the lack of consultation with the community, the inadequate environmental assessments, and the human rights violations they had experienced; they were successful in obtaining a court injunction in 2009 and the state governor's agreement to end the project in 2012 (Lowrey-Evans, 2012). The Mexican Network for Action against Free Trade (RMALC), described earlier as the counterpart to Common Frontiers in Canada, has been Mexico's link with the Hemispheric Social Alliance, which has worked to counter the proposal for a Free Trade Area of the Americas. In Mexico, RMALC and like-minded organizations of producers, human and environmental rights advocates, social and economic policy analysts, among others, including the Zapatistas, opposed the Plan Puebla Panama proposed by President Fox in 2001 to provide the physical infrastructure from Mexico to the southern end of Central America for expanded free trade (RMALC, 2004). The opposition groups were successful in having some of the proposed projects removed—for example, plans for an airport in Atenco, on ejido land near Mexico City, and all hydroelectric dams were cancelled; however, much of the plan has now been relaunched and renamed (Pickard, 2004; Proyecto Mesoamérica, 2013). Union activism in Mexico has departed from the usual nationally focused activities as illustrated in the 2006 strike by seventy thousand teachers in Oaxaca, supported by the Popular Assembly of the Peoples of Oaxaca (APPO) and the actions of the auto workers and miners unions in building solidarity with the international union movements for pressure on the Mexican state (Cockcroft, 2010). The final example of activism addresses the escalation in violence and death arising from drug-related crime and the government's militarized response to it. Citizens, including parents of young people killed, hurt, or missing because of the drug war violence, have formed the Movimiento por la Paz con Justicia y Dignidad (Movement for Peace with Justice and Dignity) to shout out their messages: "No more blood" and "We are fed up"(Giardini, 2011). The poet, Javier Sicilia (2013), whose son was killed in March 2011, is a central force in the movement, which has organized caravans and public forums, developed proposals and spoken with political officials, and thus far achieved legislation requiring the government to recognize victims of crime along with their families and to assist with their expenses.

Activism in Mexico is often met with repression by the government, and many of the movements resisting or challenging neo-liberalism described earlier have not been exempt. Gilbreth and Otero (2001) identified a form of "low intensity warfare" in Chiapas after the Zapatista uprising where, despite the peace agreement, the military presence increased—providing material aid to citizens supporting the PRI and subjecting communities in resistance to harassment and intimidation:

> These policies and the presence of soldiers...polarized communities with divided loyalties and eventually erupted into violence as government supporters, emboldened by local PRI authorities, were encouraged to form paramilitary groups to attack EZLN sympathizers. (p. 16)

The attack on Las Abejas in Chenalhó, Chiapas, on December 22, 1997, is one of the most shocking examples—while members of the pacifist group gathered in the church in the village of Acteal, government-trained paramilitary troops killed twenty-one women, fifteen children, and nine men (Kovic, 2003a; Watt & Zepeda, 2012). In early 2004 in the Zinacantán region of Chiapas, where a PRD municipal government had been elected, the authorities cut off the water supply to the Zapatista support communities (Hernández Castillo, 2006). After three months with no solution, the Zapatista supporters held a non-violent protest rally; however, on their way home they were ambushed by armed members of the PRD government, who injured twenty-nine people, destroyed several homes, and ultimately displaced 125 families (Centro de Investigaciones Económicas y Políticas de Acción Comunitaria, 2004). The communities protesting La Parota dam met with violence between 2003 and 2007 when three people were killed, three leaders of groups opposing the dam were detained, several people were injured, and others received death threats (Amnesty International, August 2007). The Federal Commission of Electricity is believed to have paid people to support the dam (Guidi, 2007), and the Guerrero state governor is thought to have been behind the use of force against protesters (Hernández Castillo, 2006). Opponents of the airport proposed on ejido land in San Salvador Atenco, north of Mexico City, in May 2006, were met with a police operation that detained hundreds of people without due process and subjected many to human rights violations, including sexual abuse of at least twenty-six women (Amnesty International, November 2007; Cockcroft, 2010). In Oaxaca, the striking teachers encamped in the city centre were attacked by state police with guns, attack dogs, and tear gas before dawn on June 24, 2006, prompting the formation of APPO and the call for the resignation of the state governor. After four months of popular occupation of parts of the city, President Fox sent in the federal preventive police, who also involved paramilitary groups in a violent repression that resulted in at least twenty deaths, including that of Indymedia reporter Brad Will (Chomsky as cited in Meyer, 2010; Libertinus, 2006). However, even with the increased militarization connected to the drug war, which has resulted in more human rights violations, Mexico's strong history of collective action prevails—this time in the form of the new Movement for Peace with Justice and Dignity, described earlier.

Oppressed Populations

AS IN THE DESCRIPTION of the Canadian context, information about particular groups facing oppression is important background for understanding their struggles for change. Again, the prevalence and realities of the poor, women, and Indigenous peoples are highlighted.

The Poor in Mexico

Mexico's Consejo Nacional de Evaluación de la Política de Desarrollo Social (National Council for Evaluation of Social Development Policy) (Mexico, CONEVAL, 2013a) measures poverty using two income lines, and the following information about those measures is sourced from their website. The minimum well-being line represents the cost of basic food needs for one person for one month, and at the 2013 year-end this was approximately MXN $840 pesos (Cdn. $70) in rural areas and MXN $1,200 pesos (Cdn. $100) in urban areas. The well-being line represents the cost of these basic food needs, plus other non-food essentials such as shelter, public transportation, health care, and clothing; at the 2013 year-end this line was approximately MXN $1,620 pesos (Cdn. $135) in rural areas and MXN $2,400 pesos (Cdn. $200) in urban areas. A person is considered to be in a situation of extreme poverty if he or she is living below the minimum well-being line, i.e., insufficient income to attain basic food needs. A person is considered to be living in moderate poverty if he or she is living above the minimum well-being line, but below the well-being line, i.e., with sufficient income to meet basic food needs, but insufficient to meet all basic needs (shelter, etc.). The total number of people living in extreme poverty, plus those living in moderate poverty, represents all people living in poverty. Vulnerability to poverty is also measured in terms of income and social factors such as inadequate housing, lack of education, and inaccessibility of essential services and social security.

In 2010, the year for which CONEVAL (2012a) has published a full report on the incidence of poverty, 46.5 percent of Mexican people were poor: 11.5 percent lived in extreme poverty and 35 percent lived in moderate poverty. An additional 34.5 percent were considered to be at risk of poverty due to income or social vulnerability factors, leaving only 19 percent of the population who were neither poor nor at risk of poverty. The OECD's (2013c) most commonly used measure of low income is 50 percent of the country's median income, which allows for comparisons of poverty across countries. However, use of this type of relative income measure is not appropriate in a low-income country like Mexico, where the median annual income for 2010 is reported by the OECD to be only MXN $39,000 pesos (Cdn. $3,250).

All six Mexican states in which case examples of collective struggles for social justice were studied for this research project had high levels of poverty in 2010, according to the CONEVAL (2012a) report. Chiapas (78.5 percent), Guerrero (67.6 percent), and Oaxaca (67.4 percent) had the highest levels of poverty in the country and, taking into account the population at risk, less than 10 percent of the population was neither poor nor vulnerable to poverty. In Veracruz (with a poverty level of 58.5 percent) and Michoacán (with a poverty level of 54.8 percent), along with Tabasco, Puebla, Tlaxcala, and Hidalgo, 11–13 percent of the population was not vulnerable to poverty. In Morelos (with a poverty level of 43.7 percent), along with Zacatecas and Guanajuato, 14–17 percent of the population was not vulnerable to poverty. These findings are consistent with data from CONEVAL (2013b) indicating the incidence of poverty in 2010 was higher in the rural areas (64.9 percent) than in the urban areas (40.4 percent).

Women in Mexico

Women's oppression in Mexico is embedded in long-standing ideologies that support machismo and patriarchy, as noted earlier. It is not surprising then that Mexico has a lower rank than Canada, placing it seventy-second of 186 countries on the UNDP (2013) Gender Inequality Index (GII) with a maternal mortality rate of fifty deaths per one hundred thousand live births; adolescent fertility rate of 65.5 births per one thousand women aged fifteen to nineteen; 36 percent of seats in Parliament held by women; less females than males with some secondary education (51 percent of females in comparison with 57 percent of males); and a lower rate of labour force participation (44 percent of females in comparison with 81 percent of males).

Very little difference between Mexican women and men's poverty levels is evident in the government's aggregate poverty data (CONEVAL, 2013b; INMUJERES, 2012). However, other research indicates that women represent less than 40 percent of the labour force (OECD, 2013d), and that in 2006 they earned only approximately 42 percent of what men earned (OECD, 2013e). It is also important to note that approximately 25 percent of households in Mexico are now headed by women without a partner (CONEVAL, 2012b). Chávez Carapia (2013) notes that this is a growing phenomenon that constituted only 19 percent of households in 2000. She explains that, to manage their costs, these women must enter the labour force and, as González (2006) corroborates, many are limited to opportunities in the informal sector, such as selling tamales in the streets.

Women in Mexico continue to shoulder most of the household tasks—forty-four hours per week for women in comparison with thirty hours per week for men (OECD, 2013f). An increased burden is also accruing to women as men migrate north, leaving them with responsibilities for work in the fields and in community roles (González, 2006). International influences for change, such as the United Nations' women's conferences, brought more attention to women's rights in Mexico with such outcomes as the establishment of federal programs—for example, the Instituto Nacional de las Mujeres (National Women's Institute) (INMUJERES). However, the Mexican women's movement recently has needed to struggle against reactionary legislation in the states surrounding the federal district, which criminalizes women who choose to interrupt their pregnancies (Cockcroft, 2010). The growing inequality in Mexico is reflected among women—the wealthiest 10 percent of whom contribute to the increasing involvement of women in leadership positions in all spheres: state, market, and civil society (González, 2006). In fact, the 36 percent of seats in the Mexican federal government held by women is substantially higher than Canada's 25 percent (UNDP, 2013). The vast majority of Mexican women, however, are outside the circles of power and vulnerable to violence in their homes and workplaces, and to femicide—particularly in locations like Ciudad Juarez—in the current environment of impunity (Cockcroft, 2010; González, 2006; OECD, 2013f). As in Canada, there is still much to be accomplished to ensure rights and equality for women.

Mexico's Indigenous Peoples

Mexico's 10 million Indigenous peoples comprised about 10 percent of the total population when the comprehensive census was conducted in 2005 (Mexico, Comisión Nacional para el Desarrollo de los Pueblos Indígenas, CDI, 2010). The CDI includes as Indigenous all people who speak an Indigenous language or are part of a household where the head speaks an Indigenous language. The numbers of Indigenous peoples and their proportion of the total population are provided in Table 3.2 for the six states in which case studies for this research project were located.

CONEVAL (2013b) reports that 72.3 percent of Indigenous peoples in Mexico live in poverty, and the CDI (2010) analysis provides a sense of the lived reality: 38 percent of Indigenous peoples live in houses with dirt floors; 30 percent don't have tap water in the house; 10 percent are without electricity; 25 percent of adults are illiterate; and the infant mortality rate is twenty-three per one thousand live births. Conditions in particular states are exceptionally difficult—for example, in Guerrero, 71 percent of Indigenous peoples' homes have dirt floors and the infant mortality rate is thirty-one per one thousand live births.

In contrast with Mexico's National Institute of Statistics and Geography (INEGI), which counts only people five years of age and older who speak an

Table 3.2

Indigenous Population in Mexico

State	Indigenous Population	Proportion of State's Total Population
Oaxaca	1.6 million	45%
Chiapas	1.3 million	29%
Veracruz	970,000	14%
Guerrero	535,000	17%
Michoacán	180,000	4.5%
Morelos	56,500	3.5%

Indigenous language, and CDI, which counts only people who live in a household where the head speaks an Indigenous language, many academics use a broader definition of "Indigenous." Cockcroft (2010), for example, considers nearly one-third of the Mexican population to be predominantly Indigenous and notes that they share a great deal of culture with the 60 percent of the population who are mestizo. He emphasizes the centrality of environmental stewardship in the identity and traditions of Indigenous peoples:

> Their demand for "autonomy" signifies not only local self-governance in accord with their traditions of collective decision-making, but also control over the lands, rivers, and other elements of nature they have long respected and understood in ways that run counter to capitalism's aggressive exploitation of these resources. (p. 91)

Tetreault (2013b) points out that the perspective of the Indigenous and mestizo campesinos, who operate small, ecologically sustainable farms, is not part of the World Bank's vision for agriculture and development as highlighted in their 2008 feature report. The World Bank promotes a singular development path based on principles of trade liberalization and privatization, citing the Mexican approach as a model for the world even though this has meant "peasants are dispossessed of the land (often violently) in order to allow large-scale enterprises to exploit natural resources for private gain" (Tetreault, 2013b, p. 193). Through the government's agricultural policies, only large and medium-scale producers have access to credit, training, and export markets with the exception of the primarily Indigenous, small-scale producers of organic coffee who have organized themselves into co-operatives.

Oppression against Indigenous peoples in the form of violence has been illustrated above in the descriptions of the low-intensity warfare in the Zapatista zones and the treatment of Las Abejas. The experience of inferiorization, as well as the intersection of multiple oppressions, was strikingly conveyed by Zapatista Comandante Ester on International Women's Day in 2001: "we are triply looked down upon: as indigenous women, as women, and as poor women" (para. 3). Political disempowerment has been evident in the the numerous examples of Indigenous peoples in Mexico not being consulted before mining concessions were granted, despite consultation being a requirement of the International Labour Organization's Convention 169 Concerning Indigenous and Tribal Peoples (United Nations Permanent Forum on Indigenous Issues, 2013).

Mexico's Indigenous peoples have been confronting the multiple forms of oppression with a reawakened pride since the Zapatista uprising (Barkin, 2006). They have interrupted the World Bank's vision of small farmers leaving the rural areas by using remittances to strengthen their extended families in the sending communities (Tetreault, 2013b). They have developed seed banks to protect native species and reinvigorated Indigenous languages (Chomsky as cited in Meyer, 2010). Organizations like the Consejo Nacional de Pueblos Indígenas (National Council of Indigenous People), created by the corporatist PRI government in an attempt to control the demands of Indigenous peoples, have been "reappropriated by indigenous people as a vehicle for those demands" (Hernández Castillo, 2006, p. 120). Finally, through international solidarity, Indigenous peoples have brought about the passage of the United Nations Declaration on the Rights of Indigenous Peoples, and their determination to utilize international mechanisms and bodies like the Inter-American Court of Human Rights (2011) has gotten them judicial protection when the Mexican state failed them.

Mexico, like Canada, has received substantial criticism from the United Nations' Office of the High Commission for Human Rights for its treatment of its most vulnerable people—the poor, women, and Indigenous peoples.

Unsurprising, the most recent peer review of Mexico in October 2013 resulted in 176 recommendations related primarily to ensuring equal rights; preventing torture, forced disappearance, detainment without due process, and violence against women; protecting the rights of children; preventing human trafficking; protecting human rights defenders and journalists; reducing poverty and upholding the rights to basic needs; and protecting the rights of specific populations: children, women, people with disabilities, Indigenous peoples, African descendants, and migrants (UN OHCHR, 2013d). Mexico responded in March 2014, accepting 93 percent of the recommendations without qualification (UN OHCHR, 2014). One hopes the acceptance will be followed by serious action. Most concerning is Mexico's non-acceptance of the four recommendations related to *arraigo penal*, which is a form of preventive custody without normal due process allowed constitutionally since 2008 in the context of the war on drugs. Mexico responded that it has taken note of the observations reflected in the four recommendations and has put forward constitutional reform restricting its use to cases of organized crime. Unfortunately, suspected involvement in organized crime is precisely the rationale that activists describe as a "clever pretext" being used in police arrests to deal with people engaged in social struggle.

Mexicans, along with Canadians, clearly face challenges in the neo-conservative ideological framework and neo-liberal economic environment of the new millennium, particularly regarding the poor, women, and Indigenous peoples. However, the insecure milieu of crime and militarization is an additional burden for the people of Mexico and one that can greatly increase the cost of involvement in some social movement activities.

The global context and the national situations of Canada and Mexico demonstrate the intensification of neo-conservative thinking and free-market capitalism, which is benefiting the elites and worsening the lives of the most vulnerable. Many injustices are evident in the circumstances of the poor, women, and Indigenous peoples. Increasing inequality has resulted in a growing underclass of poor people whose abilities and needs are not given importance in the global schemata. Despite many gains in the twentieth century, women's economic equality, political participation, and freedom from violence are now receiving less attention from governments. Indigenous peoples face threats to their communities, culture, and lands in a perspective that values short-term economic gain above all else. It is in this context of neo-conservativism—with its ideological beliefs that foster inferiorization based on race, gender, and class and its economic formula of aggressive capitalism wherein society is subordinated to the market—that struggles for social justice are taking place. ∎

2 | The Stories of Struggle for Change

THE CASE STUDIES cluster naturally as projects with similar objectives. Although overlapping objectives are common, a primary focus is generally apparent. There are four such clusters: (1) income generation; (2) health, housing, and the environment; (3) women's resources and advocacy; and (4) the broader social justice objectives of some grassroots support organizations (GSOs) and independent community organizers.

The income-generation projects include several co-operatives directly engaged in the production and distribution of such goods as coffee, textiles, and pottery. They also include some projects in which external agents are facilitating the income-generating potential of others.

The second cluster of projects relate to basic needs for health, housing, and a safe environment. Several of the communities are organizing to promote health and wellness, many using natural remedies. Other communities are dealing with housing and environmental matters in addition to health. In addition, there are Mexican and Canadian examples of communities struggling to protect their land and their health from the intentions of Canadian mining companies.

The third cluster of case examples pertains to provision of resources for women and to advocacy for women's equality. The women's resource projects are from the Mexican state of Oaxaca and from the Canadian provinces of Nova Scotia and British Columbia. The women engaged in advocacy include a Canadian example of the Raging Grannies and Mexican examples from the Christian Base Communities movement connected to the teachings of liberation theology.

The final cluster includes case examples of grassroots support organizations and independent community organizers with broad social justice objectives who are supporting the accomplishments of others. The three examples include work at a neighbourhood level, a state level, and a hemispheric level.

FOUR

INCOME GENERATION

THE CASE EXAMPLES dedicated to income generation include several autonomous co-operatives and a selection of projects where external support is directed toward the productive endeavours of others. The coffee co-operatives are the largest of these organizations and will be grouped as one category with other producer co-operatives forming a second category. The projects with external support make up the third category.

Coffee Co-operatives

THE COFFEE CO-OPERATIVE EXAMPLES include producer co-operatives at the state and regional levels in the south of Mexico and a distributor co-operative in Canada. The co-operatives pertain only to the small farm producers, not the large ranchers who work independently and are more likely to sell to multinational corporations such as Nescafé. CEPCO is the state-level co-operative, the Coordinadora Estatal de Productores de Café de Oaxaca (State Coalition of Coffee Producers of Oaxaca). The women's program within CEPCO has an Indigenous name, Ita-Teku (Flower of Life). The regional-level coffee co-operative studied is in the state of Chiapas— Unión de Ejidos de la Selva (Federation of Land Collectives of the Jungle). In reality, it is a consolidation of a number of organizations from four regions of Chiapas—the mountains, the border (with Guatemala), the jungle, and the highlands surrounding San Cristóbal. Its women's program is called Mujeres de la Unión de la Selva (Women of the Jungle Federation) (MUSA). The Just Us! Coffee Roasters Co-op, in the Canadian province of Nova Scotia, works in solidarity with coffee co-operatives by paying fair prices for their organic coffee, roasting it, and marketing and distributing it in the North. Because of the strong connection between the Mexican and Canadian examples, a more detailed description is provided for the coffee co-operatives than for the other income-generation projects.

CEPCO: State Coalition of Coffee Producers of Oaxaca

Oaxaca's state-wide association of coffee co-operatives began in 1989 "out of necessity," one of the executive members explained:

> We had to organize because of the death of the government-run Mexican Coffee Institute (INMECAFE) early in 1989. Before that the government program had purchased the coffee from the producers and taken responsibility for marketing—they did all of the work except produce the coffee. But in 1989 *the government abandoned us*. Immediately, the "coyotes" appeared and raised the historical spectre of middlemen taking advantage of producers by buying our coffee for low prices and selling at much higher prices—doing whatever they wished. So the small producers in various regions of Oaxaca began to develop a state-wide organization—an ambitious objective, given that we had no money and no experience. By September of 1989, there were thirteen regions that formed the organization. The next year, two more joined and now [2004] we are forty-two regions. So little by little, we have built a team that comes together to do this work that was done before by the government.

The organization's mission statement and objective is "the whole development of the coffee producing families—to have a better life." The vice-president explained, "It is to fight for more resources; to get education, health, and communication systems—everything that is needed for the well-being of the coffee-producing families and communities." Autonomy, democracy, plurality, and transparency are the operating principles of CEPCO.

CEPCO manages various programs and enterprises based primarily in the capital city of Oaxaca. Its programs include development, technical assistance, the women's program, organic coffee, and micro-credit. Its enterprises include the

Agricultural Marketing Agency of Oaxaca and the Credit Union of the Coffee Producers of the State of Oaxaca. Various programs overlap and assist each other. For example, the organic coffee program works together with the technical assistance program. The enterprises are conceptualized as distinct from the programs, although the enterprises bring in revenue to support the programs.

The marketing emphasis, most recently, has been on fair trade. For the export market, they have been participating with a group of fair trade organizations (TransFair USA) at trade fairs. Currently 95 percent of the export coffee is through fair trade and it is all certified organic coffee. Fair trade coffee in 2004 had a price of US $135 for a sixty-kilogram bag, nearly double the regular coffee price of $76 per bag. Internal promotion of the consumption of quality, organic, fair trade coffee continues through the nationwide coalition of small farmers. Agromercados, whose name refers to agricultural markets, is part of the Fair Trade Mexico organization. Agromercados promotes the coffee branded "Café Fértil" through agreements with chains such as Wal-Mart, Carrefour, and Coffee Factory and a system of franchised cafés. In addition, CEPCO was considering developing more of its own cafés (like Café Caracol).

At the national level, CEPCO participates with the small coffee producers' associations from five other states (Chiapas, Puebla, Veracruz, Hidalgo, and Guerrero) in the Coordinadora Nacional de Organizaciones Cafetaleras (National Council of Coffee Producers Organizations) (CNOC). Through CNOC they work together to develop the fair trade market for Mexican coffee. They also put collective pressure on the federal government to provide financial support for small coffee producers. Financial support is needed, for example, to assist farmers during the years when they are converting to organic coffee.

At the international level, CEPCO is involved with the Coalition of Central American and Caribbean Coffee producers. However, one of the executive members said it is very difficult for producers to influence the price of coffee since countries that produce low-quality coffee are not interested in participating in a supply management system.

Ita-Teku: The Women's Program within CEPCO

CEPCO's president said that Ita-Teku, the women's program, fits with CEPCO's concern for the well-being of the whole family and the mission to foster programs to benefit the coffee-producing families. He emphasized that "in coffee-producing families, the whole family works together—not just the husband, but the wife and the sons and daughters too." The women's program includes projects that support the coffee production, as well as some that diversify the farm income: developing and packaging nursery plants, preparing organic fertilizer, raising pigs and chickens, growing fruit and vegetables, as well as other farmyard projects.

The Ita-Teku project headquarters is located on the outskirts of a village north of the city of Oaxaca. It consists of a greenhouse, a nursery, and a laboratory for the development and production of plants and agricultural products, as well as for the training of women from CEPCO member communities about the plant cultivation. Overall support for the women's program is provided by an academic who has published a chapter about CEPCO and the economic context of peasant farmers (Aranda Bezaury, 2003). Some government funding has been provided for their projects.

The greenhouse and nursery operations are overseen by a female agricultural engineer, and a farm family lives at the site to manage the day-to-day operations. They are cultivating various flowering and ornamental plants as well as tomatoes and the maguey plant, which is used to produce mescal in a large greenhouse. The agricultural engineer, along with guest lecturers from the university, provides monthly training on growing these plants to women who have been selected by their regional organizations to become the technical representatives. These women then provide the training, in turn, to the members of their own communities.

A female biologist oversees the laboratory with assistance from practicum students. One of their projects is the development of a natural pesticide produced from fungus that prevents the coffee borer worm from completing its life cycle. They are also experimenting with the propagation of orchids and maguey.

Unión de la Selva: The Jungle Region Coffee Federation in Chiapas, Mexico

Although the regional Chiapas coffee co-operative's official name, Unión de Ejidos de la Selva, refers to collectively titled land, it is commonly abbreviated to Unión de la Selva (Federation of the Jungle). Its operations centre is on the outskirts of Comitán, about one hour from the Guatemalan border. The organization was formed in the 1970s, much earlier than CEPCO, when the Indigenous and peasant farmers were struggling economically because they had so little land. The land distribution program that followed the revolution in Mexico was delayed in Chiapas because of the ranchers' vested interests. Thus, the small-scale coffee farmers took over unoccupied land, but still needed to gain legal title it. The principle objective of the organization in the early years was to work collectively to help the farmers gain legal title. Some of the initial impetus for organizing came from the influence of Catholic priests and a brotherhood of lay workers known as Maristas, who brought a message to the peasant communities that God wants justice, not exploitation. The organization grew to sixty or seventy communities and it supported the communities in getting highways built and bus services in place.

In the early 1980s, Unión de la Selva began to focus on their common coffee production and marketing concerns. At that time there were middlemen known as "coyotes," who held monopoly rights to purchase the coffee from the producers, and they dictated low prices for the producers and high profits for themselves. The federal government responded to this problem by forming the aforementioned Instituto Mexicano del Café (INMECAFE), which managed the marketing process. Unión de la Selva began to provide external technical assistance as well through the coffee producers' association in Oaxaca. In 1989, when the government discontinued INMECAFE, coffee prices fell. Many member communities in Chiapas did not understand why this happened, they lost trust in the organization, and membership dropped. For a few years they kept their exports smaller until confidence was regained. Also at this time, some NGOs (non-governmental organizations) from the United States and Europe provided support. In 1992, they began to experiment with organic coffee, beginning with five or six communities. People could see that there would be growing demand for organic coffee in the future and also that organic production was better for the land. Little by little, other communities joined in and they were able to obtain better prices. Around 1994, the focus on fair trade began. Ten years later they were able to guarantee the producers US $121 per forty-five kilograms. For each forty-five kilograms sold, US $5 goes into a social fund for programs such as a medical clinic, which everyone in the community can access—not only the coffee producers. By 2004, Unión de la Selva had a membership of just over a thousand families.

The distribution centre in Comitán receives the coffee from the producers; removes the skins; separates the beans by size, quality, and colour; and roasts, grinds, packages, and ships the coffee. Some of the coffee is shipped in its raw form, some as roasted whole beans, and some is roasted and ground in half-kilo bags. The majority of the coffee is shipped as whole bean—approximately thirty thousand sixty-kilogram bags and about 80 percent of those are organically produced. In 2003, they opened a distribution centre in Rotterdam, Holland, and from there other European markets are being sought. Unión de la Selva makes its processing services available to other coffee production organizations.

The project of establishing cafés, like the Café de la Selva in San Cristóbal, also began in 1994. By 2004 there were twenty cafés to promote the consumption of good coffee in Mexico by educating consumers. That way a good portion of the coffee could stay in the country, and there wouldn't be such a dependence on foreign markets. In 2004, 20 percent of the production was consumed in Mexico and 80 percent was exported. They, along with other regional producer organizations, participate in a state-wide federation, La Coordinadora de Pequeños Productores de Café de Chiapas (Chiapas Council of Small Coffee Producers) (COOPCAFE), which operates the coffee museum and café in San Cristóbal. In addition, they are promoting diversification in production of livestock, vegetables, and honey.

Mujeres de la Unión de la Selva: Women of the Jungle Federation

Mujeres de la Unión de la Selva (MUSA) has been operating since 1991. It began out of the interest of women from three coffee-producing communities within the Unión de la Selva who did the initial organizing of the women's organization and welcomed all of the others in the region. Although MUSA's projects are decentralized in about a half-dozen member communities, the program has its own buildings for workshops and office space, as well as vegetable gardens and a sheep corral. It is named Casa de la Mujer (The Women's Centre) and is located on the outskirts of a town about forty minutes by car from the Unión de la Selva headquarters.

Programs include literacy, sewing, vegetable production from seedlings and transplanting, herb growing and production of natural medicines, bread making, cookie production for sale in the Unión de la Selva cafés, workshops on human rights and gender issues; and a summer camp for youth from Spain. Some of the communities have chosen particular specialties; for example, one has a mill for grinding maíz (corn) and another has a bakery. Unlike the projects from the Unión's social fund, the MUSA projects are restricted to members.

In May 1997, they incorporated as a civil association. Shortly thereafter, a woman from a Spanish non-governmental organization came for four years to provide leadership training for the current two staff. Each of the communities has its own coordinator—someone from the community itself who understands its problems. Two representatives from each community attend MUSA meetings every two months. As well, it is the local communities who identify what topics they want for workshops in order to develop skills for their income-generating projects and to deal with the issues they face as women.

The Just Us! Coffee Roasters Co-op in Nova Scotia, Canada

The Canadian co-operative studied that is engaged in marketing fair trade, organic coffee is the Just Us! Coffee Roasters Co-op. It is located in Grand Pré, Nova Scotia, near the city of Wolfville, where they have their roastery and store along with a café and museum. In addition to buying coffee from Mexico, Just Us! imports fair trade coffee from all over the world. Also, they sell other fairly traded products such as chocolate, tea, and sugar.

The co-operative began in 1996 with the roastery in a small house. Jeff and Debra Moore, the initiators and leaders of the co-operative, had worked with L'Arche from 1981 to 1995 and were ready for a change. They were seeking something that fit with their philosophy of working in solidarity with the oppressed. Jeff attended a conference in Cuba about fair trade and, in the September 1995 issue of the *New Internationalist*, they read about Unión de la Selva. Jeff then went to Mexico to meet with people from Unión de la Selva "to see what was possible." He went to the Unión de la Selva café in the Coyoacán section of Mexico City and spoke with Jeronimo, the café developer, who helped him to link with the co-operative's headquarters in Chiapas. This was not long after the Zapatista uprising in January 1994 and there was a heavy military presence in Chiapas. Jeronimo was suspected of being Subcomandante Marcos and needed to leave Chiapas (he was safer in his café development role in Mexico City). Jeff said he was treated well by the leaders of the Unión de la Selva co-operative and they were, just at that time, looking for Canadian partners. When Jeff returned from Mexico, he and Debra talked about a potential partnership and they decided to create the co-operative in 1996 with three of their friends. They started with the purchase of a small house in New Minas and later began the roastery near Wolfville.

By 2006 there were ten members, including employees each of whom had worked in the co-op for a minimum of two years and invested at least $2,000 personally. They have also developed a separate co-operative to raise public investment dollars for Just Us! Coffee Roasters Co-op's endeavours. They are now able to bring in large shipping containers holding seventeen tons (15,876 kilograms) of unroasted coffee. The roasting and packaging is then done by Just Us! in Canada. It took about five years for the co-operative to become profitable. For the first four years in which there was a profit (the sixth, seventh, eighth, and ninth years), Jeff and Debra, whose home had provided the initial equity, as well as two other original members, received slightly higher profit-sharing than the other worker-owners. The group felt it was important to do this in order to avoid the potential for unfair influence or acrimony. Now Just Us! is fully and equally owned by the co-operative members, and by 2006 was the largest worker-owned co-operative in English-speaking Canada.

The fair trade museum at their facility provides information about producers and coffee production, the unfair profits from free trade coffee production, the process involved in organically produced (verification) and fairly traded coffee (certification), and the benefits to the producers in the South such as those in the Unión de Comunidades Indígenas de la Región del Istmo (Federation of Indigenous Communities in the Isthmus Region) (UCIRI) who have been able to create a Campesino Education Centre in San José, Oaxaca.

The marketing of the coffee occurs through a number of means. In 2006, about 50 percent of the coffee was sold in supermarkets in the Maritimes. Another 30 percent was sold in the three Just Us! (co-operative-owned) cafés in Nova Scotia. Other stores across Canada, especially health food stores, plus other restaurants, made up the remaining 20 percent of sales. There is a reciprocal relationship with the Mennonite program, Ten Thousand Villages, which sells internationally produced crafts in some of the Just Us! cafés and, in turn, sells Just Us! coffee in its craft stores. There is a distinction, though, in that there is no fair trade certification process in craft production and, therefore, the work of Ten Thousand Villages is perhaps more accurately called "alternative trade." One other avenue of coffee marketing is through university students involved in student unions and public interest research groups.

Just Us! coffee was the first fair trade coffee marketed in Canada. By 2006 there were others such as Kicking Horse, which is well known in western Canada. In North America, sales in fair trade coffee grew substantially by the mid-2000s. Some of the big corporations like Via Rail, Timothy's, and Starbucks account for much of the growth. The Just Us! co-operative was exploring a broadening of their relationship with UCIRI in Oaxaca, Mexico, through a possible ecotourism/fair trade tourism venture. The solidarity of importer/roaster/distributer co-operatives in the North has been significant in helping coffee producers' co-operatives in Mexico to address the important issue of marketing.

Other Producer Co-operatives

THE STUDY INCLUDED four other producer co-operatives that are generating income and functioning without external support. Within the Canadian province of Nova Scotia and, more precisely, in the Cheticamp area of Cape Breton, La Coopérative Artisanale (The Artisanal Co-operative) members hook rugs and decorative items. In Teotitlán del Valle in Oaxaca, there is a weaving collective called Galvin Cuy, which means "New Life" in the Zapotec language. In addition, a collective of women potters in a rural village was studied as well as a tortilla-making co-operative in the state of Veracruz.

The Rug-Hooking Co-operative in Nova Scotia, Canada

In the Acadian community of Cheticamp, rug-hooking, using long strips of rags, was well established by 1850. The women supplemented their families' meagre incomes from farming and fishing by exchanging rugs for other household goods with the travelling peddlers. Rug-hooking was transformed into a home-based industry in the 1930s through the interest of a fine arts instructor, who introduced the use of yarn in place of rags, as well as new ideas about design and colour. She marketed the products in her showroom in New York City. The women hooking the rugs were impressed by successful cooperative ventures arising from the Antigonish movement. They recognized that by working collectively they also could eliminate the intermediaries taking excessive profits from their work, so they formed their own co-operative to market their products locally as well as in larger cities. In the 1960s, when the new highway connecting Cape Breton with mainland Nova Scotia brought many more visitors to Cheticamp, the current artisans co-operative, La Coopérative Artisanale, was formed. In 1976 the co-operative expanded to include a restaurant connected physically to the gift shop and museum; however, employees do not need to be members of the co-operative since many are not artisans.

In 2006, there were about 125 women selling their products through La Coopérative Artisanale, with flexible arrangements that allow women to participate as members or non-members and to produce on order for the co-op or sell on consignment. The co-operative elects an eight-member board of directors with a three-person executive. The manager, Diane Poirier, is included as a non-voting board member. Over the years, the board has developed proposals to improve the workings of the co-operative, which are then decisions for the membership. An example close to the time of the study was a decision to change the 15-percent remittance from members selling on consignment to the same 30 percent charged of non-members, as well as the change to sharing profits based on the artisan's sales that year. The co-operative had been earning less profit to share in recent years because of a weaker economy and fewer tourists, especially from the United States. Members maintained their optimism and indicated that the collective commitment extends beyond the economic issues to a concern for the broader well-being of the members.

Women Carpet Weavers in Oaxaca, Mexico

Women in the village of Teotitlán del Valle in Oaxaca, Mexico, are carrying on the weaving tradition that has been part of their community's heritage since pre-Hispanic times. They produce carpets and other items on large pedal looms using wool that they card, spin, and then dye using natural materials. Before the middle of the twentieth century, weaving was primarily a male craft. However, with the current economic difficulties, most of the men now work in Mexico City or the United States, and often sons who marry don't return to the village, where corn still must be ground at home to make tortillas and water is replenished for household needs only twice a week. In 1994, several of the local women came together to form the Galvin Cuy collective to produce woven carpets when the state government provided credit for income-generating projects. Unfortunately, that first experience went badly. The women invested the loans in equipment and primary materials but, although they made beautiful carpets, they were unable to sell them. They were unfamiliar with going to the capital city of Oaxaca to sell their products as the men had and, in the end, when the loans were due, many women had to sell some of their possessions to raise the funds.

The Galvin Cuy collective worked for a while on producing food and raising small livestock for consumption in their own community. They invited external women, funded through government and NGOs, to talk with them about women's issues and rights and about managing a collective enterprise. Around 2000, the women decided to try carpet weaving as their focus again. With the greater amount of experience and knowledge, they felt more confident. They tapped into the support of various organizations (an NGO supporting women, a government program supporting Indigenous development, etc.) and sought particular assistance with marketing the carpets. This has been much more successful. The program has been advertised to tourists, who are invited to visit the household production sites and make purchases that can be shipped to faraway destinations. In addition, their products are being sold in Oaxaca and beyond through the fair trade market. The group has enough funding now to begin plans for a roofed-in warehouse to store the carpets safely from insects that can damage the fibres.

The Indigenous Potters Co-operative in Rural Mexico

In a Mexican Indigenous village there is a pottery collective composed of about fifty women. They use high-quality white clay, which is found about two metres below the surface of the ground, within walking distance of the village. They bring it back to their homes, carrying it on their heads—only the amount they need because it is very heavy. They make the pottery at home, using very hot wood-burning ovens. Being able to do this work at home allows the women to carry on with their other domestic responsibilities as well. About nine of the women—those who do not have small children or husbands at home—share the vending work at their small store.

The idea for the collective began in the mid-1990s. An Indigenous woman from a nearby community talked to women in the village about the need for change. Shortly thereafter, a woman from the state capital provided a workshop in their village on women's rights. Only three women attended, but together they began to organize themselves and developed the pottery collective. When they had about seventeen committed participants, they began their work. They recovered the knowledge of their mothers and grandmothers about making pottery, and they designed and built the store at the entrance to the village by the highway. Little by little they have increased their membership to the current fifty members.

They are structured as a legal association with a president, secretary, and treasurer. They believe the effort has been worthwhile for the women, although sales are lower when it is not tourist season. A serious problem arose about a year ago, when the president (mayor) of the village built two more stores—exact copies of the stores that the collective had built—and announced to the women in the town that they could sell their products individually in the government stores. As a result, the collective faces competition and has fewer sales. Fortunately, the members have remained with the collective and they are continuing to search for solutions to the marketing problem.

One of the executive members said that the collective also has been important to the members' development as capable women with rights—"it helped them overcome their self-doubts." Furthermore, they participate in political activities at the municipal level and beyond.

The Tortilla-Making Collective in Veracruz, Mexico

The final case example of an independent income-generating project that was up and running was the *tortillería* (tortilla-producing and vending shop) in a small town in the southern part of Veracruz. The people of this community have a history of working together collectively as a result of the work of the "catechists" of liberation theology in forming Christian Base Communities (CEBs) in the 1970s. The catechists (or lay priests) led discussions about Christ's teachings from the Bible and, out of the belief that poverty is not God's will, politicized the people at the same time. The community developed an organization in which the work has been for the benefit of everyone and has been the result of everyone working together: "No es para ganar dinero; es para todo, y todo en grupo" [It's not for financial gain; it's for everyone and everyone as a group]. They have succeeded in developing many different collective projects in which the people share the benefits, for example, a butcher shop, artesanía production, and a health clinic (including herb production). Women have formed study groups and, through talking about gender relations, have brought about more egalitarian relationships. The community as a whole has become involved in political affairs and collectively supports one of the progressive parties.

The tortillería collective was able to purchase the tortilla-making equipment with a grant from Holland (MXN $60,000 pesos or Cdn. $7,500). The Mexican NGO, Equipo Pueblo (People's Team), provided the connection to the Dutch funding body. At first they worked in borrowed space, but now they have a place of their own. The tortillería was started by a group of about ten women. Some of the women left and the spouses of others joined in. Now four couples are involved in this collective. They operate two tortillerías, one larger than the other. At any one time, two of the couples operate the large tortillería, one couple operates the smaller one, and the fourth couple takes their turn to rest or to buy provisions in the neighbouring city. The tortillerías run seven days a week from 6:00 a.m. to 8:30 p.m. They produce over three hundred kilograms of tortillas each day.

The tortilla makers explained that the project is good for the whole community. Having locally produced tortillas means better-quality tortillas at better prices for the people. The four couples work collectively—they elect a president and a treasurer for a two-year period, and have been taking turns this way since 1997. In addition to the benefits for the broader community, the couples in the collective have been able to provide opportunities for their children to study in the nearby city.

Income-Generation Projects with External Support

IN THIS GROUPING OF PROJECTS where external support is integral to increasing people's ability to sustain themselves and their families, there are two projects led by civil society organizations, one that is a quasi-governmental program, and two early-stage projects that are being facilitated by committed individuals. One of the civil society organizations is the Women's Economic Equality Society in the Canadian province of Nova Scotia, and the other is a collective named Luna Creciente (Crescent Moon) in Chiapas, Mexico. The quasi-governmental program is the Casa de las Artesanías (House of Crafts) in Michoacán, Mexico. The two projects with leadership from individuals are the *amate* paper painters in Guerrero, Mexico, and an embroidery collective in Veracruz, Mexico.

Women's Economic Equality (WEE) Society in Nova Scotia, Canada

The WEE Society promotes women's economic well-being by fostering their "full participation in the social and economic well-being of the province" (WEE Society, n.d., "Our History" section). The organization was founded in 1996 by a group of dedicated women and is based on their commitment to developing community economic development (CED) opportunities that take women's realities into account. They have been seeking out avenues and partnerships in order to provide resources and learning opportunities for women, usually on a project-by-project basis. One example is IT Works for Women, which provides computer-technology learning sessions for women in a comfortable manner—scheduled two half-days a week with child care provided and refurbished computers available for those who need them.

Luna Creciente Collective in Chiapas, Mexico

Luna Creciente (Crescent Moon) is an autonomous collective in San Cristóbal, Chiapas, which earns its own income from its café, bookstore, and artesanía sales in order to assist various artisan co-operatives. One of the co-operatives that it supports is Jolom Mayaetik, which means "Mayan Weavers" in the Mayan Tzotzil language. The Jolom Mayaetik weavers do most of their work on back-strap looms with which they create such products as clothing, table runners, and wall hangings; however, some of the members use pedal looms and others do embroidery work. They began their work as a collective in 1984, but in 1996 there was a division and it is the Jolom Mayaetik weavers who continue to work as a co-operative.

They have a building in San Cristóbal with a storage room for supplies and a large work/meeting room with good light for the textile work, as well as a patio, where the cooking area and washroom are located. The women sell their artesanía in San Cristóbal, as well as in other parts of Mexico and in the United States through arrangements facilitated by Luna Creciente. The Jolom Mayaetik organization elects an executive, but interestingly, in addition to the executive roles common in the North, two of the members are elected to be "guardians" of the organization. The guardians have a leadership role in helping the group identify and address issues in order to promote cohesion and prevent division in the group.

Casa de las Artesanías in Michoacán, Mexico

The Casa de las Artesanías (House of Crafts) (CASART) in the Mexican state of Michoacán is a quasi-governmental organization that has a state mandate and funding, but is structurally separate from the state. Its mandate to promote the artisan sector is related to the state government's economic development priorities. It operates out of a former convent in the historical centre of Morelia, the state capital, where it has its main store for artisan products, a museum, and its offices. CASART works closely with an artisans organization, Unión Estatal de Artesanos de Michoacán (State Federation of Michoacán Artisans) (UNEAMICH), which it fostered in order to have a representative structure for participation by the artisans from the various communities in the marketing endeavours and in determining priorities.

The artisans involved are producers, not simply vendors, who use the traditional materials and methods practised in Indigenous communities for centuries. Their products include such things as pottery and ceramics, woven and embroidered textiles, wood carving, copper products, musical instruments, and toys. Frequently, particular communities have specialized in distinct artisan traditions—an outcome, perhaps, of the work of Vasco de Quiroga, the first bishop of Michoacán in the 1530s, who encouraged the development of communal towns around Lake Pátzcuaro (Verástique, 2000). For example, in the town of Capula, artisans make a well-recognized form of traditional pottery, and in Santa Cruz the women embroider folkloric scenes on blouses and household items. Most of the artisans incorporate their craft into their family life along with their subsistence food production and home-maintenance activities and enjoy the independence and freedom of having neither a boss nor employees.

CASART sees its role as strengthening the sustainability of the artisans' livelihood in a dialogical method where knowledge from marketing and science influences production in a manner that retains traditions as much as possible. The long history of popular markets and fairs is the basis for large shows and competitions that are widely publicized through advanced media, thus attracting many buyers. Some exhibitions are annual festivals in regular places, such as one during Holy Week in Uruapan, but additional opportunities are sought out in a variety of settings. The artisans organization UNEAMICH, comprising approximately five thousand members, is very involved in these marketing events. As well, CASART operates seven retail stores, in addition to the store in Morelia, located in other parts of the state of Michoacán, in another Mexican state, and in California.

Traditional methods are adapted, such as in the production of pots for cooking beans, which had rounded bottoms when they were used for cooking in wood fires and eating on earthen floors; now consumers need pots with flat bottoms for cooking on stoves and setting on tables. As another example, figures and sculptures made from corn cane paste require gluten from orchid bulbs, which are scarce; thus CASART's researchers are investigating means of propagating orchids in vitro and in greenhouses. In addition to research, training in using the new methods is provided to the artisans in order to continuously improve the products.

One of CASART's priorities is helping the artisan communities to obtain registered trademarks in order to protect the name and integrity of the crafts that are part of their cultural heritage. This is in response to concerns that CASART staff heard from the artisans about unfair replication and competition from outside the communities and often from countries where labour is cheap. The makers of the famous Purépecha guitars from the village of Paracho were among those expressing these concerns in the 1990s. CASART assists the producers of particular crafts to constitute themselves as civil associations and to legally register trademarks for their products. The cloth tags used on fabrics and the hologram identifiers used on pottery to display the trademark are produced for the artisans by CASART.

Two examples of artisan collectives that are member organizations in UNEAMICH as well as civil associations supported by CASART illustrate the workings of this quasi-governmental program. The first example is from a community that has specialized in making pottery. Only thirty years ago nearly all of the people were potters and there were probably three hundred family workshops; however, now there are only about eighty workshops since the materials have become expensive and products are not selling well. Producers from China came to Mexico, and the Mexican people very willingly taught them how to produce the pottery, never thinking that the Chinese people would replicate the pottery in factories and undersell the Mexican producers in their own country. Thus, the primary objective of the local potters association for becoming a legally constituted civil association was to register a collective trademark for their pottery, a process that seems to take between ten months to three years in total. Another important advantage is the potential for the civil association to receive funding for the establishment of a warehouse for storing primary materials, which will allow the association to buy in bulk and keep supplies on hand. The potter I interviewed is typical in that he learned his craft as a child growing up in this community, but he is unique in that he is educated as a physician. It is because of this dual expertise that he is also involved in promoting the production of lead-free ceramics with support from a national program. From the one remaining elder in the community, who uses totally natural materials and the pre-Hispanic method, he learned how to give the pottery a shine without using lead or the high-temperature processing used to fire ceramics. Using this technique, but with a different design, he taught this method to youth in the community. Connections to other government funding bodies for projects like this one are another valuable benefit that CASART can provide to artisans.

The second example is from a different community with its own specialization—the production of *manta* (cotton and acrylon fabrics made on traditional pedal looms). In this case, too, the artisan work is part of the heritage of the community and of the family, but since the economic downturn, which began in 2008, products have not been selling well and parents are questioning whether they should encourage their children to carry on this tradition. Some of the producers sought the assistance of CASART and constituted themselves as a civil association with hopes of addressing some of their concerns. They also had producers from another area (in their case, within Mexico) who were saying that their products were from the Michoacán town; thus obtaining the trademark now protects their products from these imitations. For this community, the primary objective of forming an association was to be eligible for assistance in establishing a storage facility for their primary materials so they could buy in bulk at wholesale prices and also avoid supply shortages. However, in 2009, lending organizations were still requiring impossible collateral (the members' homes are also part of their heritage) and high interest rates (e.g., 18 percent per year). The other concern the artisans had also hoped would be addressed through their involvement with CASART was the need for more marketing opportunities. However, there has been only one annual festival and one out-of-state opportunity for them in the past year. As a result of these disappointments, some of the original members have left the association and others feel used by the government, which promotes tourism by emphasizing the beauty of the artesanía, but offers the artisans little support.

The artisans organization UNEAMICH elects its executive and the president works with the local civil associations to understand their needs, advocate with CASART and other government programs, arrange for training courses and workshops in their communities, as well as foster marketing opportunities and coordinate the artisans' participation in exhibitions. Often the shows require the artisans to travel in a bus to a larger centre, so the president, Emilia Reyes, needs to find places for the artisans to stay while they are away from home, as well as oversee the production of promotional materials and the events. In 2009, each of the associations with registered trademarks were invited to participate in the annual festival in Uruapan as well as in one other show; however, UNEAMICH would like to see the itinerant shows increased to at least twice per year. Emilia described four dreams she holds for UNEAMICH: (1) a larger role for CASART in marketing the artesanía, such as buying more pieces from the associations and selling them in more places in North America and in Europe as well; (2) social security coverage for the artisans if they suffer a work-related injury; (3) more accessible loans for the civil associations; and (4) increased educational opportunities for the artisans' children.

Amate Paper Painters in Guerrero, Mexico

In a marginalized city neighbourhood in the state of Guerrero, many poor women earn money by painting colourful, folkloric images on paper from the bark of the *amate* tree. They depict typical scenes of everyday life in the countryside with, for example, ducks at a pond, a dog, some roosters, a *palapa* (an open-walled building with a woven palm-leaf roof), children playing, people hoeing a field, sometimes a celebration like a wedding, and always a blue sky with a brilliant sun. One of the painters, Sara, explained that normally the women can complete one of the paintings on a twenty-eight-centimetre by thirty-five-and-a-half-centimetre pre-stamped paper in one and a half hours, and complete about forty of them in a week while taking care of their family and household responsibilities. The women in the Guerrero neighbourhood have an arrangement with a merchant from outside the area who lends them the unpainted, but pre-stamped, amate papers and pays them about MXN $10 pesos per painted paper. The artisans, however, have to pay for the paint. Thus, in an average week, each woman earns about MXN $400 pesos and spends about MXN $200 pesos on paint, making about MXN $200 pesos or Cdn. $20 per week in profit for sixty hours of work. This results in about Cdn. 33 cents per hour—only half of the Mexican minimum wage of Cdn. $5.00 for an eight-hour day (67 cents per hour).

There are between fifteen and twenty artisans in the neighbourhood working with the merchant who brings the amate papers and pays them for painting them. They have been brought together by an informal community organizer to talk about their work. The painters believe that the merchant hires Indigenous women to sell the pieces at much higher prices in the cities. Several of the artisans realize it would be better if they worked together to buy the paper directly, but Sara said, at this point, they have been unable to find it. They also know there would be no guarantee that they would be able to sell the paintings if they unite to work collectively without the merchant. So, the idea of forming a co-operative is beginning to be considered and the community organizer is helping them to explore some of the questions they have raised.

An Embroidery Collective in Veracruz, Mexico

Another project that had not yet come to fruition was a women's embroidery collective in a fairly remote village in Veracruz. The secondary school teacher had been meeting with the ten women twice a week, teaching them to sew (by hand), to embroider in a variety of styles, and to crochet. As a result they were producing embroidered clothing, tablecloths, and tortilla cloths.

The problem they faced was finding a way to sell these products. They have saturated the market in the local village by selling house to house and at two annual fairs. Taking the products to nearby villages hasn't been very successful, and going to the capital city of Veracruz is expensive and may not result in sales, so this challenge remained to be solved. ∎

FIVE

HEALTH, HOUSING, AND THE ENVIRONMENT

T HIS CLUSTER OF CASE EXAMPLES pertaining to social mobilization regarding health, housing, and the environment is divided into three groups. One group comprises projects that focus primarily on health concerns. A second grouping includes projects that deal with health and a variety of related matters, including housing and the environment. A third grouping is dedicated to communities engaged in struggles to protect their environments (and, consequently, their health), specifically from the activities of Canadian mining companies.

Communities Organizing to Promote Health and Wellness

THE RESEARCH INCLUDED three projects with health and wellness as their primary focus. These include a collective of health promoters in a rural parish in the state of Guerrero, a women's collective in Mexico City that prepares medicinal products from plants, and a women's group in Cuernavaca, Morelos, which provides health services using low-cost natural remedies.

The Natural Medicine Collective in a Guerrero, Mexico Parish

A team of eight health promoters works with the support of a parish priest, Padre Pedro Felipe, in rural Guerrero to provide health care using natural medicine in their own communities and to provide training for it in the wider community. Distinct from professional naturopathy, the natural medicine (sometimes called *medicina popular* or the people's medicine) includes health promotion through natural foods and healthy lifestyles; treatment using medicinal plants in syrups, ointments, and teas; and more complex practices such as reflexology, massage, cure through energies (rooted in Eastern philosophy), and *temascal* baths (an Indigenous tradition, similar to a sweat lodge, that has been rediscovered in recent decades). Spiritual and cognitive processes are engaged as well in the accompanying prayerful ceremony and critical discussions about the economic and socio-political causes of illness.

Padre Pedro Felipe explained that health promotion fits within the social ministry responsibility of a pastor, consistent with Christ's healing actions, complementing the prophetic and liturgical responsibilities. He said that fostering knowledge of natural medicine was encouraged by Bishop Don Sergio Méndez in Cuernavaca, Morelos, who was a strong proponent of liberation theology. The use of natural medicines also has a basis in Indigenous tradition predating the Spanish Conquest. The traditional *curanderos* (healers) used copal, corn, hallucinogens, and candles in their diagnostic practices, and for treatments they used medicinal plants, massage, temascal, and ceremonial prayers. Natural medicine provides an alternative to the often expensive and distant treatments prescribed by conventional medicine.

The training for practising natural medicine uses a train-the-trainer model. Padre Pedro Felipe has trained through a university program in Mexico City and is qualified to provide instruction for beginning levels. He arranges for other trainers to come in to do the more advanced training sessions. He and his team hold conferences each year for health promoters throughout the state. It is common to hold the conferences in one of the churches where people can sleep as well as prepare meals with the produce they bring, thus keeping costs low for registrants. Guest practitioners often present free of charge, with participants covering their travel costs. Smaller workshops are offered more frequently in the coordination team members' local parishes. As well, the team meets quarterly to do their planning and share experiences in their work with their own communities. Sometimes, in order to be efficient in their use of limited time and money, one member of the team will attend a course or workshop out of town and then share what he or she has learned with the others. As a result of their training, the priest stated that "these health promoters are doing very good work now."

The coordination team began their work in 2004. It is composed of men and women, although the majority are women, and they elect their own executive. They are considering charging more for some of their services, rather than often providing the consultations and some of the prepared medicines for free or below cost. Currently, "the people pay what they can." However, Padre Pedro Felipe noted, the health promoters need to cover their costs for the medicines, which would be around Cdn. $2–$3 per treatment. Some community people might not be able to pay, but others could afford Cdn. $10–$15. This would balance out in the end and would provide the team with money for some of their workshops and other projects.

A Mexico City Collective Preparing Medicinal Products from Plants

A women's collective in Mexico City grows medicinal plants, prepares medicines and body care products, and sells them in various markets, as well as in their own massage and production centre. The project was initiated by Margo, a Mayan woman who had been involved in community organizing work in Guatemala and came to Mexico as a refugee. The women she brought together were interested in finding a way to address their families' economic needs. Margo suggested some options, including doing large-quantity cooking together, and the women chose the idea of working with medicinal plants. Once the core group had selected a focus, they invited others who were interested in working with them. Each woman brought a plant that she already knew to the next meeting and they shared their knowledge. As a group they went into the countryside to look for plants that they recognized. They then looked up scientific studies about the plants to learn more about the various uses, contraindications, etc. In follow-up discussions, they ensured that every woman's opinions were heard and that time was always provided to share what was happening in their lives as women.

They studied together to learn more, such as how to prepare the medicines and what the recommended dosages are. Some left because they wanted to earn money rapidly and didn't have the patience for such a long-term project; others who had the necessary commitment joined them. They also took time to develop their consciousness about the earth, nature, and the environment. They reflected on how their ancestors saw nature, what happens with the garbage now, the relationship between different parts of the universe, and how we are affected if, for example, we don't have water. This emphasized the importance of their common interests that were much greater than economic interests alone. Some left, but those with the common interest remained. It takes time to build a committed group for a long-term project, Margo said.

The women found land to grow their plants; did the planting, harvesting, preparation of the medicines; and looked for people to work in solidarity with them, particularly in marketing the products. They work every other day in the greenhouse or the centre and they meet weekly as a group. By 2009, they had been operating for six years. Their elections are every two years and they have an executive with a president, a secretary, a treasurer, and a person who is in charge of the stock and distributes the project's earnings among the members. The members feel it has been beneficial to them and their families, as well as to people in the larger community who purchase the natural products.

The Cuernavaca Group Providing Natural Remedies in Morelos, Mexico

The final example of a group that came together to provide low-cost natural health care is a women's group in Cuernavaca, a city in the state of Morelos. Their leader, Yolanda, said their work also arose from meetings in the local Christian Base Communities. The members did their analysis of the realities of the communities and concluded that one of the biggest concerns was the many illnesses among people who had no resources for medical care. The parish priest encouraged them to study natural health care methods at a church-related centre in Cuernavaca, where they learned about methods from Chinese medicine to detect organ problems, Bach flower therapies, and footbaths to detoxify the body. After four years of training, and while they continued their learning, eighteen of the women began to offer non-profit consultations three afternoons a week, even though many of the women needed to do other low-paid work to contribute to meeting their families' needs. They continued their learning through the Centre for the Study of Medicinal Plants at the University of Morelos, which has an herb nursery. There they had classes every Sunday and learned about the curative uses of various plants. They took field trips into the countryside to learn to recognize the plants, see how they grow, and hear from the Indigenous elders and curanderos about how they are used. They went to Indigenous communities near Cuernavaca to tap into the traditional knowledge about systems of the human body, various illnesses, personal characteristics, and interpersonal dynamics, as well as traditional practices regarding the use of particular plants, aromatherapy, fresh-air exercises, massage, various therapies, iris analysis, and cleansing baths such as temascal. This was a very broad program of study that took another three years. However, fifteen women completed it, even though some of them were older. They continue to take up training opportunities when they arise—more recently in laboratory analysis and Chinese acupuncture.

In 2009 four of the women were working in a collective and the other eleven were working out of their homes, although the full group of fifteen continued to come together for meetings and training workshops. The collective was given space, rent-free, where they provide consultations, treatments (including massage), and traditional herbal medicines that they have prepared. They have a listing of suggested prices, which are set at levels that are intended to be affordable for the community. However, no one is turned away. When people cannot afford the suggested prices, they are invited to pay what they can. Occasionally that is nothing at all. A portion of the income is used to purchases materials for their clinic. The remainder is divided equally among the four women. Unfortunately, it is still not enough to cover the women's living costs and they need to take on part-time paid work. But, Yolanda said, the women are not concerned that the clinic doesn't provide them enough to live on. Their motivation, from the beginning, has been to provide a much-needed community service. "The important thing is that they cure them." The church has always been their inspiration and source of support.

Communities Dealing with Health and Related Matters

IN THE STUDY there were three examples where the communities were dealing with health and related matters. The first example is a team of women promoting human and environmental well-being in Tejalpa, Morelos. The second is the Casa de Salud Popular (People's Health Centre) in a marginalized neighbourhood within a city in southern Veracruz. The last example is a neighbourhood association in a marginalized community on the outskirts of a city in the state of Guerrero.

The Tejalpa Health and Environmental Well-being Project in Morelos, Mexico

Six women comprise the Equipo de Promotoras Ambientales de Tejalpa (Tejalpa Team of Environmental Promoters)—Tejalpa being a town adjacent to the larger city of Cuernavaca, Morelos. The team operates a health and wellness centre, as well as a recycling centre for their community. The team, led by Estela Bello Soto, began their work in the 1980s as a women's centre, organizing women in the community to develop collective projects to generate income and holding workshops on gender issues and natural medicines.

One of their first projects was a community garden, collectively owned by the women, to grow corn and soy for their families' consumption. However, industrial contamination of the water soon meant that irrigation of crops was no longer possible. This raised the community's consciousness of environmental issues and they developed the recycling program. They provided educational programs about separating household refuse, established a collection program, and obtained a storage and packaging depot. Now they are selling the separated materials to the industries that can use them.

The team became incorporated under its new name in 1995. The original women's centre was replaced by the Casa de Salud Malintzin (the Malintzin Health Centre), which was built with the help of architecture students from the University of Washington. The students came for three months at a time for two years in a row, and they provided their knowledge, their financial support, and their physical labour. The centre offers health consultations and treatments using homeopathy, herbal medicines, reiki, massage, and temascal baths. For women, workshops are offered on nutrition and gender issues, as well as self-help groups. The team member who leads these activities explained that women in their community are often stressed—some because their husbands have gone north to work and others because of the strong patriarchal traditions; through the natural healing methods, the women are able to recover their power. There are services for children with problems in learning, language development, and emotional well-being, as well as workshops on parenting. There is also a group for older people that deals with issues they face like abandonment, and supporting projects they take on such as a vegetable garden with an organic water-purification system.

The team has been able to obtain funding from foundations for some of their programs, such as the one for children, which has allowed them to hire some specialized staff. The health services and products are provided at cost to their clients. However, the collective sometimes has to use revenue from other projects to finance the health centre. For example, they have a machine that they use to prepare the plastics for recycling, which they rent out for other recycling centres to use. The six-member team manages the affairs of the organization with rotating executive positions and a consensus model of decision making. Although they are heavily involved in the work, the six team members do not draw a salary: "Nos mantenemos" [We maintain ourselves], Estela said. This commitment to the community is particularly generous, given the time the women have invested in preparing themselves for this work and the time they have needed to spend away from their own families.

Casa de Salud Popular: The People's Health Centre in Veracruz, Mexico

The People's Health Centre is located in a marginalized neighbourhood on the outskirts of a southern city in the state of Veracruz, where people without adequate housing participated in a land takeover and subsequently settled and obtained title to the land. At the time of its founding in the early 1980s, the community received tremendous support from a Catholic priest, who lived very simply and taught the community the principles of liberation theology, and that they could accomplish much if they were united. The women formed working groups to produce and sell goods like honey and fruit preserves, and became committed to working together to help the community as a whole. Many community members were inspired by this priest and, after he died very young, they have continued to deal with their challenges collectively.

The first large issue they took on was the sickness that resulted from flies carrying pathogens from the adjacent garbage dump to their kitchens. Mountains of garbage were brought to the dump by establishments from all over the region, including the hospital. One woman recalled seeing a dog chewing on a human arm. Because of the contamination of their food, many people became sick and babies got diarrhea and died. The community asked the municipality to ban further dumping in their residential area. The municipality refused, stating that the garbage had been there before they had moved to the neighbourhood. The community felt incensed—"it was as if the garbage had more rights than we as people"—so they kept a vigil at the entrance to the dump for nine years! Finally the municipality gave in and built a proper landfill site in a non-residential area and covered the remaining garbage in the neighbourhood with truckloads of earth.

After the garbage problem was solved, fewer children died, but some still did due to malnutrition and other poverty-related problems, so the women decided to develop a health centre for the community. They worked to obtain title to the land where the garbage had been. While some were constructing the initial consultation room, others learned what they could from the Indigenous peoples and others about elementary health care. In the spring of 1994, they opened the People's Health Centre. In 1996, with some funding from Canada, they were able to obtain the necessary equipment to do Pap tests, which are then analyzed by a laboratory outside the community. Bit by bit, the women have expanded the building and their services. By 2004 the centre included, under one roof, an open-air reception area; three consultation rooms that are also used for Pap tests and acupuncture; a small pharmacy with natural and homeopathic remedies; and the most recent addition, a meeting room for approximately thirty people with a kitchen, as well as washrooms. Separate from the main building is a dry latrine—the waste from this is used as fertilizer for plants.

The centre is open three days a week in the primary neighbourhood and two afternoons a week in a palapa in a nearby neighbourhood, staffed completely by community volunteers. Volunteers must participate in training at the centre for three days every month for twelve months in order to become health promoters. After they are trained, the health promoters continue to meet as a full group of about twenty on a Friday every three months to do their planning. The people who come to the clinic need to pay for the medical materials, but the services are free. About once every six months the health promoters all receive an honorarium, and once every year they do a program evaluation. Some of the health promoters, along with other volunteers from the neighbourhood, engage in volunteer work outside of the consultation hours to support the health centre. One important task is preparing the natural remedies and, one Monday morning, I observed four women clean the centre thoroughly and prepare syrup from honey and aloe vera, which they poured into sterilized jars. Other working groups generate income so the centre can purchase homeopathic medicines and meet its other costs, such as utilities. Making amaranth cereal bars and embroidered items were some of the fundraising activities I observed. Most of the women work as domestic help on the other days of the week when they are not volunteering at the centre.

Addressing housing needs was the third project undertaken by the women in the Veracruz neighbourhood. In the mid-1990s, there were several households in the neighbourhood with very inadequate housing; by 2004 six houses had been built through their collective efforts. I visited three of the households and learned that previously each of them had been living in one-room buildings made of corrugated sheet metal. One of the community members sought out information through the Unión de Colonos Inquilinos Solicitantes de Viviendas del Sur de Veracruz (Southern Veracruz Union of Tenant Settlers Seeking Housing) (UCISV Ver), which has an office in the state capital. She discovered Habitat for Humanity, but there was a slow process (six years) of learning the requirements for receiving loans and getting to the top of the priority/waiting list. In the end they received loans of approximately Cdn. $4,000 for building materials for each house, which each household is repaying at about Cdn. $25 per month.

When the community received the Habitat for Humanity approval, they were able to proceed with one house per year and they needed to decide whose house was the greatest priority. The first priority was a family of four with a six-year-old daughter who had experienced a lot of sickness. The second priority was a family of seven in which the husband had not been consistently responsible in contributing to the family. The third one was a tiny, single woman getting on in years. On average, it took about three months to build each house. All six of the women helped with each house, and husbands and other family members participated when they were available. The resultant houses are sturdy and dry, but modest. Much of the cooking and washing continues to be done outside using the shelter provided by the original corrugated metal structures. The community is looking at helping with houses for two other households in the neighbourhood. In the meantime, they have also been fighting for municipal water and sewers.

The organization was operating very informally, but entirely democratically, in 2004. One of their members, Maria de los Angeles Prieto Linares, functioned as its coordinator, but had no formal title. She was chairing the group's meeting when I asked if I could study the program. She was leading a women's weight-loss group when I visited one morning, and providing medical consultation for a community member on another occasion. She is credited by the other community members with being the person who has located the resources and provided the leadership that has made their accomplishments possible. She is single and lives in a simple house with another single woman who has paid employment. This housemate pays all the bills and Maria de los Angeles does the domestic work—she described it as a form of sharing that works for them. The organization was beginning the process of formalizing to become a legally recognized civil association, so that it could receive funds in its own name and feel secure about the organization's longevity beyond the contribution period of the current core members.

The Neighbourhood Settlers and Community Founders in Guerrero, Mexico

Another example of people taking some marginal land on the outskirts of a city to settle and build a community is in the state of Guerrero. When I met with some of the community founders in 2009, the earliest settlers told me they had arrived twenty-two years earlier in 1987. Some had been involved in an urban dwellers movement out of which a specific non-profit organization was formed to fight for ownership of the land they now inhabit. The non-profit organization, in turn, sold it in parcels at very affordable prices to people who wanted to be part of the community. Cástula, a feisty woman of seventy-nine years, showed me a certificate that she had received in recognition for her struggles on behalf of the community in the 1980s. One of the young men involved in the struggle had been assassinated, and she had been held in jail, although only for two hours.

The land was covered in thorn bushes and the community members had to work with machetes to clear the scrub to build their houses and create walking paths. The initial houses were built with sticks, wooden boards, and cardboard. The men worked together, using picks and sticks, to dig a well. After four months they had a well about nine metres deep that they could draw water from using buckets. The next task was to create an entrance into the community and widen the paths to prepare a roadway, which was necessary before any services could be put in. Again they worked "like ants," everyone co-operating together to help however they could.

They were without electricity for two years—before that they depended on candlelight. They approached the federal electrical commission and had to provide documentation to prove the size of the population and the financial viability of the project. The commission paid for some of the costs, but the community, together, had to ensure that the rest of the costs would be paid. Again, the community co-operated to ensure that this project would come to fruition. The process to get municipal water was similar, but required more work. A more detailed study was needed to document what was needed and they had to put a lot more pressure on the water commission to get them to respond. Community members demonstrated their conviction by occupying the commission's office daily. They took turns in groups of seven—it wasn't confrontational, but it was continuous. Finally, after two years, a water pipe brought water into the community. A commission employee arrives daily to turn on the tap. Each street receives water once a week, and they have organized it so that each street knows which day is theirs. The people go with their pails and carry the water home to fill their drums and other water containers. Still, this is not drinkable water; for drinking, they have to purchase purified water in large jugs.

After acquiring water, the community worked together to establish a kindergarten. In order to accomplish this, they had to do a census of the kindergarten-age population. The next struggle was to establish a primary school in the community. Group members described how Mexico has many qualified teachers and many children needing education. What is lacking is an adequate budget for school buildings and teachers' salaries. Sometimes teachers will work in a salaried position for one shift in the day and as volunteers in the other shift (children go to school from 7:00 a.m. to 1:00 p.m., or from 1:30 p.m. to 7:30 p.m.). The community members approached the education ministry, and some teachers came door-to-door to register the children. There were enough children of primary-school age to justify a school with six teachers. The federal and state governments agreed to a tripartite cost-sharing arrangement with the community to proceed with building the school. Each family paid about Cdn. $30 as their share of the materials cost and contributed manual labour. After three years the school was ready for children to attend. Although education is free, there is still a Cdn. $2 entrance fee, plus the cost of uniforms and notebooks. They are pleased with these achievements and their most recent one, which was to obtain public transportation. Volkswagen vans, called *combis*, drive through the neighbourhood, transporting people between workplaces, senior schools, markets, services, and their homes.

The community members said that they still lack a health centre. Here, they said, one could die from a scorpion bite. However, they worry that the community is losing its spirit. Partly, this is a sense of disillusionment that their previous political candidate didn't work out for them. Another problem is that the community has grown from the original 140 parcels of land (usually one family each) to include another estimated thirty families in the extended area. It has been difficult to include these people in the neighbourhood and instil the same sense of community. That is one of the challenges that lie ahead.

Communities in Conflict with Canadian Mining Companies

THE FINAL GROUP in the health and environment cluster includes two communities engaged in struggles to protect their health and environments from the activities of Canadian mining companies. For both communities, their human rights and cultural continuity were at stake. In the Mexican state of Guerrero, an ejido (a community with collectively titled land) was dealing with a Canadian mining company that had a concession for the minerals beneath their land. In the Canadian province of British Columbia, a First Nation community was fighting a mining company's proposal to turn a lake in their territory into a tailings pond. These are the two examples in which data collection included participant observation, so they are described in greater detail than others.

An Ejido Struggles against Canadian Mining in Guerrero, Mexico

Exploitation of gold from the land of the Mexican people dates back to the colonial era of enrichment for the Spanish Empire. Mexico's War of Independence (1810) and Revolution (1910) were fought to bring the country's resources under the control of its people. However, the current global neoliberal arrangements have encouraged changes in Mexico's Constitution and legislation such that ejido lands can be sold and mineral rights can be granted to foreign companies, as noted in Chapter 3.

The Guerrero community studied is located in a gold belt, where a concession held by a Canadian mining company is estimated to contain Cdn. $2.5 billion worth of gold. Although the Mexican government grants rights to subsurface minerals, access via surface land must be negotiated with the property owners. In this ejido, each of the 110 families received about Cdn. $18 for the first three years of exploration. However, the *ejidatarios* (people who collectively own the ejido lands) are peasant farmers and they began to experience neurological, gastrointestinal, and skin problems and noticed that plant and animal life had deteriorated as well. They had their water tested and concluded that the damage to their health and the environment was due to the presence of arsenic at 11.5 times acceptable levels. They sought help from a man and, after he became ill, his daughter in the nearby town to read and explain the mining company's offers and contracts. The ejidatarios demanded that the company not do mountain explorations upstream from their living area. However, their pleas to the company and various government departments were fruitless, and members of the community heard that the state governor's family has financial interests in mining machinery. In 2005, the federal government granted exploitation concessions to the mining company. Two ejidos formed a coalition, but the company created divisions. The company "bought" one of the ejido leaders, who accepted less than half of what the community requested. Similarly, the company negotiated separately with the other ejido, successfully splitting the coalition. Non-violent protests were staged by people from the contaminated ejido. In 2008, they blocked the entrance to the mine, preventing trucks and equipment from entering. Families took turns at the blockade and it was then that the threats, shootings, and detainments began. Unfortunately, these are not unusual. Although not all the Canadian mining companies are behaving badly, a McGill research group suggests that thirteen of the 520 Canadian projects operating in Mexico at the time of their study resulted in open conflict (Frechette & Studnicki-Gizbert, 2010).

In the winter and spring of 2009, I was told about the threats being made to the family of the father and daughter who had assisted the ejido and I was asked as a Canadian if there was any way I could help. In April 2009, a private members' bill, C-300 (Corporate Social Responsibility of Mining, Oil, & Gas Companies in Developing Countries) came before the Canadian Parliament for second reading, and I began to advocate for its approval. The bill, introduced by Liberal John McKay, was intended to require Canadian mining companies to respect environmental and human rights in their operations in developing countries or forgo public funding through Export Development Canada and the Canada Pension Plan. In Mexico, Red Mexicana de Afectados por la Minería (Network of Mexican Communities Affected by Mining) (REMA) was active in mobilizing people against the environmental and human rights abuses that were occurring in relation to mining in many parts of the country. However, as described in Part I, Mariano Abarca, an activist opposing the Canadian Blackfire exploration mining operation in

Chiapas, was assassinated prior to hosting a REMA meeting in August 2009, and another REMA activist, Bety Cariño, was assassinated in April 2010 while taking part in a humanitarian mission in Oaxaca.

In the Guerrero ejido, in August 2009, one of the community members who was engaged in protest against the mine was shot in what seemed to be set up to look like a conflict between families. However, while the man was recuperating in hospital, military and police personnel surrounded the hospital and, when the man was discharged, he went into hiding out of fear that they would kill him. Shortly thereafter, twelve to fourteen heavily armed police in state police vehicles arrived in the ejido village and violently removed men of the injured man's family from their homes and arrested them without warrants. When the father came into the house and asked why they were taking his son, the police asked if he, too, was a family member. When he said yes, the police said, "Then you're coming too!" In the winter of 2010, nearly two dozen ejidatarios and the young woman assisting them went to the state human rights office to report the ongoing threats, and while they were there giving their statement, the officer received a telephone threat that someone in his family would be injured if he continued to take their statement.

In the winter of 2010, some of my students and colleagues were in Mexico with me for a ten-day field trip. I was able to bring the young woman and two of the ejidatarios to our location to share their story with us. I had previously received updates subsequent to the spring of 2009 from the father through email and by reading a Mexican national newspaper, but it was important for me to hear it in person. While arranging for the meeting, I became increasing aware of the danger the young woman and the ejidatarios were facing, and that it was possible for them to make the trip only when accompanied by non-governmental human rights workers. After hearing their testimony, some of my students and colleagues were committed to participating with me in advocacy in Canada to stop the environmental and human rights abuses. I kept in touch with the Guerrero community through the human rights NGO that had accompanied them because of the high likelihood that the telephone and email messages of my contacts in the community were being intercepted. Since we had videotaped material from the meeting with the Guerrero community, I briefly considered requesting a meeting with the mining company at their Toronto headquarters. However, I realized that identifying myself to the company could endanger me and my associates during future trips to Mexico. Furthermore, the original mining corporations had already sold their interests to a new corporation, which, in turn, had changed its name since the purchase. If the rights abuses were a surprise and a concern to the Canadian company, they could simply sell to another company and the abuse could continue.

Instead, we engaged in advocacy for approval of Bill C-300 at its third reading in the fall of 2010. We spoke with all three of our local federal representatives, showing them the video of the testimony we had heard, and we participated in a letter-writing campaign along with members of a Canada-wide coalition for socially responsible mining. In the end, Bill C-300 was defeated during third reading in a 140-to-134 vote in the House of Commons with all Conservative members of Parliament voting against the bill and all Opposition members voting for it or absenting themselves from the vote.

In Guerrero, it appears that the majority in the ejido have decided to accept the agreement proposed by the mining company. This should come as no surprise given the low incomes of Mexican peasant farmers and the troubles that befall those who protest mining activities. The young woman appears to have been pretty much isolated, and her father spends most of his time in the United States. At least this is the best information I have been able to confirm through discussions with the human rights NGO, which completed its work with the protest leaders in 2011. The father and daughter who assisted the ejidatarios needed to change email addresses and cellphone numbers frequently because their pursuers were intercepting their communications so, regrettably, I have lost contact with them.

A First Nation Contests a Mining Proposal in British Columbia, Canada

In the Chilcotin territory of the British Columbia interior, Taseko Mines proposed a gold and copper mine that involved draining a glacial lake, known as Teztan Biny (Fish Lake), and using the lake as a tailings pond for the poisonous mining waste. The mining company intended to build an artificial lake and airlift twenty thousand of the over eighty-five thousand trout from Fish Lake into it. The Xeni Gwet'in, one of six First Nations communities that comprise the Tsilhqot'in (Chilcotin) Nation, were adamant that the poisons would make their way into the river systems with devastating consequences for the Indigenous culture, the fish and wildlife, and the environment of all Canadians.

Prior to 2002, disrupting a fish-bearing lake was not allowed. Now Schedule 2, which was added to the *Fisheries Act* regulations, allows for the reclassification of natural water bodies as tailings impoundment areas (Council of Canadians, 2016). In 2005, the provincial government of British Columbia endeavoured to encourage more mining activity by simplifying the claim-staking process through online access. These initiatives are in addition to free-entry legislation, stemming from feudal law, which was initiated in the gold rush era to increase settlement in the Canadian frontier (Carter-Whitney & Duncan, 2008). The free-entry legislation gives the mining industry the opportunity to stake a claim on the minerals below the surface of any land area—normal land ownership pertains only to the surface. Now, over half of British Columbia's 203 First Nations have claims staked on their territories, the government review process is speedy, and limited resources are provided for First Nations participation. When Fish Lake was studied in the spring and summer of 2010, the provincial government had already given its approval to the Taseko Mines proposal, and the federal government's Environmental Impact Assessment was underway.

The Xeni Gwet'in people and the broader Chilcotin Nation have a long history of struggle for their rights. In the legendary Chilcotin War of 1864, the Chilcotin defended their territory from gold rush incursions. In 1989 the Xeni Gwet'in, who are centred in the Nemaiah Valley, made the Declaration of the Nemaiah Aboriginal Wilderness Preserve in which they stated there would be no logging or mining or other use of the land in their territory unless the Xeni Gwet'in were involved in the decision and agreed that it was compatible with their traditional way of life, which honours both the environment and their culture (Xeni Gwet'in, 1989). In 1992, the Xeni Gwet'in and other Chilcotin First Nations established a roadblock at Henry's Crossing to stop a lumber company from cutting trees in their area, a success they celebrate annually on the first weekend in June. In 1998, the Chilcotin Nation filed their title case based on their trapline. In 2007 the judge's decision came down and the Chilcotin were found to have rights to use of the land, but title was not declared. It was the Chilcotin's appeal of the 2007 decision that led to the landmark Supreme Court ruling in 2014 recognizing Indigenous title to their unceded ancestral lands (Blaze Carlson, 2014).

Much of the Xeni Gwet'in's recent struggle has received a tremendous amount of support from numerous organizations and committed people. The Friends of the Nemaiah Valley (FONV) has been supportive since the 1980s in dealing with logging incursions and the Aboriginal Wilderness Preserve declaration. The FONV helped with raising awareness and funds for the title case and conducted a wildlife assessment in 2002, which culminated in the Xeni Gwet'in declaring the wilderness preserve also a Wild Horse Preserve. Several individual members of FONV are involved in other organizations that have also supported the Xeni Gwet'in. One example is Respecting Aboriginal Values and Environmental Needs (RAVEN), which has charitable status and is thus able to issue receipts for income tax purposes. RAVEN's focus is broader—for example, it is also concerned with the impact of the tar sands. One of RAVEN's directors is Jack Woodward, who is an authority on Indigenous law and has represented the Chilcotin on many of their cases, often pro bono. The executive director is Sue Smitten, who directed and produced the film *Blue Gold*, which describes the Xeni Gwet'in's traditional uses of Fish Lake. Similarly, one of the FONV members has created a website with a singular focus, *Protect Fish Lake*, which includes the *Blue Gold* film.

The Council of Canadians sought out the Xeni Gwet'in when they learned of Taseko Mines' proposal for Fish Lake, and the local chapter in Williams Lake, where the environmental impact assessment hearings were centred, has been very supportive. The national office of the Council of Canadians has engaged in promoting public awareness about the mining proposal in Fish Lake, and on May 27, 2010, national chair Maude Barlow visited and did a public panel presentation with Xeni Gwet'in Chief Marilyn Baptiste in Vancouver. Similarly, Mining Watch has been involved in creating public awareness and, along with the Council of Canadians, has launched a lawsuit regarding the *Fisheries Act* regulations (Schedule 2), which allow water bodies to be reclassified as tailings ponds.

Professional expertise has been provided through people like Tony Pearce, an environmental consultant, and Amy Crook, employed by the Centre for Science in Public Participation (CSP2), which "provides training and technical advice to grassroots groups on water pollution and natural resource issues, especially those related to mining" (CSP2, 2016, "What We Do" section). Amy Crook had a central role during the hearings of the federal environmental impact assessment panel in identifying potential experts and coordinating the presentations.

Networking and outreach efforts of the various organizations, especially FONV, resulted in connections with people like Karen Hurley, an instructor at the University of Victoria. In helping her students to understand the environmental impact assessment process, Karen Hurley had them look at the Fish Lake example, and some of the students did a presentation to the environmental impact assessment panel. In addition to the many organizations and individuals who were helpful, the Xeni Gwet'in and their supporters made the national media, including the Canadian Broadcasting Corporation (CBC), aware of the issues.

The Xeni Gwet'in's actions in convincing the federal environmental impact assessment panel of the problems inherent in the Taseko Mines proposal for Fish Lake were quite remarkable. In advance of the hearing, they worked diligently with their consultant Amy Crook to develop the terms of reference for the review, including ensuring that the panel held hearings in all Chilcotin communities and not only in the city of Williams Lake. With Amy Crook's assistance, they also updated the baseline assessment studies incorporating the traditional knowledge about water-flow patterns in documentation for the panel. They ensured that neighbouring First Nations communities also had an opportunity to describe the concerns beyond the Chilcotin territory, including the fear that contaminants escaping the proposed Fish Lake tailings pond enclosure would go from Fish River to the Taseko River, the Chilcotin River, the Fraser River, and into international ocean waters with impacts on the fish, and particularly the salmon, in all of those waters. The community also arranged for representation by the Union of British Columbia Indian Chiefs and the national Assembly of First Nations.

Roger Williams, former Xeni Gwet'in chief and 2010 band councillor, described some of the strong arguments that the community put forward. Although the mining company has promised to monitor the Fish Lake tailings pond for twenty years after the mine has ceased operations (following five years for preparation and twenty years of exploitation), the community's knowledge suggests that within fifty to one hundred years, the contaminants will reach the adjacent Big Onion Lake and from there, the downstream rivers. The Chilcotin people have strong doubts about the viability of an artificial lake—in fact, one elder said that making a lake is the Creator's job (Findlay, 2009). At the hearing they pointed out the discrepancy of Taseko's proposal that indicates the artificial lake would be refreshed by pumping in clean water when there is no plan to continue provision of electricity after the end of the forty-five-year program.

Marilyn Baptiste, the Xeni Gwet'in chief in 2010, communicated regularly with the community through meetings, newsletters, and informal opportunities to keep people informed about everything related to the mining proposal and to counter misinformation. Chief Baptiste tried to prepare the community for the environmental impact assessment panel hearings by continuously talking with people and encouraging them to come as groups to the hearings, to spend time there, and to convey the stories of the elders and ancestors, such as portraying the rituals with the fish and showing where the traplines are placed—the people's lived experiences. The Xeni Gwet'in leaders advocated strongly for permission to open the hearings with a traditional ceremony because this is important to the healers and the elders. The panel allowed them to bring in their hand drums, so they were able to do the drumming, two songs, and a prayer in the Chilcotin language. The mining proponents countered by opening with "O Canada."

All of the students from the Nemaiah Valley school (which includes all grades through to Grade 10) participated in the hearings. The senior class made submissions. The intermediate class created and performed a play for the panel in which some of the students wore masks representing wilderness animals that had died, while others were narrators who explained what was happening. The primary students were given the option of submitting their work but, as their teacher said, "they wanted their voices to be heard." Thus each of the primary students did a brief presentation at the hearing. The chief described how her five-year-old niece spoke passionately with only quick references to her few notes. Two of the youth who are in their final years of secondary school in Williams Lake (where they face opposition from people who favour the mine) recited poems that they had written.

At the conclusion of the panel hearings, the Xeni Gwet'in invited the federal government representatives to see Fish Lake for themselves. On a late June day, several made the journey—two hours west from Williams Lake along the highway, forty minutes south along a gravel road, twenty minutes along a dirt access road beside a steep river basin to Fish Lake, and a canoe ride to the island in the midst of the lake surrounded by snow-topped glaciers.

On July 2, 2010, the Canadian Environmental Assessment Agency (CEAA) released the report of the government-appointed environmental impact assessment panel. They reported that the mine likely would have "significant adverse environmental effects," as well as negative impacts on several aspects of the territory, including fish, fish habitat, grizzly bears, and First Nations' use of the land for traditional purposes (Canada, CEAA, 2010a, p. ii). At this point I participated in advocacy for a federal government decision recognizing the findings of the panel and rejecting the Taseko Mines proposal. Having stayed with a Xeni Gwet'in family and canoed on Fish Lake, I understood their commitment to preserving the lake and all that it entailed.

Over the summer, *The Globe and Mail* provided considerable coverage of the issue, identifying that it was controversial and that much was at stake. One article covered a news conference in Ottawa, at which Xeni Gwet'in chief Marilyn Baptiste was accompanied by the leaders of the Assembly of First Nations and the Union of BC Indian Chiefs. Chief Baptiste was quoted stating that First Nations people were willing to sacrifice their lives to stop the mining project. She referred to a comment by one of the elders to the Environmental Assessment Panel that if a roadblock was necessary, she would be there on the road in her wheelchair with her shotguns (Stueck & Curry, 2010). The news media also presented the perspective of those who favoured the mining project. Comments from the mining company, the Chamber of Commerce in Williams Lake, and the premier of British Columbia, Gordon Campbell, emphasized their belief that the mining project would bring jobs and economic resources to a region of the province that was suffering from the devastating effects of the pine beetle infestation on the already sluggish lumber industry (e.g., Stueck, 2010). On November 2, 2010, Environment Minister Jim Prentice announced the federal cabinet decision to reject the Prosperity mine proposal (Canada, CEAA, 2010b). Interestingly, within the next two days, Prentice resigned, as did BC Premier Gordon Campbell, whose provincial government had given its approval to the proposal (Fong, 2010; Whittington, Brennan, & Delacourt, 2010). ∎

SIX

WOMEN'S RESOURCES AND ADVOCACY

THE THIRD CLUSTER of case examples from the research includes the collective undertakings that deal with women's resources and advocacy. There are three groupings within this cluster. The first group contains women's resource centres or projects, the second group consists of advocacy endeavours, and the third group relates to a church-based women's program in Chiapas.

Women's Resource Projects

THERE ARE THREE CASE EXAMPLES in the women's resource projects grouping. One is the Rosario Castellanos Women's Group in Oaxaca, the capital city of the Mexican state of Oaxaca. The other two examples are from Canada—the Antigonish Women's Resource Centre in the province of Nova Scotia, and the Kamloops Women's Resource Group Society in the province of British Columbia.

The Rosario Castellanos Women's Group in Oaxaca, Mexico

The Rosario Castellanos Women's Study Group is named after a feminist writer and poet from the state of Chiapas. Its mission, according to the poster at the entrance, is "to transform society into one more just and equal that respects the rights of women." The group works toward this through the Casa de la Mujer (the Women's Centre), which is the direct services part of the operations, and an array of other programs, including sexual health, legal consultation, psychological support, research, education, and communication. They are a group of twelve women associates who form the board of directors and the full organization. Each of the associates brings a particular expertise and takes responsibility for an area of service: two lawyers (Gabriela Gutiérrez, who coordinates the women's centre, and the other, who is the organization's secretary; in addition, both provide legal advice); three psychologists/sociologists, who provide direct service and conduct research; one historian, who is one of the founders of the organization and its treasurer; one video producer; three medical doctors, who provide consultation related to the health education programs; one accountant; and one teacher. They are not a membership-based organization with fees and an annual election of a board of directors as would be typical in the North. When one of the twelve members of the board/organization is unable to continue, there is a search for a replacement. Some of the associates receive a monthly stipend for their professional services and some provide their services as volunteers. They also have a small staff: a receptionist/secretary; a social worker, who does intake and assesses fees based on ability to pay; a librarian, who is in charge of the documentation centre; a writer, who works on publications; and an accounting assistant.

The Women's Centre component of the organization includes the documentation centre with its journals, books, and videos; the speakers series; and the direct services in the psychological and legal areas. The speakers series was the initial program of the organization. A theme is chosen for every month—for example, the themes in the winter of 2004 were about women's heritage, women and politics, and children and gender perspectives. Every Wednesday at 6:00 p.m. there is a speaker addressing an aspect of the monthly topic. The psychological consultations are provided by three specialists, who each offer about four hours per week. They address issues of low self-esteem, family violence, emergency contraception, child development, and couple issues. The legal services are provided by the lawyers and focus on such issues as family law, violence, divorce, and income security entitlement. The Women's Centre has an attractive physical presence in the front half of an old *casona*, a large house organized around two courtyards, close to the city centre. The space includes the reception and office area, as well as the conference room for the speakers series at the front of the building; the documentation centre; and the various consultation rooms surround the peaceful courtyard.

The health program deals with sexual and reproductive health. A program to reduce risks during pregnancy is provided in co-operation with other organizations. Two other programs focus on preventing maternal death in pregnancy and childbirth with specialized material for Oaxacan women and immigrant women from northern states working in tomato production. The education program includes a scholarship fund for about a dozen grants to women entering university with excellent grades and a record of work with women. The communication program produces material in video, audio, and print forms. They produce the journal *Entrelineas* (Between the lines) approximately twice a year with input from an editorial committee with representation from other organizations. The communications committee produced a three-part series of videos in 1997 called *Nuestras Vidas Compartidas* (Our Shared Lives): *If It Weren't for That . . . We Would Be Equals*; *Perhaps This Happens to Many of Us*; and *These Times of Trembling Are Now Over*. Another video, *Step by Step—Toward a Pregnancy Without Risks*, was produced in 2001. The videos are approximately twenty minutes each and have been purchased by organizations and government departments, including some outside of Oaxaca. They have also produced radio programs and workshops for which the scripts and materials are printed as booklets.

The organization is active in the socio-political sphere through participation in the electoral process and offering educational workshops and conferences for elected officials. During state election campaigns, the organization has asked candidates to clarify their platforms with respect to gender issues, and they made the candidates' positions known by publishing their comments. After the elections, they have co-hosted workshops and conferences for elected officials on gender issues. Each year they take a leadership role in organizing the International Women's Day events. They also participate in networks with other organizations working on women's issues or civil society concerns.

The Rosario Castellanos Women's Study Group was started in 1977, not long after the first United Nations' World Conference on Women in 1975 in Mexico City. A special twenty-fifth-anniversary edition of *Entrelineas* celebrates this accomplishment. The long-standing presence of the organization and the reputation of the associates themselves are what they believe have contributed to the credibility of the organization. The current challenges the organization's representatives identify are decreased funding and a difficult policy context. Financial support from the Mexican government and US foundations had decreased in the early 2000s. At the same time, the election of conservative parties has resulted in public policy with less attention to gender equality. But their good relationship with the press provides them with access to the broader public and gives them opportunities to increase public sensitivity to women's issues.

The Antigonish Women's Resource Centre in Nova Scotia, Canada

The Antigonish Women's Resource Centre & Sexual Assault Services Association in Nova Scotia developed out of women's participation in a 1982 discussion series at St. Francis Xavier University. The women decided to form the Antigonish Women's Association in order to create a space for women to organize for social change. As a complement to the community-organizing activity, they opened the Antigonish Women's Resource Centre in 1983 to provide services for women. From its beginning, the organization has held the dual objectives of fostering social change and providing needed services. Although the two names and distinct boards of directors were maintained for twenty-six years, the organization changed its name in 2009 to clarify its role in providing sexual assault services and amalgamated all of its functions, including the social change work, under one board.

The centre initially received core financial support from the Women's Program of the federal Secretary of State, but by 1998 this funding ended. The Nova Scotia Department of Community Services has provided funding for social services, but not for activities to promote social justice. Funding for the social change component has been an ongoing challenge. From the original core group of fifteen women, the organization has grown to over one hundred members. The board of directors consists of twelve to sixteen women, including a balance of university women and "born-and-bred" locals. The centre is engaged in individual, group, community, and social change programs. Individual and group services include information, support (crisis and ongoing), advocacy, accompaniment, health care, and sexual assault support. Community support programs include help for low-income women, such as income tax preparation, emergency financial support, and provision of Internet access. Social change work includes a program to involve rural women and girls in resisting violence, providing input to government by submitting briefs and participating on committees, and promoting social assistance reform. The centre takes an active role in working with the community to address poverty and violence against women.

The social assistance reform project has been a very interesting one. It is a joint project of three women's centres in Nova Scotia, begun in 2001, and carried out with funding from Status of Women Canada. Research in 2005 involved in-depth interviews and focus groups with ninety-one women on social assistance in eleven different regions of the province and was reported to the Nova Scotia government. In May 2006, a two-and-a-half-day session was held in Halifax with some of the women from the focus groups in order to prioritize the recommendations and flesh them out. On the final day, senior staff members from the Department of Community Services were asked to join a working group that included community organizations, as well as women with the lived experience of being on social assistance, to learn about the findings. All those involved described this as a very powerful experience and the media provided good coverage.

Another noteworthy social change activity of the Antigonish centre was the 2006 Valentine's Day campaign. Hot-pink valentine postcards were printed for women to forward to their federal and provincial elected representatives. The postcards were packaged in a larger card that included a fact sheet highlighting how poverty is created by specific policies related to minimum wages, employment insurance, income assistance, education and training supports, pay equity, and pensions. The campaign was endorsed and promoted by a broad coalition of women's organizations in Nova Scotia. Service users in many organizations took dozens of the packages and helped to distribute them. Although the impact was not yet known, nearly ten thousand of the packages were sent.

The executive director, Lucille Harper (who was one of the founding members of the association), described the "pressures to depoliticize" in the current sociopolitical context, where funding mandates and critical needs push the organization toward service delivery. The emphasis on service delivery creates pressures for a more professionalized, non-engaged relationship with the women requiring services. However, the organization is committed to building its actions on the needs identified by the women and, furthermore, staff see advocacy and empowerment as central to their role. Lucille has received recognition for her long-time, dedicated work toward women's equality—in October 2010, she received one of the five Governor General's Awards in Commemoration of the Persons Case.[1]

---

1. Since the fiftieth anniversary in 1979 of the Persons case, which declared the word "person" included both women and men, the Governor General of Canada has conferred five awards each year to deserving citizens in memory of the "Famous Five" through a nomination and selection process administered by Status of Women Canada.

The Kamloops Women's Resource Group Society
in British Columbia, Canada

The Kamloops Women's Resource Group Society (KWRGS) in British Columbia was born out of annual women's conferences that were held at the local university in the early 1980s. The need for a women's centre and a local rape crisis centre were identified there. Two separate organizations have come into being: the Kamloops Women's Resource Group Society, which opened its women's centre in 1984, and the Kamloops Sexual Assault Counselling Centre. Members told me that the women's centre was probably at its peak in the 1990s, when funding provided for drop-ins and employment programs, but the BC government ended their $47,000 per year funding in 2002, and the federal Status of Women's program funding of $25,000 per year was cut in 2006. One of the local elected representatives in the provincial legislature responded to protests about the cuts, asking, "Why would we fund women sitting around drinking coffee?" The group's subsequent publication of the stories of local activist women in the area was given the title *Not Just a Tea Party* as a retort.

Although staff never increased beyond two core positions, plus project staff, the society can now afford to pay for only ten hours a week of coordinator services. Similarly, the centre moved to smaller quarters and revised its focus to "recording women's herstory, holding events to raise awareness, working to improve women's rights, and referring women to resources within the community" (KWRGS, n.d.). Without the drop-in facilities, many women phone the centre for information about resources, especially legal matters since government-funded legal aid has also been cut dramatically. Other service requests pertain to housing, employment, completion of forms, health issues, needs of children with disabilities, addictions, and homelessness. The organization is now considering seeking charitable status.

The KWRGS is committed to networking with other organizations, including other women's centres, in order to continue their endeavours. Members stated that working toward legislative change is very difficult in the current environment, but it is possible to complete specific projects and to participate in the initiatives of other organizations and jointly address what is needed. Participating in the local peace walk and in an event for seniors are examples of collaboration. Outreach to new members and supporters is also important in keeping the organization vital. Some of the projects, like the *Room Full of Missing Women* art exhibit, attract like-minded women. Similarly, the coordinator, Evey Chursky, noted that it is hoped that the women who have been helped by the KWRGS may become the women who will later be involved in changing pertinent legislation. The attention to collaboration may also include more involvement of men as allies in the struggle for women's equality. Men have participated in the Walk for Justice, worn T-shirts stating, "My strength is not for hurting," and expressed their appreciation, as fathers of daughters, for the organization's support of women's safety. In looking ahead, the Kamloops Women's Resource Group Society is seeking the kind of project that could be mounted collaboratively and that a large part of the community could get behind; they are exploring whether addressing women's health needs might be workable this way.

Women Engaged in Advocacy

THE STUDY INCLUDED three examples of women engaged in advocacy. One is a Nova Scotia gaggle of the Raging Grannies, and the other two are women who are leaders in the Christian Base Communities movement with separate involvements in Morelos, Mexico.

The Raging Grannies in Nova Scotia, Canada

The focus of the Raging Grannies' activism includes, but is not limited to, women's equality. The Raging Grannies are women who arrive unexpectedly at public events dressed outrageously as older women in big, bright hats; they take the stage by surprise, sing critical ditties to familiar tunes, and disappear as quickly as they arrive. The first group formed in Victoria, British Columbia, in 1987, to protest the arrival of US warships in their coastal waters (Roy, 2004). Their witty strategy was soon copied across Canada and in other countries across the world. Below is a song on the pay equity theme written by the Victoria Grannies and sung to the tune of the Newfoundland folk song "I's the B'y That Builds the Boat" (Raging Grannies, 2009):

> We're the women who did the work
> So men could get the credit.
> We said leave it all to us
> And wished we'd never said it.

No, I don't mind staying late
I'll make that last correction.
No I don't want extra pay
You deserve perfection.

That was then, but this is now
We're wiser and we're older.
Some might mellow as they age
But Grannies just get bolder.

We're prepared to do the work
But we want more than credit.
Equal pay for equal work
We'll sing until we get it.

A member of the Wolfville, Nova Scotia, gaggle of the Raging Grannies shared some of her Granny knowledge and experiences with me. The Maritime gaggle includes groups from Fredericton, Wolfville, and Halifax; there are "Granny gaggles" all over Canada and some of them come together at the national Grannies' Unconvention. Some gigs performed by the Wolfville Grannies prior to my June 2006 visit were: a roast at a federal election all-candidates forum; a presentation of a child-care petition to their member of Parliament; a protest of plans for open-pit mining along the shoreline; and an exposition of unfair labour practices at Wal-Mart. In instances where police have been called, the officers are often reluctant to be seen using force against apparently harmless, older women or perhaps to have to confront their own mothers, aunts, or grandmothers. On one occasion the police responded so slowly that the Grannies had left the event and were calmly and inoffensively enjoying coffee in a nearby café by the time the police arrived and found "no grounds for arrest."

The Wolfville gaggle gets together for a practice/meeting every two weeks. When I was in Nova Scotia, they were working on their marching skills in order to sharpen their entrance and timing. In their meetings, the group members educate each other regarding current issues—they want to be sure they have their facts straight before they put them out publicly in order to ensure a high level of credibility. They take time to consider dilemmas regarding their practices. An important question has been: "Should the Grannies accept invitations?" By doing so, would they be optimizing an educational opportunity or would they be preaching to the converted? In the end, the group decided that they would accept invitations if the occasion served their purpose of social change activism. A recent invitation that the group accepted was from the Kings County farm women's organization, which they found to be a great audience to engage with regarding ideas about genetically modified foods and buying local. The Grannies not only sang, but described the Raging Grannies movement and its history, and each member spoke about why she has chosen to be a Granny. Decisions about actions are made collectively by the gaggle. If one member has an idea, they post it on the group's listserv and others offer their opinions. A decision not to act was made regarding the beauty pageant that is part of the Apple Blossom Festival. Many different views were put forward and in the end, the group decided that crashing the pageant might be misinterpreted and interfere with the group's interest in building connections with the youth. The Wolfville gaggle generally has been positively represented by the local media; however, some Granny gaggles have been less positively received in other circles. Through the *Granny Grapevine* newsletter, members have learned how gaggles in the United States have shown up at military recruiting offices asking to be enlisted for service in lieu of the young people, which in some cities has resulted in arrests. Even in Canada, apparently the Canada Security and Intelligence Service has listed some Grannies as potential terrorists.

Licha's Work in Tejalpa and the Mexican State of Morelos

Alicia Arines, whose nickname is "Licha," is one of many Mexican women whose community organizing work arose from their involvement in the Christian Base Communities (CEBs). She described how thirty-five years ago, when she arrived in the state of Morelos from the state of Guerrero, Tejalpa was a beautiful area with fertile land and a clear river where many Indigenous peoples farmed. In the 1970s, however, it became the industrial zone of the Cuernavaca valley and large manufacturing companies from the United States took over the farming land, consumed a great deal of the water, and contaminated the river. Many impoverished people from the state of Guerrero immigrated in search of employment, but living conditions in the town and surrounding area deteriorated.

Licha joined the efforts of the Catholic priests, who were encouraging the development of Christian Base Communities. She was one of the lay workers in this movement who invited people in the neighbourhood to weekly two-hour Bible study sessions that focused on their own local issues. The meetings followed Freire's (1968/1984) process: see, think, act, and celebrate/evaluate. They observed the problems resulting from the contaminated water; reflected on God's direction to care for the earth; acted by joining together with other CEBs to form an ecological organization to educate, protest, and initiate recycling programs; and celebrated their accomplishments.

Licha described how the Christian Base Communities, though initiated by the priests, have been organizations composed entirely of laypeople. The focus is on respect for all human beings and engagement in a social ministry that works toward human rights and transformation of society. The CEBs gained renewed inspiration from the Latin American Episcopal conference held in Puebla, Mexico, in 1979, which emphasized the "the preferential option for the poor." This motivated them to respond in solidarity with the struggles of the poor in other Latin American countries who were facing government repression. The CEBs and similarly motivated organizations sent supplies to the people in the conflicted countries and, with encouragement from the bishop of the Cuernavaca diocese in the state of Morelos, Don Sergio Méndez Arceo, received many people as refugees. Although Bishop Méndez was replaced by more conservative bishops after he retired, and liberation theology lost favour within the Catholic Church hierarchy, the principles of liberation theology and the Christian Base Communities movement have endured in many parts of Latin America.

Licha is now busier than ever with numerous community organization projects. Her children are grown and her second husband is very supportive of her community work. In fact, he is involved in campesino/farmer struggles, as well as Indigenous and environmental movements. Together they participate in a national network for economic solidarity and help organize fairs for producers to sell products and promote fair trade. Another major project that Licha currently heads is a community kitchen that prepares nutritious and inexpensive midday meals in a neighbourhood with many low-income people. She is also involved in human rights work, particularly women's right to live free of spousal violence.

One of Licha's passions is her work with Católicas por el Derecho a Decidir (Catholic Women for the Right to Decide) (CDD), which promotes women's freedom of choice to be in relationships, to engage in sexual relations, and to have children or not. It is an international organization that was established in 1970 in Washington, DC. The Mexican branch established its offices in 1994 in Mexico City. Licha is the *promotora* (promoter/leader) in the state of Morelos, reaching out to women in the CEBs, traditional health programs, youth groups, and municipal offices. The national organization provides training and development courses in human rights and feminist theology for the promoters/leaders. There are two- or three-day workshops every three months addressing various topics, including common themes such as women's dignity and self-esteem, and more controversial ones such as abortion and the right to express diverse sexualities. All the costs for travel, accommodation, and meals are covered for the promoters, and Licha has been very pleased with the quality of the training. At the state level, Licha leads a nine-woman team of volunteers that she selected for the outreach work in Morelos. They get together monthly to share material and plan events at the state level. There are always at least four events per year: March 8, International Women's Day; May (because of Mother's Day), a focus on voluntary motherhood; September 28, a day for the decriminalization of abortion; and November 25, international day for the elimination of violence against women. Sometimes the events are held in co-operation with other organizations. They are affiliated with some state-level organizations, such as Red de Convergencia del 8 de Marzo (Network of Gatherings for the 8th of March) and Cocofem: Comité contra los Femicidios en Morelos (Committee against Femicide in Morelos), and with a national one, Red Nacional para los Derechos de Todos y Todas (National Network for the Rights of All).

One of the biggest challenges for CDD is that the church hierarchy opposes their work, especially in relation to abortion. An anti-abortion group known as Por Vida (Pro Life) is aligned with the church hierarchy and the PAN (conservative) party. CDD doesn't face too much opposition in Morelos, but in Mexico City there have been threats and aggression directed at the national office, the organization, and the director. It has been very helpful to have received public recognition and prizes at the national and international level for their work. These acts of solidarity strengthen them and provide protection through public awareness. The contemporary conservative family-values ideology is problematic, as well as the traditional view of women in Mexican society. Many women themselves accept the machismo norms and thus are *machistas*. They are very traditional because of their culture and education, and they accept their role as an obligation.

Licha said that the gatherings, the workshops, the training opportunities, and the materials are all very important in overcoming these challenges. These help the women to open their minds to new ideas. The organization also uses the *Canónicas* (canon law) of the Catholic Church regarding the rights of the baptized to criticize and dissent as an important point of reference in their work. The practice of thinking critically and forming one's own opinion is familiar to the Catholics in Morelos because of the teaching of the highly respected former bishop, Don Sergio Méndez Arceo.

Agustina's Work in Cuernavaca, the State of Morelos, and Beyond

As with Licha's community organizing, Agustina Reyes Estrada began her work in the Christian Base Communities, and there are many similarities in their backgrounds and experiences. For this reason, the description of Agustina's work will focus only on her most recent involvements, which are distinct from Licha's. I asked Agustina to share the story of her experience as part of the protests at the September 2003 meeting of the World Trade Organization (WTO) in Cancun. She describes it as one of the most poignant of her experiences in social movements. She was one of the representatives of the Frente Auténtico del Trabajo (Authentic Workers Front) (FAT) who participated—about forty-four people, half men and half women, who travelled on a bus together from Cuernavaca to Cancun. In Cancun, they joined with other union representatives at international levels, including Indigenous peoples, farmers, workers in *maquiladoras* (untaxed factories), and others from across the globe. They participated for several days in many educational and informational forums related to the objectives of the WTO.

The final day, all of the social movement groups joined together in a large march protesting the agreements proposed at the WTO meeting. The march concluded with a huge cultural meeting outside the buildings where the WTO was in session. There was a tall chain-link fence separating them from the formal meeting. One of the Indigenous women invited other women, who wished to, to come forward and form a circle in front of the group. Agustina and one of the other women from the FAT (their lawyer from the national office, in fact) chose to participate. The women, from all over the world, with their arms interlinked, moved up to the fence. Some had wire cutters to cut holes in the fence and climbed through. The guards hit them with batons and the women retreated. Then some of the students, who were behind the women, threw eggs at the guards and the guards retreated. The women put scarves through the fence links and together were able to pull the fence down. Men, standing behind the women, handed them white flowers, which the women gave to the guards. For the guards, this created a great confusion that Agustina compared to the story of the Tower of Babel. Women, speaking languages that the guards couldn't understand, were handing them white flowers that they clearly knew represented peace. At that precise moment, the press came out of the building where the WTO was meeting and saw the amazing demonstration of peaceful resistance.

Agustina also described her involvements in the human rights movement between 1996 and 1998, when militarization in the state of Morelos was very intrusive. The army had an even heavier presence in Chiapas, but it extended into Oaxaca, Guerrero, and Morelos as well. She was part of a group of about fourteen people and they called themselves La Comisión Independiente de Derechos Humanos (Independent Human Rights Commission). The majority were women (ten at the peak) and the rest were men. Some members of the group were the observers and data gatherers, and others communicated the information to the government's human rights commission. Agustina's involvement was as an information gatherer. Every Saturday and Sunday, she went with her comrades into the Indigenous communities that were being watched by the Mexican army. The soldiers entered the community under the pretext of offering health programs. But they were really gathering information about how many people were in the community and what they were doing, particularly where the men were working. They controlled the entrance to the community and required the women to wash their clothes and provide them with food, which they paid for. Some members of community didn't mind because it brought them more income. But others said the soldiers disturbed their peace and calm and they felt their daughters were at risk, especially when they pestered them to come and clean their quarters. In the human rights work, Agustina said they worked as a team with a more circular structure. Agustina and her group from the church collected information, others disseminated the information—preparing and distributing bulletins, for example.

Agustina said she also enjoys helping in the socio-economic transformation of vulnerable families—families who are separated because the fathers are working in the North as well as families headed by single mothers. Her priority is women because they are often marginalized and violated in terms of their human rights in the macho culture in Mexico. She listens to them and helps them to learn about their possibilities. She tries to raise their spirits so they don't isolate themselves and to motivate them to try different things. One woman, who is raising three children after leaving an abusive husband in the state of Guerrero and living in very humble circumstances in one of the Cuernavaca ravines, is one of these mothers who is working very hard to help her family get ahead and receives support from Agustina. This, says Agustina, is her volunteer contribution now. Sometimes it is as simple as seeing a specific need and asking her sisters if they have any clothing their children have outgrown that she can deliver to a struggling family.

The Women's Council of the San Cristóbal Diocese in Chiapas, Mexico

THE COORDINADORA DIOCESANA DE MUJERES (Women's Council of the Diocese of San Cristóbal) (CODIMUJ) organizes meetings with opportunities for planning and learning for the representatives of the various regions and zones within the diocese. Within the zones, there are leaders who facilitate the development of women's groups at the community level. Three components of this work in the state of Chiapas were sampled. One is the coordination leadership, CODIMUJ itself. The second is a community-level group in a humble neighbourhood on the outskirts of the city of San Cristóbal. The third is a community-level group in a poor and rural town in Chiapas.

The Coordination Leadership for CODIMUJ

The central coordination for the diocese women's program is located in San Cristóbal. One nun is the coordinator for the whole diocese, which includes seven pastoral zones in the eastern part of the state of Chiapas. Another nun works with CODIMUJ in San Cristóbal in particular. A combination of nuns and lay workers provide the leadership at the regional, zone, and community levels. One of the nuns described the different realities in the rural parts of Chiapas and in the city of San Cristóbal:

> In the rural communities of Chiapas there is a long tradition of solidarity—
> a strong feeling of community. They make decisions by consensus, wherein
> everyone must be in agreement before they proceed. If someone doesn't agree,
> they continue the discussion until they find a decision that everyone can accept.

She said that in the city (San Cristóbal), it is different. The people have come from many different communities with many different experiences. The conflicts since 1994 have created divisions among the people, and many of those who come to the city tend to be more individualistic. This, in turn, makes the work of CODIMUJ in the city more difficult. In the city, there are many very poor women, both Indigenous and *campesina* (farm women), who have to work every day to survive. Many of them sell their products and others work as domestics for very low wages. Because the poor women in San Cristóbal are fully occupied with their individual economic survival activities, the nun said, it hasn't been possible to organize collective employment initiatives. However, they still look for ways to work collectively. For example, they have helped young single women who are working as domestics to get together to rent a room and share the costs.

They also work in many neighbourhoods providing reflection groups that are based on Bible study and liberation theology. They work slowly and patiently, inviting and encouraging the women's participation. They recognize that the life of women in the cities is very difficult due to the poverty and the abuse by husbands, many of whom drink very heavily. They work from the Bible, with the word of God as the base to liberate the women, to help them appreciate their self-worth and to learn to defend themselves. From this patient work, there have been many successes. One woman, whose husband abused her economically, strongly identified with the burden of the woman from Cana and understood through the group discussion that Christ wanted women to be valued and not exploited. She then returned to her parents' home until her husband was willing to change. She reported to the group that he had come to visit her and brought his laundry for her to do. The group discussed the central question—"What would Christ want in this situation?"—and supported her decision to refuse to do his laundry until he treated her with equal respect. In another group discussion, one about the Bible story in which Jesus reproached the crowd for treating the prostitute badly, one of the women shared her secret of working as a prostitute and, through the group process, was able to overcome her sense of shame and develop her self-esteem. In other examples, women who were physically abused by their husbands have been able to stop the abuse by telling their husbands that this is not how Christ would want them to be treated. In other situations, in which the husbands did not stop the abuse, the women have left to go to a women's shelter known to CODIMUJ.

In early February 2004, CODIMUJ held one of its two-day quarterly meetings for about one hundred leaders (both nuns and lay workers) from the zones and regions of the diocese. I attended and observed how the coordination developed the leadership within the organization. The meeting was held at a modest retreat centre in a peaceful area on the edge of the city. As well as a spacious area for the full group sessions, there was a kitchen and dining area, and cabins for the representatives from the different zones. The full plenary sessions included songs that had both Christian and feminist themes, some exercises that could be replicated in the communities, descriptions of topics for discussion in regional groups, and reports from the breakout groups. Translation from Spanish into three Mayan languages was provided in the plenary sessions, but was not necessary in the breakout groups, which met in regional clusters. Because of the warm weather, the breakout groups found quiet places outside to spread their shawls and sit on the ground for the discussions.

Numerous topics were addressed during the two-day meeting. After meeting in their regional groups first on the Friday morning, the groups reported back to the plenary on what was happening in their communities: many new developments were described and there were some examples of discouragement. A Bible text for group study was provided and the coordinator emphasized that "in whatever biblical text we examine, it is necessary to discover 'where is the woman' (whether she is named or not) with our own eyes, minds, and hearts as women." Groups reported back and identified many similarities between the group leadership experience of Mary (the mother of the disciple John) in the time of the Roman Empire and the experience of women group leaders in Chiapas today. After lunch, there were some information updates about a women's centre that the organization was working on that would be able to accommodate future meetings, and about some other organizations holding meetings to contest neo-liberalism, which the women were invited to attend. An assignment for the small groups was then described and I joined one of the central groups working in Spanish, although they produced primarily diagrams rather than written summaries of their discussion. In response to the question "What customs do we have today that undermine the dignity of women?" the group identified three: the obligation to marry in their early teens, the abuse of alcohol by men during festivities (often resulting in violence against the women), and the discrimination against female children and wives. In response to the question "What can we do to change this?" the group suggested education about the equal worth of girls and boys, education about the effects of alcohol, and working in a respectful way with the whole family.

On the Saturday morning, there was a review of the ten-year process since the Zapatista uprising in 1994 with attention to the role of women in this process. The discussion was facilitated by a person from an external group working toward peace in Chiapas. She brought colourful posters with visual images for each year and asked with regard to each: "Why is the movement important?" and "Where were the women in this period?" Some of the responses were: "The movement wakes the people up despite the government's desire that the people be left asleep"; "The women spoke out about the injustice"; and "Some of the women were killed." The regional groups convened to consider the situation now, ten years after the uprising. Divisions in the communities were identified, including among the women, because of the pressures to participate in government programs rather than in the CODIMUJ activities. In presenting the findings in the plenary, each group showed their pictorial representation of their situation and it was suggested that the divisions might be a government strategy. During the lunch break, I joined a group of women who were looking at photographs that some of the women brought back from the protests at the WTO meeting in Cancun. Two of the women from this particular region had attended to participate in the demonstrations for fair trade. The full group reconvened after lunch to further examine the current situation. The discussion leader provided a vivid visual context by drawing an uphill highway on the whiteboard. She then placed vehicles of various sizes and shapes on the highway, heading uphill—civil society organizations, the Church, the EZLN, and political parties. Then she introduced larger vehicles heading in the opposite direction—the government, the paramilitary, and others (multinational corporations?). She made the point that if everyone is heading in the same directions, there is no problem; however, when people are heading in opposite directions, there are collisions. The women were asked: "What is it that we are really searching for?" They were then asked: "What do we need to do to achieve this?" Their responses are included in Part III in the discussion about strengthening organizations. In the final part of the afternoon, a facilitator from the Mexico City–based organization, Mujeres para el Diálogo (Women for Dialogue) (2011), led an interactive session with the full group that helped to distinguish gender characteristics attributable to culture, and sex differences attributable to biology. It was a very simple, sometimes humorous, yet compelling exercise that the participants could use in their communities.

The CODIMUJ Women's Group on the Outskirts of San Cristóbal

One of the San Cristóbal neighbourhoods with CODIMUJ-linked women's groups came into being in 1994, shortly after the Zapatista uprising in Chiapas. About 440 people (including the children), who left the conflicted rural areas, settled in the community on the outskirts of the city, building the houses, the school, and the church. The houses are wooden with dirt floors, water is carried from various taps in the community, and electricity has been strung to the houses but there is no street lighting. The leader of the women's program in this community told me that there are two women's groups in the community—one that holds its meetings in Tzeltal (her first language) and one that holds its meetings in Spanish. She told me that the Spanish-speaking women's group had been talking about a collective income-generating project; however, the person leading that initiative had fallen ill, so nothing further had happened yet.

On the Thursday evening, I was welcomed to the home of another community member for the Spanish-speaking women's group meeting attended by women of all ages, including two with small babies and two teenaged girls, as well as one man who was using crutches after having been hit by a car. There was much friendly discussion and exchange of advice about common experiences while waiting for the choir to arrive—a group of teenaged boys with guitars, a mandolin, a bass, and an accordion. The meeting began with prayer, the choir led some hymn singing, and one of the teenaged girls read the Bible passage. A discussion followed based on the questions: "What does this story have to say to us about how we live together in our community?" and "What are some of the things that we need to do?" After the discussion, there were two more songs, a closing prayer, and informal discussion over coffee and pastries.

The CODIMUJ Women's Group in a Rural Chiapas Town

In a rural Chiapas town, another women's group gathers weekly in the late afternoon on a weekday in the parish hall. When I visited, about twenty women were seated on wooden chairs in a circle, dressed in their traditional clothing and speaking their Mayan language. The nun who facilitates the group spoke in Spanish and one of the members translated. The meeting began with prayer and songs that had references to the struggles of women and Indigenous peoples in Chiapas.

One of the women spoke about a recent situation where she needed health care. It sounded like a health care worker who had some medicine available would provide assistance only if the ailing woman made some kind of commitment that she would affiliate with their evangelistic group. The woman described how she considered this and declined the service. As a result, she needed to let nature take its course with the illness and was left for a while with only beans and vegetables to eat because she hadn't been well enough to work.

The discussion focused primarily on what the group might like to do on International Women's Day in their town. The nun said they could celebrate with a mass, they could protest some of the conditions that bother them—the decision was theirs. She was very animated in describing these options. She asked them if they are content with everything or if they want to protest some issue—for example, that they pay for electricity but often have none; that the army has had a menacing presence for the last eight months, checking for arms along the highway; or that there is no health care in the village (one could be dying and there is no doctor here). She talked about a politician who visited town on Sunday evening and handed out cakes to the people. She said this is a very corrupt man who has been responsible for many deaths, has raped young women, and is involved in the drug trade, yet she heard that the people applauded when he spoke. "Qué vergüenza! [How shameful!] Are we really like trained animals that jump for little treats?" she asked, as she demonstrated the posture of a jumping circus dog. International Women Day, she said, provides an opportunity for us to show others that we are not stupid; we are critical thinkers who are capable of analyzing our situation. ∎

SEVEN

GRASSROOTS SUPPORT ORGANIZATIONS AND INDEPENDENT COMMUNITY ORGANIZERS

SOME GRASSROOTS SUPPORT ORGANIZATIONS (GSOS) and independent community organizers with broad social justice objectives are
providing resources and supporting the work of others, rather than
engaging in specific projects of their own. Three case examples in
this study fell into this category. TADECO is a formal organization engaged
in community development in the state of Guerrero. The second is quite
unique—a couple doing informal community organizing in their neighbourhood. And the final example, COMPA, which is located in Chiapas, is a network of organizations contesting the imposition of the neo-liberal economic
paradigm in the Western hemisphere.

The Community Development Workshop (TADECO) in Guerrero, Mexico

THE TALLER DE DESARROLLO COMUNITARIO (Community Develop-
ment Workshop) (TADECO) is located in Chilpancingo, the capital city of the
state of Guerrero. It is a grassroots support organization dedicated to working
in a participatory manner with communities to engage in critical analysis and
to transform society into one that is more just and egalitarian. The organization is composed of five associates with training in sociology, education, and
economics. They have a true storefront operation, selling corner-store items to
neighbourhood customers, plus an Internet café with related services such as

printing and copying. In addition, they produce newsletters, films, and music related to Mexican culture, social issues, and protest activities, which they sell at their office and at their kiosk in the city centre. They reject the current politico-economic system, which privileges a few and marginalizes the great majority of the population in Mexico, and they are committed to working with the people to find alternatives using such vehicles as liberation theology.

The director described the huge problem of rural malnutrition that has links to earlier pressures on farmers to change to growing monoculture cash crops. Prior to that, mixed farming was common and farm families and communities had access to their own farm-produced eggs, poultry, milk, etc. Mixed farming also provided organic manure, which in the last fifteen years has been replaced with chemical fertilizers in keeping with the strategy of agribusiness. TADECO is part of the movement to confront this trend and help farmers recover the *milpa* (farmyard garden for the family's consumption). More recently, as described in Part I, free trade agreements pressured the Mexican government to end the protected collective ownership of lands redistributed after the revolution and the tariff-protected food crops. The harsh competition from US grains has led to many small-scale Mexican corn producers being unable to sell their crops at a profit. Now former ejido lands are being registered as separate parcels and sold. This is a big change from the former collective ways of the Indigenous peoples. TADECO tries to support the Indigenous communities in their efforts to preserve their traditional ways and to unify in the face of these neo-liberal economic trends.

TADECO works toward gender equality through discussion groups that are led by two or three couples from the community. The organization provides resources such as films, poetry, and music with gender-equality messages, as well as learning tools that make the process fun and enjoyable. TADECO also works with youth because they will be the builders of the new society. Together with youth leaders, they organize one-day conferences to discuss youth rights and provide opportunities to be involved in collective activities to work toward these rights.

TADECO also has a political committee that examines what is being done by the different governments and political parties. They critique government programs and participate in observing the elections, but they don't believe the party system has the potential to resolve the problems. Their struggle is against the corruption that the parties engage in, but people vote for these parties even when the party's platform is contrary to the people's interests.

TADECO engages the community in working toward transparency in the political processes.

At one time, TADECO participated in government-funded programs; one project increased their staff to thirty-seven; however, many of the staff didn't share the same ideology and TADECO doesn't want to repeat the experience. A lot of their projects are accomplished with the support of community volunteers and collaborators who support their work, but in order to maintain its freedom to criticize government, TADECO has made a conscious decision to remain independent of government funding.

TADECO also supports organizations that are working on behalf of people whose rights have been abused. One example is the Comité de Familiares y Amigos de Secuestrados, Desaparecidos, y Asesinados en Guerrero (Committee of Families and Friends of the Kidnapped, Disappeared, and Assassinated in Guerrero). The TADECO director's very good friend, Jorge Gabriel Cerón Silva, who was a leader in a sister organization, is one of the people who has disappeared. The TADECO director explained that the government has "criminalized the social struggle." When people involved in the social struggle go missing or are injured, he added, the government claims that the person was involved in the drug trade and that is why something happened to him or her—"it is a clever pretext." The committee has documented twelve hundred forced disappearances between 2005 and 2009 in the state of Guerrero. TADECO is also involved in many networks and alliances working to promote transparent democracy, human rights (including rights to land and resources), and an end to violence against women. A recent collaborative project examining the reality of Mexican undocumented agricultural workers in the United States and their families remaining in Mexico included a United Nations committee on human rights, the government of the state of Guerrero, the Universidad Autónoma de Guerrero (the Autonomous University of Guerrero), and three local NGOs.

Two Independent Neighbourhood Organizers in Guerrero, Mexico

TERE CRUZ AND AMADO BAHENA are a couple who engage in community organizing based on their own personal convictions. They are not employed by an organization, nor have they formed a civil society organization under the auspices of which they carry out their practice. They don't receive any remuneration for their work; rather, they live simply and in solidarity with their neighbours.

Tere is a trained social worker and a former nun; Amado had studied to be a priest. Both concluded that they needed to move beyond the institutional church in order to do the kind of work they felt was important. They now live in the humble neighbourhood on the outskirts of a Guerrero city that was described earlier in the examples of the settlers and the amate-paper painters. They have lived in the neighbourhood since the land was first subdivided and parcels were made available at very low prices. Tere arrived in the year after the land was first occupied, and Amado joined her eight months later. They helped the community unite to make the demands for water and electricity, etc. But they made it very clear to me that they don't see themselves as community leaders; they consider themselves to be cultivators of the leadership abilities in others.

Their house is constructed very simply of wood with a dirt floor. The water they use in the kitchen and for bathing is collected afterward for the plants and trees that shade the house. There is a fire pit behind the house for cooking and the ashes from it are used to cover the waste in the dry latrine. The furniture is rustic and sparse, but the walls are filled with their paintings, and a drum for traditional dance is in the centre of the living room area.

Tere and Amado provide painting classes for youth in the community, as well as classes in traditional dance. The drum in the centre of their living room is decorated with a design that is typical of the Tlacuilos (Aztec scribes and artists). Although they have been invited to be part of public performances, they prefer to focus on the dancing for the benefit of the youth so that they develop an appreciation of their cultural traditions. Tere also helps community members learn the benefits of traditional medicines and, in addition, she is the informal community organizer mentioned earlier who is encouraging the amate-paper painters to consider forming a collective. They no longer affiliate with any political party. They believe that this could alienate members of the community and interfere with their work. They have put some of their thoughts into writing and poetry that they share with members of the community. They don't publish it in commercial venues or newspapers. Instead, they said, they prefer to work "in the shade."

COMPA: Convergence of People's Movements in the Americas

THE CONVERGENCIA de Movimientos de los Pueblos de las Américas (Convergence of People's Movements in the Americas) (COMPA) is a network of organizations and movements in North, South, and Central America, as well as the Caribbean that are engaged in struggles against neo-liberal capitalism. It provides a means of communication through its website and opportunities for members of the movements to come together in periodic assemblies or congresses to develop common strategies. COMPA does not have any paid staff, but the volunteer coordinator in 2004 was a woman employed by Alianza Cívica (Civic Alliance) in Chiapas with whom I met.

The organization was formed in 1999 at an assembly in Washington, DC. At its second meeting in 2000 in San Cristóbal, Chiapas, COMPA established its six strategic directions: (1) to struggle against the proposed Free Trade Area of the Americas; (2) to struggle against militarization and specifically the Plan Colombia; (3) to struggle against the external debt and imposition of structural adjustment programs; (4) to struggle for gender equality; (5) to struggle for territorial rights and the rights of Indigenous peoples; and (6) to struggle for sustainable and just rural development.

The structure was established recognizing five major regions: the North (Mexico, the United States, and Canada), Central, Caribbean, Andean, and Southern Cone, with two representatives from each region. For the North, the representatives are from Mexico and the United States; there are participating organizations in Canada, and one of those is Low Income Families Together (LIFT). Obtaining greater representation from the South, as well as balancing representation from large grassroots organizations, was still to be worked out.

In the third continental conference, which took place in Cuba in November 2002, the focus was on clarifying the norms and practices of COMPA. They discussed the functioning of the continental coordination and the development of a support team for the coordination. They also considered the progress on the various strategies and decided to reinforce the efforts regarding gender by holding a continental meeting with the sole focus on gender. In preparation, numerous local sessions were held to prepare reports on the status of women in various areas. In Mexico, for example, they developed a group, COMPA México Mujer (COMPA Mexico Woman), which created a questionnaire, adapted to various contexts, in order to gather data in preparatory sessions in various states. The continental women's meeting was held in November 2004 in Nicaragua, and subsequent general assemblies were held in Venezuela in 2005 and Honduras in 2009 (COMPA, 2011).

The coordinator is clear about her objectives in this role. She saw her first priority as consolidating the network. Her second concern was to promote the development of popular education in ways that identify and respect particular cultures. Print, visual materials (including drawings, photography, art, and videos), as well as audio cassettes, are media in which they are developing support materials. Her third objective was to facilitate the work toward developing alternatives to the neo-liberal strategies. For this, she said, social mobilization and education are necessary in order to have informed participants who can then think about what else is possible.

The description of the case examples in the four clusters—income generation; health, housing, and the environment; women's resources and advocacy; and grassroots support organizations (GSOs) and independent organizers—along with the earlier contextual information, provide the essential background for discussion of the social mobilization themes in Part III. ∎

3 | Themes and Theories in the Struggles for Justice

WITH THE CONTEXT OF THE STRUGGLES set out and the individual stories of struggle and change recounted, the focus in Part III of this book turns to the social mobilization themes that emerged from the experiences and the related theory. Some of these themes in the struggles for justice appear to be fundamental and have universal relevance; others are specific to their particular context and their transferability to other situations will need to be assessed. The themes are located within the existing literature from across the social sciences and various practice disciplines interested in social mobilization.

Social movement theories from sociology have much to offer in building knowledge from the experiences of social movement communities, particularly now that the synthesis of insights from different paradigms such as resource mobilization, political process, social construction, and new social movement approaches is respected in academia (Buechler, 2011). Gramsci's political theory about civil society activists countering the hegemony of the state is useful, as well as knowledge about appropriate structures of organizations and effective leadership from the seemingly disparate field of organizational behaviour. Practice theory is utilized from the social work profession's community organizing methodology, as well as from the fields of international social development, community economic development, theology-based social ministry, and the pedagogy of popular education.

The themes pertain to four overarching categories. The first of these categories relates to the purposes of the various communities and collectivities with reference to the challenges inherent in their current context and the motivating influences for the collective projects they undertook. The second focuses on the nature and structure of the collective work and attends to their common objectives, the manner of working and organizational configuration, the resources required for the work and the related challenges, as well as the shared benefits of their work together. The third category deals with the means of mobilizing and taking action for the collective good, such as the targeted concerns and the strategies and methods utilized. The final category encompasses the challenges encountered, the outcomes achieved, and some overall conceptualizations for bringing about greater justice.

EIGHT

THE PURPOSES OF THE COLLECTIVE ENDEAVOURS

THE PURPOSES of the collective endeavours arose from the challenges experienced in the contexts in which the actors were embedded. Closely linked to these purposes are the motivating influences underlying the collective responses to the challenges.

The Challenges of the Context

CONTEXT IS CENTRAL to people's life chances, their understandings of their experiences (Thompson & Tapscott, 2010), as well as the opportunities for and constraints upon change initiatives (Green, 2008). Furthermore, as both Wichterich (2000) and Wilson (2009) remind us, change strategies must be adapted or constructed for the particular context. The challenges experienced by the communities and collectivities studied are connected, of course, to aspects of the context presented in Part I. However, illustrations of the specific realities of the communities and collectivities are foregrounded here.

The Economic Consequences of the Neo-liberal Model

The globalization of neo-liberal capitalism has reached even the most remote of the communities included in this study. The former liberal welfare-state economy in Canada and the former state-led developmentalist framework of Mexico have been replaced by the dominant free-market paradigm of our global economic context. Several aspects of the neo-liberal model have created fundamental challenges for the communities. The three pillars of the WTO's 1995 Agreement on Agriculture that Desmarais (2007) identified—"market access, export competition, and the reduction of domestic support"—emerged as significant across a broad range of products.

The reduction of state support in Mexico was most sharply experienced in the agricultural sector and the rural communities (Cortez Ruiz, 2010). The secretary of CEPCO, who had been involved with the state-wide coordination organization of small-farm coffee producers in Oaxaca from its beginning, spoke with emotion about the dramatic change. Earlier, he explained, INMECAFE (the government-run Mexican Coffee Institute) had purchased the coffee directly from the producers and did all of the marketing work until 1989, when "the government abandoned us."

Free trade under NAFTA required the partner countries to open their borders and provide access to their domestic market for the producers in the other countries. However, the United States, as the more powerful partner, was able to avoid the expectation of subsidy-free export competition and continued to heavily subsidize its agroindustry (Acuña Rodarte, 2003). For Teotitlán del Valle, Oaxaca, where the Zapotec people traditionally found economic gain in both weaving and agriculture, the low prices of US grains now sold in Mexico have made their own agricultural pursuits unviable. As a result, many of the young men have gone north in search of work, leaving the weaving enterprise primarily to the women. These women now must shoulder the family and community responsibilities without the traditional male contribution, as well as the role of selling the woven carpets, even though they had little marketing experience and most had seldom left their village previously.

The Environmental Context

Threats to the environment from industrial contamination and mining activity were all too common in the case examples. In the unregulated free-market economy, accounting ledgers do not deduct ecological and social costs from profits, and the Canadian government allows the extractives sector to play a predator role in the global South (Kuyek, 2011). The government's actions in removing protection of waterways are making Canada vulnerable to this same exploitation and devastation. The Xeni Gwet'in First Nation in BC's Nemaiah Valley recognized this in their opposition to Taseko Mines' proposal to use an existing lake as a tailings pond and to create an artificial lake for the fish. They were clear that the artificial lake could not support fish life, and that the poisons from the tailings pond would leech into the river systems. The UN's World Commission on Environment and Development (1987) called for sustainable development "that meets the needs of the present without compromising the ability of future generations to meet their own needs" (Chapter 2, para. 1). Past Chief Roger William demonstrated the centrality of that wisdom among Indigenous peoples in his first comment to me about the mining proposal: "We are taking too much away from future generations—what are we doing?"

The Political Context

The political context presented constraints to the possibilities for the communities in both Canada and Mexico. As Khagram (2002) concluded in his analysis of the struggles of people displaced by India's Narmada Valley Dams, a democratic context allowing protest and providing an autonomous judicial system was one of the prerequisites of success. Certainly, Canada's Indigenous peoples confronting a mining company's proposal had the advantage of a more democratic government and a more functional judicial system than did the ejidatarios dealing with a Canadian mining company in Guerrero, Mexico. This is borne out in the categorizations of the Economist Intelligence Unit (2013), which measures democracies in terms of pluralism, civil liberties, and political culture and ranks Mexico's democracy above that of many authoritarian regimes, although it is seen as flawed in comparison with Canada's full democracy (which, in turn, continues to lag behind that of most Scandinavian countries).

The impartial rule of law was blatantly absent in the treatment of the Guerrero mine protesters. The state police's arbitrary arrests of members of one family without warrants followed the common pattern documented by Human Rights Watch that was detailed in Chapter 3. At first, the state prosecutor's office denied that the state police had arrested the men; the community members eventually were able to learn where their comrades were being held, but even one of the human rights officers received a threat if he continued to assist them. Layton, Campillo, Ablanedo, and Sánchez (2010), who studied advocacy to reduce maternal mortality in Mexico, also encountered some powerful authoritarian state governments and noted that "the opportunities for and the impact of citizen engagement have been severely curtailed" (p. 105).

People in other Mexican communities spoke of government corruption and rights violations as well. In one of the Chiapas villages, members of a women's artisan collective described a municipal election after the 1994 Zapatista uprising when people wanted to see an end to PRI rule. They were adamant that the PRD had won the election; however, the ballots were burned and the PRI maintained control. Also in Chiapas, I learned from a women's organization that Indigenous girls from rural villages attending secondary school in San Cristóbal had been raped by soldiers operating military checkpoints. Daughters of leaders in the Zapatista movement were known to be at particular risk, so measures to protect them had been taken. According to Cockcroft (2010), many activists lament the "ubiquitous corruption" (p. 133) in Mexico and expect that an immense transformation will be required to restore democracy. Although the minimum requirements of democracy described by Diamond and Morlino (2005) are met in Mexico's universal suffrage and recently fair elections, the rule of law is not consistently applied to all citizens, the police force is not respectful of citizens' rights, and corruption is not sufficiently detected and punished to measure well on the first of the dimensions they suggest for assessing the quality of democracy.

A more covert form of government control was evident in the experiences of the Canadian women's centres. The Antigonish Women's Resource Centre in Nova Scotia has experienced pressure to depoliticize and to emphasize professionalized services through cuts to government funding and narrow funding mandates. The Kamloops Women's Resource Group Society in British Columbia has suffered similar funding cuts that required restructuring of their services and consideration of seeking charitable status despite its inherent constraints on advocacy. This constriction wrought by government was observed by Hammond-Callaghan and Hayday (2008) in their volume examining social movement activism in Canada, calling it the "hegemony of the liberal order" (p. 15).

The Socio-cultural Context

Examples of the realities of poverty, remote location, patriarchal structure, power imbalance, and traditional relations illustrate the socio-cultural context of several communities. Michael Cernea (1993), in his international advisory role as a sociologist, notes that socio-cultural factors, in addition to economic and environmental factors, are crucial to sustainable development.

In the south of Mexico, the depth of poverty was evident in people's living conditions. For example, dirt floors were common in many of the humble homes, and the people dug trenches around the outside to prevent the rainwater from running in, but even then, they explained, the humidity comes up from below the ground and makes for a very muddy floor. Health issues are a major challenge in marginalized communities (Layton et al., 2010) and this is most tragically evidenced in children dying of preventable diseases (Ife, 2010). The leader of the women's group on the outskirts of San Cristóbal had raised her family in a Tzeltal village in Chiapas, and she told me that she had given birth to twelve children, but due to illnesses like measles and a cough with fever, only six of them are still living. Likewise, I heard from the director of TADECO, the organization fostering community development within the state of Guerrero, that many of the children are malnourished and full of parasites and, therefore, they can succumb to minor illnesses very easily.

In some of the remote villages, the people needed to travel three hours to get provisions from the nearest town. For the Xeni Gwet'in in the Nemaiah Valley of British Columbia, it was a three-hour drive to Williams Lake, and for the Indigenous peoples living in the Sierra de Santa Martha in Veracruz, it was a three-hour walk to the town of Soteapan. The extent of poverty and the remoteness of many Indigenous communities contribute to the "shortage of surplus time" (p. 139), which Friedmann (1992) identified as a barrier to participation in social mobilization activities.

For women, patriarchal structures created a further barrier to participation. At the CODIMUJ meeting in Chiapas, participants in the discussion sessions identified practices rooted in ideologies of male dominance in their communities, such as men dictating the marriages of their daughters, who were fourteen (or sometimes younger), and the expectation that women's role is to maintain their husbands. In a Veracruz town, one of the community organizers highlighted the challenge that women face in the machismo culture, where they are expected to be in the home. This was expressed in the quote "Sus esposos no les dejan salir" (their husbands don't let them go out), which I also heard in Teotitlán del Valle, Oaxaca. Christine Kovic (2003b), in her study of CODIMUJ, similarly reported hearing about the courage women needed to participate in collective endeavours in the face of criticism for not remaining at home.

A significant imbalance of power exists between Canadian mining corporations and the Indigenous communities living on the land desired for mining purposes. The mining industry has successfully lobbied government for legislative change, making it easier for mining companies to meet environmental standards. Typical of other Canadian Indigenous communities, the Xeni Gwet'in First Nation, in the British Columbia example, lacks the political influence, money, and technical expertise of the Taseko Mines corporation. The Chamber of Commerce in Williams Lake and then premier Gordon Campbell favoured the Taseko Mines proposal and, in early 2010, the BC government granted permission for the proposal against the Xeni Gwet'in's wishes. Past Chief Roger William described how the government had sent several proposals to the Xeni Gwet'in for review since their 1989 Declaration of the Nemaiah Aboriginal Wilderness Preserve, but the government set impossible deadlines, didn't provide adequate funding to hire technical experts to review the material, and, in the end, ignored the community's opinion. For the 2010 federal environmental impact assessment, which led the federal government to reject the Taseko Mines proposal, substantial participation from community members of all ages, as well as from partner organizations, needed to be mustered to counter the claims of Taseko Mines.

On the positive side, the socio-cultural characteristic of strong community bonds served many of the study sites well in their struggles for social justice. This was exemplified in the description provided by one of the CODIMUJ leaders of the "long tradition of solidarity" in the rural communities of Chiapas, where discussion of issues typically continues until everyone is comfortable with the outcome. Similarly, in the Veracruz urban neighbourhood that began by tackling the garbage problem, the community organizer stated that they "work in solidarity with the children and for the children." The way the six families worked together to construct each of their houses, one by one, with Habitat for Humanity funding was an example of these community bonds. The ·Women's Economic Equality (WEE) Society is an example of women in Nova Scotia working together in solidarity for economically marginalized women. A collective of four women work in a non-hierarchical fashion from their virtual offices in their own homes to develop and run innovative employment services for women with a core group of long-term project staff, even though there sometimes are gaps in funding during which the collective and staff are not paid. Oxhorn (1995) has written about the benefit of community solidarity in civil society organizing, emphasizing the notions of mutual self-help and community participation in the concept of *vecino* (neighbour) in the poor neighbourhoods of Latin America. Although these bonds were more naturally occurring in the Mexican rural and poor neighbourhoods of this study, there certainly were examples of such solidarity in Canadian projects with a strong commitment to the social justice work as well.

The Motivating Influences

THE PEOPLE INVOLVED in the collective struggles for social justice spoke with passion about their endeavours and, consequently, the key influences that motivated them emerged as a strong theme. Motivation has been recognized as an important element in collective action since the early developments in social movement theory that looked at participants' motivations as a form of cost-benefit calculation in making rational choices (Olson, 1965). More recently, Pinard (2011) has offered a model for considering motivation in collective action that suggests three potential internal motives: grievances, aspirations, and moral obligations. As the data from the projects studied will show, this model has some merit for understanding social mobilization in the current Canadian and Mexican contexts. Two distinct types of motivating influences were observed in the examples—necessity and ideals.

Acting Out of Necessity

I was quite struck to hear several of the communities begin their story by telling me that their organizing was "out of necessity," something that they clearly had to do in order to survive. There was urgency for the Chiapas and Oaxaca coffee farmers "abandoned" by the government to find a new way to market their crops, for the people in the Veracruz neighbourhood by the garbage dump to protect their babies from dying due to contaminated food, and for the settlers in the Guerrero neighbourhood to get water and electricity into their community. Overall, the necessities pertained to income, living conditions, land, environmental conditions, health problems, gender oppression, and fear. Although Thompson and Tapscott (2010) raise questions about the applicability of social movement theory in southern contexts where desperation drives people to collective action, analysis below of the present examples suggests that despite the protagonists living on the margins of survival, they did engage in conscious and sophisticated framing of options and selection of strategies.

An income issue that often needed to be addressed was the exploitation by middlemen who bought products at prices barely above cost from producers like the coffee growers, the amate-paper painters in Guerrero, and the artisans in Nova Scotia, then sold the products at much higher prices for their own excessive profit. Another injustice related to income was the unfair competition experienced by artisans in Michoacán whose guitars and pottery, for example, were being replicated in countries with cheap labour and sold internationally with labels implying the products were made by the famous Mexican craftspeople.

Improved living conditions constituted a necessity for families who lived in one-room corrugated metal houses in the Veracruz neighbourhood and wooden structures made with sticks in the Guerrero neighbourhood. But the crowded living conditions were secondary to the families' initial need to find and gain title to vacant land that they had found. Land issues were even problematic for farmers who held collective title to ejido land; the neoliberal changes making this land available for sale had led to conflict in the communities in the Guerrero region that TADECO serves—in one instance, eight campesinos being pressured to sell their land were assassinated in a village of only fifteen families.

The necessity of organizing to deal with environmental issues was obvious for the two Indigenous communities struggling against the Canadian mining corporations. It was also the motivation for the groups in the Tejalpa area, the industrial zone for Cuernavaca, Morelos, which became so contaminated that food and livestock could not be produced there and children could not be bathed in the tap water. The two community organizers from Tejalpa who were interviewed, Estela and Licha, brought additional motivations that intersected with the need to address environmental problems—on Estela's part, a feminist commitment, and on Licha's part, a feminist commitment and a liberation theology imperative. However, in both cases, the initial community project they described to me dealt with the ecological concerns.

Dealing with the health issues emanating from the garbage dump in the Veracruz neighbourhood was paramount for them. Ending the contamination of their food by the flies from the rotting garbage was truly a matter of life and death. That strong a resolve motivated them to take turns in maintaining a round-the-clock vigil at the entrance to the dump for nine years until the municipality finally relented and created a landfill site in a non-residential area. The communities studied also included examples of health promoters using natural medicines and traditional practices. Padre Pedro Felipe in the state of Guerrero and a Christian Base Community (CEB) in Cuernavaca, Morelos, were motivated by the needs of many community members who were ill but had no resources to cover the cost of conventional medicine. In both of these examples, as well as in a few similar ones, the leaders engaged in intensive study themselves and provided or arranged for the training of others and, as a result, a growing group of practitioners are providing an affordable means for people to recover their health. One final example of motivation arising from health-related necessity is apparent in the work of the potter/physician from the Michoacán town specializing in pottery. Because of his medical training, he recognized the effects of lead on families making pottery, and he is now teaching youth in his town a pre-Hispanic method of applying a shine to pottery without the use of lead.

The need to address women's inequality was the fundamental motivation of many of the collectives and organizers. All three of the women's resource projects arose from discussions about women's oppression in the late 1970s and early 1980s among women connected to their local universities. The Rosario Castellanos Women's Study Group introduced themselves to the wider public in 1979 through a weekly radio program addressing such themes as violence against women, abortion, rape, and the history of feminism in Mexico. British Columbia's Kamloops Women's Resource Group Society and the Kamloops Sexual Assault Counselling Centre were developed in response to needs identified in annual women's conferences in the early 1980s. Similarly, the Antigonish Women's Resource Centre & Sexual Assault Services Association in Nova Scotia was born out of women's participation in a 1982 discussion series. The founding of these three organizations is consistent with the findings of many analysts of the women's movement that much activism and program development followed the first World Conference on Women in Mexico City in 1975, which, along with the related United Nations declarations, provided legitimacy for women's demands (Eschle & Maiguashca, 2010). Three decades later, these programs and new ones continue to pursue the rights of women.

MUSA, the women's program of the jungle and highland region coffee co-operative in Chiapas (Unión de la Selva), runs training programs every two months focusing on skills for their income-generating projects and on struggles they face as women. Workshops were being held, at the women's request, on alcoholism (since men's heavy drinking often resulted in women being beaten) and on human rights (since the women often encounter resistance from their husbands when they seek greater equality and leave their homes to participate in collective enterprises). Wichterich (2000) notes that the slogan "Women's rights are human rights" builds on universalizing norms; the advantage of this in a very machismo setting suggests a highly astute framing decision on the part of the MUSA organizers. Licha, whose organizing work in relation to environmental issues in Tejalpa was described earlier, is currently the lead for the state of Morelos in the movement for women's reproductive rights through her participation in Católicas por el Derecho a Decidir (Catholic Women for the Right to Decide). Again, the international legitimization of women's rights and maternal health objectives has been important in the Mexican context, where for many women, seeking abortion was against the law (Layton et al., 2010).

The final matter commanding redress out of necessity was the fear related to "low-intensity warfare" in Mexico. The apprehension created by the military checkpoints in Chiapas was discussed by members of a CODIMUJ women's group in a rural Chiapas town, as well as in relation to girls attending secondary school in San Cristóbal. The knowledge that the soldiers had raped other Indigenous women heightened their fear and raised the matter as a possible focus of protest for the upcoming International Women's Day. Fear was also a motivator for people involved with TADECO in Guerrero, who worked in collaboration with the Committee of Families and Friends of the Kidnapped, Disappeared, and Assassinated in Guerrero because partners in the social struggle had been disappeared along with hundreds of others in the state for whom the government frequently used the pretext of the drug trade to disguise its own complicity. Interestingly, there seems to be very little about the impact of fear on motivation in the academic literature.

In the numerous issues that motivated the communities to act out of necessity, one finds evidence of grievances, as suggested in Pinard's (2011) model identifying three internal motives for collective action. Pressing needs related to poverty, land, the environment, health, gender oppression, and fear constituted grievances that prompted social mobilization to struggle for solutions.

Ideals That Propelled the Collective Action

Ideals, including fundamental principles, core values, and the central tenets of distinctive worldviews, were at the root of much of the collective action. The principles of liberation theology, the values of social justice and democracy, as well as the precepts of an Indigenous worldview, were ideals that the organizers and social movement communities cited with conviction in describing why they mobilized. As with the influence of urgent needs mentioned earlier, often there are overlapping ideals present simultaneously.

Liberation theology was referenced in Part I as central to the socio-cultural context of Mexico, and in Part II in the telling of specific stories, particularly in Mexico. Kovic (2003b) has noted how the Catholic Church in Mexico was profoundly influenced by the meetings of the Second Vatican Council in the early 1960s and the Latin American bishops meeting in 1968, which "emphasized the structural roots of poverty and called on the church to take corrective actions and to end injustice" (p. 131). Others, such as Cortez Ruiz (2010) and Tetreault (2013a), have connected the influence of liberation theology with specific social movements, such as the Zapatista movement in Chiapas and the agroecology movement in the south of Mexico, respectively.

Organizers and communities motivated by liberation theology and its "preferential option for the poor" were abundant. Since illustrations of how their beliefs played out in their work were provided in the stories in Part II, here I focus on the remarkable commitment of some of these leaders to living a non-materialist life in solidarity with the poor. The relevant message of Christ is recorded in the Bible's New Testament:

> Do not lay up for yourselves treasures on earth.... Do not be anxious about your life.... Look at the birds of the air: they neither sow nor reap nor gather into barns, and yet your heavenly Father feeds them. Are you not of more value than they?...Consider the lilies of the field, how they grow; they neither toil nor spin; yet I tell you, even Solomon in all his glory was not arrayed like one of these.... Will he [God] not much more clothe you?...Seek first the kingdom of God and his righteousness, and all these things shall be yours as well. (Matthew 6: 19, 25–33; Revised Standard Version)

Several of the leaders in the projects studied had chosen to live humbly and not worry about assets or income. Still, for the sake of brevity, I must exclude some who also inspire me and will highlight only those where the subject was explicitly discussed.

Maria de los Angeles, who is the coordinator of the health centre in the Veracruz neighbourhood, receives only a small stipend for her work and she doesn't have other employment—her housemate pays the bills and Maria de los Angeles does the housework. She told me that she simply doesn't need money—she doesn't worry about having things and she always has what she needs. When the Just Us! Coffee Roasters Co-op in Nova Scotia began in 1996, it was comprised of Jeff and Debra and three of their friends. Jeff and Debra offered their home as equity for the original roastery in a small house, and it took five years before the co-operative became profitable. But, they said, the fair trade project fit with their philosophy of working in solidarity with the oppressed and they trusted that their material needs would be met as they always had been in the past. Tere and Amado in the Guerrero neighbourhood are the final example. Tere told me that she and Amado had decided it would be too difficult to live this simply in the same manner as the poor if they had children and, therefore, the many children she has encountered in her work have been her "children in her heart." I asked how they live without paid employment and Tere said that members of her family have been generous to them, and a liberation theologian, who recently died, had provided them with a regular stipend for many years. As well, she said that they have done some contract work when needed. Amado explained, "God always provides for us—we get by on very little and we are never in need."

Social justice is a core value that was pivotal to the purpose of many of the social struggles studied. It overlaps, of course, with the principles of liberation theology discussed earlier, as well as with those of many other religious belief systems, professional practice disciplines, and other people involved in social development work. The global definition of social work, for example, contains the phrase "Principles of social justice, human rights, collective responsibility and respect for diversities are central to social work" (IASSW & IFSW, 2014, para. 1). Wilson, Calhoun, and Whitmore (2011) analyzed the work of nine activist groups across Canada led by people with varied academic and practice backgrounds, and found that activists from all of the groups identified broad social and environmental justice goals.

The Antigonish Women's Resource Centre & Sexual Assault Services Association in Nova Scotia, since its beginning, has been committed to social justice objectives as well as to providing needed services. Although it has been an ongoing challenge to fund the social change activities, they remain dedicated to working for women's equality. In the marginalized neighbourhood in the state of Veracruz, the women had worked long and hard to obtain title to the land, to have the municipality establish a proper landfill site in a non-residential area, to establish and operate a health centre using preventive and traditional approaches, and to replace inadequate housing with sturdy homes. Next, they were preparing to fence in the property from animals and considering the development of a recreational space. Some comments from various women participating in the community's projects convey the centrality of social justice in their efforts: "I enjoy being part of this group, working with natural medicine, struggling for justice, and doing human service" and "We are women who feel good about fighting for our rights—we enjoy the struggle," as well as "The struggles have been tremendous because we were dealing with powerful people. However, they weren't too much for us because we are women who can do what we want to in order to move forward."

The importance of democracy was also a common reason given for the social mobilization actions. Bartra and Otero (2005) have documented the Indigenous struggles in Mexico for land, autonomy, and democracy. This study revealed unresponsive governments and unfair political party practices being disputed in the small towns and marginalized neighbourhoods as well. In the rural Chiapas town, where a women's group was fostered by CODIMUJ, there was discussion of a protest on International Women's Day focusing on one of a number of problems they experienced with government and politicians. This included the frustration that, despite paying for public utilities, electricity is often not provided. In the under-resourced neighbourhood studied in Guerrero, the founders described a time before they had a community tap, and one of the political parties came in weekly with a water truck, but, they provided water only to their party members. "These were ugly months," one of the founders said of the party's attempt to buy votes from desperate people and create division in the community; however, in time the people responded by uniting and successfully pressuring the water commission for a water pipe for the entire neighbourhood. In Canada, the Raging Grannies are often eager to appear at political events to expose some of the shortcomings in Canada's democratic life. The Wolfville gaggle, in an all-candidates forum, introduced each of the contenders in song and roasted them equally; they highlighted politicians' common difficulty in remaining true to their stated positions (a clear reference to their own MP having changed sides in the House of Commons in the prior sitting). These efforts, motivated by the desire to move closer to the ideal of democracy and the understanding that further efforts will be required, are consistent with Daniel Schugurensky's (2013) perspective that "democracy should not be perceived as a static structure but as a long historical—and probably endless—process shaped by the struggles of subordinated groups for freedom and equality" (p. x).

The final ideals that gave impetus to collective action in the examples studied are the precepts of Indigenous worldviews. McKenzie and Morrissette (2003) provide a helpful understanding of the beliefs and principles of Indigenous culture as distinct from the dominant Euro-Canadian culture. Fundamental Indigenous beliefs are that the spirit of the Creator is present in all of nature and living things, including humankind, and that all things have an interconnected role in ensuring balance, harmony, and overall well-being. Arising from these beliefs are principles for living in a sacred relationship with the earth: "not as separate from the natural world; rather, [as]...an extension of the same world" (p. 259) and in communal and reciprocal relationships with one another. Altimirano-Jiménez (2013) highlights the importance of colonial structures in shaping Indigenous places, so we are reminded of the greater mixing of Indigenous and Spanish cultures in Mexico, where campesinos who may not be considered Indigenous by virtue of their spoken language may still be living on communal lands with profound commitment to living in harmony with the land. However, there is relevance to the Indigenous peoples' worldviews in both Canada and Mexico, and in Altimirano-Jiménez's statement about the problematic neo-liberal perspective on economic development in which "nature and natural resources are almost exclusively depicted as economic potential, a depiction that does not always match Indigenous peoples' understandings of their place-based relationships with nature" (p. 6).

The clearest examples of adherence to Indigenous worldviews were from the Guerrero and British Columbia communities fighting to protect the land, water, vegetation, fish, wildlife, and people from the poisons produced in mining operations. In Guerrero, the ejidatarios blocked the entrance to the mining area after they found unacceptable levels of arsenic in their water and that their pleas to the company and to the government went unheeded. In British Columbia, the Xeni Gwet'in First Nation made their case to both provincial and federal environmental impact assessment hearings that the proposed mine would be severely detrimental to the water, fish, wildlife, and their own use of the land for traditional purposes. Similarly, in the Michoacán CASART program supporting the artisans through trademark protection of their craft and marketing opportunities, the motivation was also to protect the artisans' cultural heritage and way of life. Many of the artisans are continuing traditional methods from pre-Hispanic times, and many of the producer collectives date back at least to Bishop Vasco de Quiroga's organizing work in the 1530s. Hence it is totally consistent with their Indigenous worldview that the artisans want to protect their crafts, which they describe as part of their heritage. Nor are they willing to borrow large sums to build warehouses, for example, by risking their homes and land as collateral—they saw these not as commodities, but as part of their heritage too. Thus, their motivation is to protect their traditional way of life in a manner that fits with their Indigenous worldview.

In summary, the principles of liberation theology, social justice, democracy, and the Indigenous worldview were ideals that motivated many of the communities to mobilize. These correspond to the moral obligations identified by Pinard (2011) as one of three internal motives for collective action. The other internal motive Pinard suggests is aspirations, and clearly, aspirations are the corollary to grievances arising out of necessity and they are the goals of actions based on moral obligations or ideals. Thus, Pinard's internal motives of grievances, aspirations, and moral obligations in collective action are substantiated in the finding of necessity and ideals being the primary motivating influences in the struggles for social justice documented in this research. These motivating influences, which arise from the challenges of the neo-liberal context of present-day Canada and Mexico, together constitute the purposes of the collective endeavours. We should not be too surprised, then, to find many of these same aspirations in the declaration of the Zapatista National Liberation Army (1994/2002) upon their uprising, which coincided with the implementation of NAFTA: "We, the men and women of the EZLN … ask for your participation in and support of the plan that struggles for work, land, housing, food, health care, education, independence, freedom, democracy, justice, and peace" (p. 220). ∎

NINE

THE NATURE AND THE STRUCTURE OF THE COLLECTIVE WORK

THE NATURE AND THE STRUCTURE of the collective endeavours were important in the lives of these social movement communities. Aspects of this include the objectives of working together; the manner of doing the collective work; and the supports and shared benefits of the work.

The Principles, Objectives, and Commitment to Working Together

THE PEOPLE INVOLVED in the social movement activities spoke about the principles that guided their work and the collective objectives they held. In addition, a very strong theme throughout the collective work studied was the importance of working together as a community.

The Principles and Objectives of the Collective Work

Many of the participants in the collective enterprises spoke of the principles of co-operation and sharing for the benefit of the whole community, which guided their work together. In the Veracruz town with the tortilla collective, a community organization had developed out of the liberation theology discussions, which had created numerous collective projects—all for the benefit of everyone. One of the long-standing members of the organization described the co-operative, non-competitive way this community has been able to work together. For example, she said, "When someone must be sent as a delegate to a meeting, there is a friendly discussion about who would like to go." An organizer from one of the NGOs that had worked to obtain resources for this community substantiated this claim, saying that when project funds were obtained, the community had similarly amicable discussions about who needed the assistance the most and where they should begin. The state-level coffee producers' coalition in Oaxaca operates according to the same principles—working together to find solutions to the problems confronted "for the well-being of the coffee-producing families and communities."

Collective objectives were established in keeping with the specific challenges the particular communities were facing. The Xeni Gwet'in, in their 1989 declaration, made it clear they would not allow any logging, mining, or other land use in the British Columbia Nemaiah preserve without their agreement. Employees of CASART, the quasi-governmental organization in Michoacán, were confident that their approach in facilitating the creation of formal civil associations by artisans collectives was the most effective and sustainable way to support the artisan sector. The collective objective of the artisans in the legally recognized civil associations of Michoacán was to register a collective trademark for their products. In addition, many of the artisans collectives, in Michoacán and beyond, worked together so that they could buy their inputs, maintain storage facilities, and market their goods jointly.

The Commitment to Working Together

Strongly connected to the principle of co-operation and the objectives of the collective work was a belief in the importance of working together. The former chief of the Xeni Gwet'in emphasized that their community had been united for a long time as a result of previous struggles and achievements. One of the CASART staff indicated this was true of the Indigenous communities of Michoacán as well, which had been working together in their own forms of organizations for centuries—it was only the formation of legally constituted civil associations that was new. The founders of MUSA's belief in the value of working collectively was described by one who is now a staff person: "We had the same idea as the Unión de la Selva: as a group we can accomplish more than individuals; as individuals it is slower and more difficult to succeed." The leader of the community organization in the marginalized Veracruz neighbourhood gave credit for the people's commitment to the priest who had brought them together in the 1980s: "He taught us that we can accomplish much when we are organized; each person acting on his/her own—no, but organized—yes!"

Some of these principles and beliefs in collective work in Mexico no doubt arose from the teachings of liberation theology. Samuel Ruiz, the former bishop of Chiapas, remarked on the new producer co-operatives and the growing sense of social responsibility among the Indigenous peoples, "seeing a need to act for peace and justice together...[and] increasing solidarity" (Menocal & Ruiz, 1998, p. 100). There may also be a greater proclivity among women's groups, not only in Mexico, to hold strong commitments to working collectively for the benefit of the community. Tinker (2000) found, in her study of poverty alleviation projects, that community development programs run by women tend to be broader, creating "a democratic space where community residents could both form ties with each other and develop as individuals" (p. 237) while working to better the community. These shared values, beliefs, and sense of purpose characterize the collective identity, which Caniglia Schaefer and Carmin (2005) note are present within particular social movements and Kutz-Flamenbaum (2012) describes as unifying in ways that make the collective action possible.

The Manner of Doing the Work and Structuring the Organizations

THERE WERE A VARIETY OF WAYS in which the collectivities did their work together and variations in how they structured their organizations. In both of these areas, approaches were found in Mexico that were not observed in Canada.

The Ways of Working Together

The manner of doing the collective work varied in terms of simplicity and sophistication; whether the workers were volunteers or employed staff; and the roles of members, organizers, spouses, and experts. One of the simplest practices was the Raging Grannies' routine of dressing up in outlandish hats and singing two or three stinging songs before dashing away. The practitioners of alternative medicines emphasized the simplicity of their work and that they "have learned how to help people get better with very little money," but in reality, they have invested a great deal of time in learning about the properties of various herbs and the preparation of the remedies. Sophisticated knowledge is used in the biology lab in Oaxaca, where the women's program of CEPCO was developing, for example, an organic herbicide to fight the coffee borer.

Most of the people power put into the work of the various projects was contributed by volunteers. This is not surprising in collective activities that are for the benefit of the participants' own community, like the Xeni Gwet'in's struggle against the Taseko Mines' proposal, although the persistent need to fend off such attempted incursions must surely be taxing. And it is usually the case that members of boards of directors are volunteers, although in work that is countering powerful forces, the time commitment is usually substantial. What is surprising is the amount of unpaid work people are contributing to their community or organization. The health promoters in the Veracruz neighbourhood, for example, volunteer a day or two each week, receiving only a small honorarium every six months, with many working as domestic help on the other days to support their families. In the Oaxaca women's centre, each of the twelve board members is chosen for her expertise and is responsible for the centre's work in that area—some entirely as volunteers and some receiving a small monthly stipend. This level of unpaid contribution was not found in the Canadian cases. In some of these examples, the children of the volunteers were involved as well—the students from British Columbia's Nemaiah Valley school at the environmental impact assessment hearing, and the older children in the Veracruz neighbourhood at the vigils to stop trucks from dumping garbage. A combination of volunteer and paid workers is also occurring in organizations because of decreased funding for paid positions, as in the case of the coordinator in the Kamloops, British Columbia, women's centre whose paid hours have been reduced to ten hours per week, but she continues to put in many more hours each week as a volunteer to ensure that the important work gets done.

In many organizations there is a blend of volunteers and employed staff. At the Oaxaca women's resource centre, in addition to the board members who provide professional services as volunteers, there are paid employees running the centre and working on publications and multimedia resources. Similarly, Catholic Women for the Right to Decide has a paid team of six women, plus an executive director at the national level; however, the promoters and representatives at the state level are volunteers. Only in the income-generating projects and co-operatives are nearly all of the participants paid for their work. In some of the co-operatives the board or executive positions are unpaid, whereas in others, some members of the executive are paid to perform managerial tasks. The producers or workers not in managerial positions are generally reimbursed according to the goods or work they provide, and they consider themselves to be collective owners or members rather than employees. Some of the co-operatives, like the artisans in Cheticamp, Nova Scotia, allow non-members to sell their products on consignment, but not to participate in profit-sharing. Children of members are now employed in some of the coffee co-operatives. The co-operatives are particularly pleased when the young people, with their first-hand knowledge of producer issues and their abiding cómmitment to the community, pursue education in areas that benefit the organization. The manager of marketing and the manager of the roastery at Unión de la Selva in Chiapas, as well as the manager of the greenhouse and nursery operations at Ita-Teku, the women's program of the Oaxaca co-operative, are examples of this.

The manner of doing the work also varied in relation to the roles and levels of participation. Family responsibilities affected the potential involvement of collective members. Many of the income-generating projects provided an opportunity for members to do their work from their homes. This is obvious in the case of the coffee producers and the members of the associated women's programs who were growing new plants to diversify their cash crops. However, in all of the co-operatives that included women with young children, accommodations were made in arranging for the responsibilities ancillary to the actual production. For the women diversifying the family's dependence on coffee income, the training sessions held outside of their local community were attended by representatives without child-care responsibilities, who, in turn, trained the other women in their community upon their return. For products that required women from the community to be involved in marketing beyond their own home, it was women without young children who ran the stores or sold the products in the streets and parks of tourist areas and in artisan fairs. Variation in the intensity and type of participation in the collective work also occurred in relation to the level of commitment as seen earlier in the influence of ideals and in relation to skills, as in the design work by one of the members of the artisans co-operative in Nova Scotia.

There were important expert roles in the collective work, some of which were played by members of the collective itself and some by people who were external. Examples of internal experts were the academics, lawyers, and professionals in leadership positions in the three women's resource projects. Some of the external experts were the scientists, lawyer, and videographer who assisted the Xeni Gwet'in.

The role of husbands was important in the women's collective endeavours. In two different Veracruz communities, husbands participated in particular projects—for example, constructing the houses built with financial support from Habitat for Humanity and running the tortillería. In one of the Canadian women's resource projects, a staff member told me that her husband is proud to wear his "Vagina Monologues" t-shirt, and that it promotes discussion of women's rights with his friends and family. Conversely, three of the women who were leaders of social movement organizations in Mexico told me that their marriages had ended because their husbands were not supportive of their work and were not willing to collaborate in domestic responsibilities. In relation to coffee production, the Oaxaca state-level co-operative emphasized that the whole family works together, not just the husband, but the wife and the sons and daughters. Staff of the women's program of the Unión de la Selva in Chiapas concurred, saying that they foster "the importance of the whole family's participation in the production of the coffee and in the benefits of the production."

The Ways of Structuring the Organizations

Various types of organizations and entities were active in mobilizing for social change. There were also numerous ways of structuring the organizations in relation to the degree of formalization, whether membership was open or closed, the existence and role of a board or executive, linkages to a larger organization or federation, and the decision-making process.

Typologies in the academic literature help to distinguish the various kinds of organizations and collectivities, although there is variability in how many of the terms are used. As described in the introduction, this research employs a broad definition of social movements and has adopted Staggenborg's (2013) concept of a "social movement community" to include entities that are not organizations. Thus, this study includes several people who are not affiliated with a particular organization, although the collective activities they foster led to the development of organizations. In Mexico, this includes people like Agustina and Licha, who work outside of organizations, as well as through more than one organization. In Canada, this is exemplified in the work of the women who came together after discussions at their universities to create the women's programs in Antigonish, Nova Scotia, and Kamloops, British Columbia. The other social movement communities were organizations and they all fit the broad category of civil society organizations (CSOs), which are also known as non-governmental organizations (NGOs).

Society can be conceptualized as being comprised of three sectors: the private sector (the market), the public sector (the state), and the voluntary sector (civil society). From this perspective, it is quite apparent that the individuals and organizations involved in the social movement communities studied are neither private sector businesses nor public sector governments—they are operating in the voluntary sector, and the organizations are civil society

Figure 9.1

Civil Society Organizations

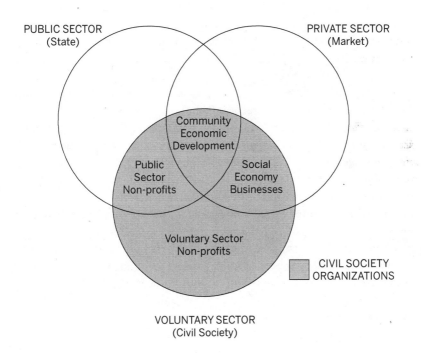

PUBLIC SECTOR
(State)

PRIVATE SECTOR
(Market)

Community
Economic
Development

Public
Sector
Non-profits

Social
Economy
Businesses

Voluntary Sector
Non-profits

CIVIL SOCIETY
ORGANIZATIONS

VOLUNTARY SECTOR
(Civil Society)

Source: Adapted from Quarter, Mook, and Armstrong (2009), p. 7.

organizations. The complexity begins when we acknowledge that organizations may receive revenue from more than one sector and are more accurately located within three intersecting circles. This is illustrated in Figure 9.1 in an adaptation of what Quarter, Mook, and Armstrong (2009) called the social economy.

Civil society organizations are defined as organizations with a social mission, and they are represented by the full circle of organizations based in civil society, including those that intersect with the private sector and the public sector since they may or may not receive revenue from the private or non-profit sectors. Voluntary non-profits are those CSOs that do not overlap with the private or public sector. The voluntary non-profits in the study are CODIMUJ in Chiapas, all three of the women's centres, the Raging Grannies in Nova Scotia, and COMPA located in Chiapas. Social economy businesses are CSOs that earn revenue in the private sector. In this study, the social economy businesses are the co-operatives studied (the coffee and other producer co-operatives, the collectives directly engaged in income-generating projects, and the health-related projects. Community economic development (CED) organizations receive revenue from both the private and the public sector as government-funded micro-enterprise development programs do. The WEE Society in Nova Scotia and CASART in Morelos are examples of CED organizations since they use public funds to assist women and artisans, respectively, to generate income from the private market. The last category, public sector non-profits, includes CSOs with substantial amounts of public sector funding. The two communities struggling against Canadian mining companies—the ejido in Guerrero and the Xeni Gwet'in in British Columbia—can be said to represent this category. Although a strong case can be made that these communities are local-level governments and, therefore, public sector entities, they do not have autonomy over approval of mining projects on their land, and they are involved in social movement activities with social, health, and environmental objectives.

Any model, of course, is based on ideal types and real-life examples do not always fit one ideal type precisely. The health promotion projects in Mexico fall primarily in the social economic business category because their revenue comes from sales of the natural remedies and alternative treatments they provide. However, the promoters are not generating an income from this activity; its purpose is to assist community members who cannot afford conventional health care and prescription medicines. This service objective has a great deal in common with the objectives of many voluntary sector non-profits and in a

Canadian context, where charitable donations are more readily available as a reliable source of revenue for such services, these projects would more likely be voluntary non-profit organizations. Another example of imprecision is the categorization of CASART. It is considered to be, essentially, an example of CED because its operations include UNEAMICH, the state union of Michoacán artisans, whose members' incomes are generated through their sales in the private market. However, UNEAMICH aside, CASART would be a public sector non-profit and a specific subtype—a quasi-autonomous, non-governmental organization established by government with a government mandate and funding, but operationally independent.

Another means of distinguishing different types of organizations is by identifying their level of operation: local, regional, provincial/state, national, or international. At the local level, one finds community-based organizations (CBOs), which are also known as grassroots organizations. The marginalized neighbourhood on the outskirts of a city in the state of Veracruz now operating a health centre, and the marginalized neighbourhood in the Guerrero city that had won land title, water, electricity, and a school are examples of CBOs. The Unión de la Selva coffee co-operative in the jungle and highlands portion of Chiapas is an example of a regional-level organization, and CEPCO is an example of a state-level organization. Catholic Women for the Right to Decide (CDD) is a national organization in Mexico, which Licha represented in Morelos, and Convergence of People's Movements in the Americas (COMPA) is an example of an international organization.

One more type of organization needs to be identified here and these are grassroots support organizations (GSOs). Boglio Martínez (2008) defines GSOs as "development NGOs providing services and resources that enhance the capacity of impoverished communities and their organizations to build sustainable alternatives to their challenging life conditions" (p. 341). This is the kind of activity carried out by TADECO in Guerrero and by Tere and Amado as independent organizers in Guerrero.

Beyond organizational types based primarily on source of revenue, organizations also vary in how they are configured in terms of formality, openness to additional members, a board or executive function, connection to larger bodies, and decision making. Formality is often clustered with centralized and hierarchical organizational forms and contrasted with, at the opposite end of a continuum, organizations that are informal, decentralized, and egalitarian (Buechler, 2000). The most informal entities studied were, of course, the individuals and couple who were working outside of a particular organization and the amate-painting and embroidery collectives that had not yet come to fruition at the time they were studied. Of the functioning organizations, the most informal was the marginalized neighbourhood in Veracruz, which, by 2004, had operated for twenty years without any elected officers and recognized Maria de los Angeles as their leader, but one without need of an official decision or title. They were beginning the legal process of registering the organization to enable them to apply for funding in their own name and to ensure the longevity of the organization. All the other organizations were formalized, although to varying degrees. CASART was probably the most formalized organization with legislation affirming its quasi-state mandate, its centralized location in the state capital, a hierarchical structure of multiple divisions and departments reporting to a director, and a mandate to assist community-based artisans collectives to become legally constituted civil associations so they can register collective trademarks for their products.

The organizations also varied with regard to openness to additional members. The civil associations fostered by CASART were constitutionally obliged to include all interested artisans engaged in the same craft. Invitations were similarly extended to other interested people in the community by Margo's group in Mexico City after they determined their focus on preparing natural medicines. In contrast, the women's centre in Oaxaca invites only specific women to join them, based on their professional expertise when one of the current twelve decides to resign. In the same fashion, the Just Us! Coffee Roasters Co-op in Nova Scotia invites only employees to become worker-owners after they have worked there for two years.

The existence of boards of directors or executives and the related roles also varied across the organizations. Some of the boards or executives were membership-based. For example, the board of the women's centre in Nova Scotia was composed of ten to fifteen people elected by the membership of about one hundred. On a smaller scale, the fifty members of the potters' collective in Chiapas elect an executive composed of a president, secretary, and treasurer. In contrast, other boards and executives were exclusive. The women's centre in Oaxaca mentioned earlier does not have a membership that elects the board—the centre comprises solely the twelve-member board, which changes only when a replacement is needed for someone who resigns. Similarly, the Tejalpa health and environmental project in Morelos has no membership or election of an executive; they simply comprise a team of six who rotate through three executive roles. This exclusive structure, which serves the latter two organizations in Mexico very well, was not found in any of the organizations in Canada. The most common executive positions were president, secretary, and treasurer. A unique executive role called "guardian" was identified in Mexico, but was not found in Canada. The textile workers co-operative in Chiapas had two additional executive members who were described as the official guardians and heart of the organization with responsibility for facilitating well-functioning relationships among the members of the collective. The executive of the coffee co-operative in Chiapas also included a guardian position. This is probably an especially important role in a situation where the community organizer is unable to speak the Indigenous language of the members of the collective.

Connections to larger organizations were important features of some of the organizations. In three of the cases in Mexico, organizations were linked to parent organizations. Both of the coffee producers' co-operatives had women's programs that were affiliated with the primary organization. Similarly, the state union of Michoacán artisans, UNEAMICH, was fostered by and works closely with CASART. Another type of linkage is the federated structure whereby organizations at the local level send representatives to the regional level, and the regional level sends representatives to the next level, and so on. This is the structure of the women's organizations comprising CODIMUJ from the community to the diocese level. It is also used in the coffee producers' co-operatives. Unión de la Selva encompasses the local and zone co-operatives up to its level as a region, whereas CEPCO is situated one level further at the state level; the state-level organizations belong to the CNOC—the National Council of Coffee Producers Organizations in Mexico. In Canada the Xeni Gwet'in are part of a federated structure through their membership in the Chilcotin Six Nations, the British Columbia Assembly of First Nations, and the Canada-wide Assembly of First Nations. Although there isn't an example of a federated co-operative in the Canadian examples studied, tiered producer co-operatives in Canada date back to the efforts of Moses Coady in the Antigonish movement, which led to the creation of the United Maritime Fishermen in 1930 (Lotz & Welton, 1997).

The final characteristic of the ways that the organizations structured their collective work relates to their decision-making processes. Cecilia Díaz (1997) describes participation in organizational planning as important democratic practice that strengthens the participants and the collectivity. The organizations studied demonstrated commitment to the principle of involving their membership fully.

Some of the organizations hold an annual meeting to bring the members together. The artisans co-operative in Nova Scotia discusses recommendations from the board for any major changes at their annual meeting. In Oaxaca's state-level coalition of coffee producers, meetings are held monthly with the representatives from the regional coalitions, and they engage in problem-solving together, as the president described:

> The life of an organization is not easy. Yes, it is marvelous what we have created; however, there will always be problems. We can never forget about the importance of communication. For each problem, it is necessary to work together to look for the solution. We do this using our meetings; every month we talk about the problems we are facing and we search for solutions together amongst everyone.

Members of the Wolfville, Nova Scotia, gaggle of the Raging Grannies are able to post their ideas for appearances on their listserv so that all members can provide their input and be involved in the decision.

There is a variety of methods for making decisions: by lack of response, by authority, by minority (leaving many uninvolved), by majority through a vote, by consensus (ensuring all can live with it), and by unanimous consent (Schein, 1999). Most of the organizations studied described working in non-hierarchical ways, making decisions by consensus, and ensuring that executive roles did not overload individual members, although election of the executive was often done by vote. The women operating the WEE Society programs in Nova Scotia work together in a very egalitarian structure, respecting each other's contributions and skills and, in keeping with this commitment, Doreen Parsons, whose role is similar to that of an executive director, is not willing to use that title. The Tejalpa and Cuernavaca alternative medicine collectives have three common executive offices: president, treasurer, and secretary, which the six and four members of the respective collectives rotate through. The women's resource centre in British Columbia is structured with the same three executive positions that are determined on a year-to-year basis to keep the roles from seeming too onerous for women who might otherwise be afraid of a longer-term commitment.

The organizations, in general, appear to have adopted structures that are consistent with their principles of equality and participation. They have created mechanisms to ensure communication and effectiveness without the bureaucratization that Choudry, Hanley, and Shragge (2012) caution can divert valuable energy from important social change objectives.

The Resources, Challenges, and Shared Benefits of the Collective Work

ALSO FUNDAMENTAL to the nature of the collective activities were the resources, the challenges, and the benefits of working together. These relate to the collective work specifically—the challenges and the outcomes of the mobilization process will be discussed later.

Resources: Support and Financing

The resources for the collective activities were primarily financial and human and they were from both internal and external sources. Reductions in funding, so characteristic of neo-liberal environments, were problematic for several of the projects. Another important resource mentioned by project leaders was a place of their own.

Internal income generation is the raison d'être of most co-operatives as Quarter, Mook, and Armstrong (2009) note: "A co-operative is an autonomous association of persons united voluntarily to meet their common economic, social, and cultural needs and aspirations through a jointly-owned and dem-ocratically-controlled enterprise" (p. 51). As the Just Us! Coffee Roasters Co-op in Nova Scotia illustrated, it may take some time for the co-operative to become profitable—in their case, five years. However, as well as providing incomes for the members, there can be benefits for the larger community. The artisans co-operative in Nova Scotia allowed non-members to sell their hooked articles on consignment in the co-op's gift shop, and the jungle and highland region coffee co-operative in Chiapas helped with developing transportation between villages and providing access to credit. Working collectivity also made it possible to increase marketing opportunities. UNEAMICH, operating at the state level, arranges for artisan fairs in Michoacán and beyond, providing transportation for the artisans and their products. The projects providing alternative health services and natural remedies were not initiated for income-generating purposes; however, some of the teams are considering charging more to people who can afford to pay more so that they can generate income for themselves through this work. Also in Mexico, where charitable donation is less common than in Canada, voluntary non-profit organizations have found creative ways of generating income. TADECO in Guerrero funds its community organizing work through its storefront office services, and Luna Creciente in Chiapas funds its artisan support work through its café and shop.

The human resource contributions of the numerous committed individuals in these programs were quite astonishing. Several of these were described earlier in relation to the ideals that motivated them. In addition, readers are reminded of Licha's involvement in the collective kitchen and advocacy for women's freedom from violence in addition to her state leadership role with the Catholic women's right to decide campaign—all unpaid work. As well, it is noteworthy that although the British Columbia resource centre can pay for only ten hours a week of coordinator services, the coordinator volunteers many more hours—sometimes putting in full-time hours. This is consistent with Kuyek's (2011) observation that "some activists develop lifestyles that free them from the need for full-time work" (p. 133), sharing income, accommodation, child care, etc., and working part-time or taking turns working so they have more time for organizing.

External support from powerful third parties can provide important resources to social movement organizations (Nepstad & Bob, 2006). Acceptance of some types of support, however, can constrain the organization's autonomy. Government funding, while ideal when recognizing a responsible role in the interests of citizens, can be unpredictable and interfere with advocacy (Wharf & Clague, 1997). An example of helpful government support and funding is evident in the assistance provided by CASART, the government-mandated organization in Michoacán, which helps artisan communities to get trademarks for their products and obtain financial backing from other government bodies, such as FONAES (the National Assistance Fund for Enterprises in Solidarity) for infrastructure loans. In contrast, TADECO had a negative experience with a government-funded project that they didn't wish to repeat—a need to hire many more staff, including people who didn't share their perspective and, in addition, a loss of freedom to criticize the government. Canadian provincial governments generally have been helpful with funding for community economic development (CED) projects like those provided by the Women's Economic Equality (WEE) Society in Nova Scotia. Even neo-liberal governments can rationalize investment in human capital to enhance labour market participation. Researchers who have examined CED emphasize that it is only realistic to expect that external funding such as government grants is necessary, in addition to market revenue, to sustain projects that assist employment-disadvantaged people (Conn, 2006; Shragge, 2003).

Insufficient funding was one of the greatest challenges facing the social movement organizations. The problem that the WEE Society experienced, with gaps between grants leaving the core staff unpaid, is consistent with Toye and Chaland's (2006) critique of government funding in Canadian CED projects. They took issue with government funding because often it is only short-term, limited to projects with measurable outcomes, and focused on economic self-sufficiency rather than social empowerment. The women's centres in Mexico and Canada alike experienced significant cuts in federal funding. The centre in Nova Scotia, Canada, receives some provincial funding for services that are critically needed, but as Cheryl Hyde (1989) indicated is often the case, the funding mandate calls for the employment of professionals and "those clinically oriented, may be less likely to engage in or support political actions" (p. 175). The centre in British Columbia needed to consider seeking charitable status even though they recognized this would constrain their advocacy abilities—an important component of social justice work. In the neo-liberal policy context, Choudry, Hanley, and Shragge (2012) lament the redirection of many social movement organizations toward "institutionalization, professionalization, depoliticization, and demobilization" (p. 15), referencing Andrea Smith's (2007) chapter in the aptly named book, *The Revolution Will Not Be Funded*. Financial support from a foreign government can be unproblematic, as in the case of Canadian funds for the health centre in Veracruz to purchase medical equipment. However, the Chiapas coffee co-operative identified a negative consequence for them as a result of German assistance for Guatemala with machinery that gave Guatemalan coffee producers a competitive advantage over Mexican producers.

NGOs and foundations provide the financial, material, and technical support that Friedmann (1992) noted is typically needed by marginalized communities. In Mexico, the feminist organization, Mujeres para el Diálogo, was providing support to women's organizations in very remote areas. Their publications were being used in the community organization rooted in liberation theology in a Veracruz town, and they were providing training at a workshop for women leaders in the southeast of Mexico as well as at one of the quarterly meetings of CODIMUJ for leaders of women groups throughout the San Cristóbal diocese. The Xeni Gwet'in in British Columbia faced a formidable opponent in the struggle against Taseko Mines and they benefited from the support of a number of NGOs. The Friends of the Nemaiah Valley (FONV) raised funds to bring in technical experts to report at the environmental impact assessment hearings. The Centre for Science in Public Participation (CSP2) provided the assistance of Amy Crook, who acted as "a bridge," blending traditional knowledge with science—for example, incorporating important Xeni Gwet'in knowledge about the water-flow patterns. Two national NGOs—Mining Watch and the Council of Canadians—broadened awareness of the Fish Lake issue and participated in a nationwide coalition to stop the use of fresh water for dumping toxic mining waste. This exertion of additional pressure on opponents is another aspect of third-party support that Nepstad and Bob (2006) recognized as important to social movement success.

Foreign NGOs and foundations, similarly, were external agents providing resources to the civil society organizations studied in Mexico. It is important to examine critically the motivations and methods of NGOs engaged in international development, given the too frequent reproduction of imperial and colonial relations (Snyder, 2012). However, helpful support was described in several Mexican cases that fostered the strengthening and independence of the organizations in achieving their own objectives. It was an NGO from Spain, for example, that provided a staff person to the fledgling Mujeres de la Unión de la Selva—the women's program of the Chiapas coffee co-operative—to train the two local young women who now lead the organization. Habitat for Humanity is an example of an international NGO that was helpful in Mexico by making affordable loans available to the marginalized neighbourhood studied in Veracruz, which enabled the community to replace inadequate housing with concrete-block homes.

Other external support has come from the Church, educational institutions, and committed individuals. The influence of the Catholic Church, through champions of liberation theology, was emphasized as an impetus in the creation of the Unión de la Selva regional-level coffee co-operative in Chiapas and for the development of the neighbourhood organization in Veracruz. In both examples, the communities were taught that God does not want exploitation, and that collective work to overcome it is necessary. Priests' involvement in the founding coffee co-operatives was corroborated by former Chiapas bishop Samuel Ruiz (Menocal & Ruiz, 1998). Educational institutions were also identified as providing important support. Two educators from St. Francis Xavier University in Antigonish, Nova Scotia, provided consultation to the Cheticamp women, leading to the establishment of the current artisans co-operative, La Coopérative Artisanale, in 1963. Board members of the women's resource centre in Kamloops, British Columbia, who were faculty members at the Thompson Rivers University were able to access grants for academic work related to the centre's program, and to enlist the support of other faculties for particular projects, such as help from visual arts faculty with the *Not Just a Tea Party* publication. The University of Morelos Centre for the Study of Medicinal Plants, through an arrangement made by a parish priest, provided Sunday classes for three years to the Cuernavaca collective, which now offers traditional health care. The contributions of committed external individuals were exemplified in Mexico by the women from nearby similarly Indigenous communities who inspired the pottery collective and the weavers collective in Mexico. In Canada, the Xeni Gwet'in in British Columbia received external support from numerous generous and committed individuals, for example, Jack Woodward, the lawyer who has done a considerable amount of pro bono work for the Chilcotin Six Nations, and Sue Smitten, who produced the film *Blue Gold* about the traditional uses of Fish Lake.

A final valued resource for many of the collectives in Mexico was a place of their own. The women in the marginalized Veracruz neighbourhood had constructed the Health Centre themselves—the framing, the concrete work, and the roofing—and it was a material symbol of their ability to achieve their goals. CODIMUJ was in the process of constructing a place where they could host their own conferences and have office space in San Cristóbal, Chiapas, similarly relying on volunteer effort from their own members for at least some of the building work.

The Challenges Encountered in the Collective Work

The challenges encountered in the collective work addressed here are distinct from the challenges faced in the midst of the mobilization process, to be discussed in Chapter 10. In addition to the challenge related to insufficient financing noted earlier, the communities identified related problems with loans, as well as difficulties with marketing. Loans included materials in the example of the amate-paper painters in Guerrero. As detailed in Part II, the unpainted papers were lent to the artists by a woman who paid them

MXN $10 pesos per painted paper when she returned—a net gain to the painters of only about 33 cents per hour. Formal bank loans are accessible to artisan groups who are legally constituted as civil associations. In Michoacán, CASART facilitated this legal process, but artisans continued to be faced with unreasonably high interest rates and requests to use their homes as collateral. One of the potters was proposing to fellow members of his village potters' association a type of collective revolving loan fund that could be accessed through a national foundation as a means of circumventing the above loan constraints.

The experience of the weavers collective studied in Oaxaca provides insight to the challenges related to both loans and marketing. As recounted in Part II, when the women took out their first loans in the mid-1990s, they were successful in making beautiful carpets, but they had difficulty leaving their village to sell them. When the government called in the loans, some of the women had to sell jewellery and other personal possessions to raise the money. Others had to appear at the government offices in the capital city of Oaxaca, which was very intimidating for them, especially for those who had seldom left the village. The Oaxaca state government has a much more suitable program in place now that encourages tourists to visit the rural villages to see the artisan specialty of each village and observe the traditional processes the artisans use. Tourists can purchase products while they are in the villages and arrange to have them shipped home. Women are able to integrate their weaving with their other family responsibilities (which are especially onerous for the large number whose husbands are working in the North) without needing to carry heavy woven goods into the capital city, where they feel uncomfortable.

Marketing opportunities for artisans are organized by CASART in concert with UNEAMICH, the state union of Michoacán artisans. They operate a large store at their headquarters in a historic building in the state capital, as well as itinerant artisan competitions specialized for each particular product at state, regional, and local levels and a large festival for all the artisan collectives with registered trademarks during Holy Week, when most Mexicans have a vacation. The artisans, however, would like more of these shows and an increased role for CASART in marketing the products internationally. In Veracruz, by way of contrast, no state program to promote its artisans' work was evident, and the women's embroidery collective located in a remote village was struggling at the time of the interview to develop a feasible marketing plan. Even worse than no government help, there was the example of a village mayor who created a problem for the women's pottery collective by building replicas of the collective's store and inviting women to sell their products individually in the government stores. The marketing area was a vulnerable aspect of the producer collectives' enterprises across the many examples.

The Shared Benefits of the Collective Work

Participants in the collectives spoke effusively about the value to them of working together. They spoke of benefits to members of their organization and to the larger community. Some of the aspects they emphasized related to collective objectives and others were at a more personal level.

As Choudry et al. (2012) remind us, "local organizing work begins with people where they live and the issues they face, and can contribute to the building of a wider oppositional culture" (p. 2) when there is an organizational commitment to social change. In all of the income-generating projects and in most of the co-operatives, the purpose of the collective work was to provide needed income to the members of the organization. Resolving problems related to marketing and obtaining registered trademarks were especially important member benefits in some of the communities. In other projects, the collective work was for the benefit of the broader community. In the health promotion projects of Mexico, the objective was to provide affordable treatments for anyone in the community using traditional and natural remedies, and the environmental projects were intended to ensure cleaner air and water for all residents. Tere and Amado were facilitating the full community's efforts to obtain electricity, water, and a school in the humble neighbourhood of a Guerrero city, and TADECO works to help people in south-central Guerrero to survive in the current crisis and to recover their vision of the future. The three women's resource centres and the WEE Society in Nova Scotia were working for women's rights and equality in the larger society.

The benefits of the shared work were intended for both the members and the broader community in several of the projects. Agustina explained the mutual benefit of the work for those involved in organizing programs and services in solidarity with the oppressed:

> The work itself is a circular process—as you help to transform the lives and communities of the people, you find yourself transformed. In essence, you transfer your happiness to others and the reverse happens as well. You are communicating that the happiness or sadness of others is yours as well.

The tortillería collective in Veracruz was generating income for the members that made it possible for their children to continue their education while, at the same time, they were making high-quality tortillas available at an affordable price in their town. The Cheticamp artisans co-operative in Nova Scotia shared annual profits among members, but welcomed non-members to sell their products on consignment in the co-operative gift shop.

Many of the programs paid attention to the child-care responsibilities of collective and community members. The marketing tasks and attendance at training programs out of town were not assigned to co-operative members with young children. Workshops at the Tejalpa health and well-being centre in Morelos provided child care for attendees, and the meetings of the Chiapas weavers collective welcomed the members' preschool children as well.

Many of the collectives were described as family-like environments that provided strong personal support for the members. Margo, in the development of the natural medicines collective in Mexico City, described how the time for discussion in small clusters at each of their sessions had resulted in very deep friendships. A leader in the Nova Scotia artisans co-operative spoke of how tremendously supportive the members have been of her in her new life stage as a widow, and that the collective commitment extends beyond the economic issues to a concern for the overall well-being of the members. In the Veracruz neighbourhood collective operating the health centre, women said they are a very cohesive group—"like sisters," "like family." These examples illustrate the nurturing of emotional connection, which Fabricant (2002) describes as important in building resilient communities that can withstand the individualizing tendencies of neo-liberal globalization.

The final aspect of shared benefits from the collective work that emerged in the interviews was the creation of shared hopes. For members of UNEAM-ICH in Michoacán there were ideas for a products catalogue, educational support for members' children, and a social security system for artisans. Members of the women's centre in British Columbia were beginning to envision a women's health and wellness centre in their town using a partnership model. All of the programs arising from liberation theology, TADECO in Guerrero, and the three women's centres were very clear in their assumptions or mission statements, and the others, if less explicit, certainly were very active in transforming current society into one that is more just and egalitarian. ∎

(TEN)

THE MEANS OF MOBILIZING
FOR THE COLLECTIVE GOOD

THIS CHAPTER DEALS with the means of mobilizing and organizing for justice. Important facets of this are the targeted concerns of the mobilization activities and various organizer roles, as well as aspects of mobilization strategy.

The Focus of the Mobilization Activities and the Organizer Roles

IT IS USEFUL TO LOCATE THE CONCERNS that were the focus of the mobilization activities within the social mobilization and community organizing literature in order to understand their place within larger movements for social change. Similarly, the roles of the leaders and organizers who were observed in the communities studied illustrate various aspects of leadership described in the literature.

The Concerns of the Social Justice Struggles

The targeted concerns of the mobilization activities studied included needed services, inadequate income, gender issues, environmental problems, human rights, and political oppression. For each of these there is pertinent literature.

Several of the social movement communities were engaged in providing direct services to meet people's basic needs. Joan Kuyek (2011), a Canadian academic whose organizing experience includes work with women and Indigenous peoples, has noted that holistic approaches to community organizing can be effective in creating "sustainable alternatives for the provision of food, shelter, energy, transportation and the care of children, the disabled and the elderly; they re-create and protect the *Commons*" (p. 13). In the marginalized Veracruz neighbourhood, basic needs had been addressed sequentially—obtaining land and erecting provisional shelter, selling products collectively, dealing with the garbage that was contaminating their food, establishing a health centre with low-cost services and natural medicines, and building sturdier houses to protect family members from the elements. Their activities are reflective of what Peggy Antrobus (2004) has described as "organizing in defence of place" in which women in a particular locality join together in struggles for personal safety, secure livelihoods, and community well-being.

All of the income-generating projects, the producer co-operatives, and some of the health promotion programs were addressing the community members' need for adequate income. As Shragge (2003) observes, community economic development (CED), in its various forms, seeks "to find ways to revitalize local economies, ameliorate poverty through training and job creation, and to involved residents and other local actors in these processes" (p. 123). The Women's Economic Equality (WEE) Society in Nova Scotia, after listening carefully to women across the province, involved educators, employers, community-based providers, and government funders to help women prepare for and obtain jobs in fields with skill shortages.

The coordination leadership for the Women's Council of the Diocese of San Cristóbal (CODIMUJ) in Chiapas, along with all the women's resource centres and some of the individual women's advocates, assisted women in dealing with a variety of critical matters related to gender oppression, including spousal violence. Wichterich (2000) described how women in grassroots initiatives, like those of CODIMUJ, addressing local women's survival needs "have learnt to see their individual suffering as the symptom of a wider structure of injustice" (p. 145). Antrobus (2004) similarly reports that through networking with other women's groups, the women have been able to join together to confront concerns at a global level. This phenomenon was evident in the current research as well. Two Indigenous women from rural Chiapas communities representing their regions at the CODIMUJ workshop had participated in the NGO protests of free trade at the WTO meeting in

Cancun in September 2003. Agustina, as well, had attended with a group from Morelos and had participated in the much-publicized demonstration in which women from all over the world pulled down the perimeter fence and handed white flowers representing peace to the surprised guards.

Several of the communities in the study had mobilized to confront serious environmental concerns—two Indigenous communities fighting against activities of Canadian mining corporations, and people in Tejalpa, Morelos, combating industrial contamination. In the Tejalpa example, about eight representatives from each of five CEBs formed an ecological organization, which, in addition to raising awareness and promoting recycling, demonstrated against factories releasing contaminated water and pressured authorities to require treatment. Wise, Salazar, and Carlsen (2003), writing about popular resistance to neo-liberal globalization in Mexico, suggest that community control of natural resources would be preferable to the current model of exploitation. Similarly, the Council of Canadians (2013b) promotes the recognition of safe drinking water as a human right and supports the Xeni Gwet'in in their struggle to save Fish Lake.

Human rights issues of various types were being addressed in the communities. Certainly the unwarranted arrests of members of the ejido, along with threats against the lives of the organizers in the struggle contesting water contamination by the Canadian mining operation in Guerrero, were the most blatant rights abuses. Ife (2010), however, reminds us that a comprehensive view of human rights includes social, economic, civil, cultural, environmental, spiritual, and survival rights. He encourages an approach to community development that attends to human rights "from below"—in a dialogical and mutually respectful relationship with the affected community whose context is appreciated and whose own conception of their needs and rights is foregrounded. In this sense, the Just Us! Coffee Roasters Co-op in Nova Scotia is engaged in human rights work in its attention to the economic rights of the farming communities whose products it markets in Canada, and in its recognition of the cultural rights of the coffee co-operative in Oaxaca, Mexico, with whom it was exploring a means of supporting a community-directed tourism venture.

The final category of concern targeted for collective action was the need to deal with political issues. These mobilizations varied from the flash appearances of the Raging Grannies in Nova Scotia, through the nine years of vigils to end garbage dumping in the Veracruz neighbourhood, to the seemingly endless need for the Chilcotin Six Nations in British Columbia to protect their land from loggers and prospectors. The past chief of the Xeni Gwet'in described the community's frustration with government review processes that set unrealistic timelines, didn't provide adequate funding to hire technical experts, and, in the end, often disregarded the community's opinion. Their position on the unacceptability of the Taseko Mines' proposal, however, after enormous efforts to demonstrate the potential detrimental effects on the environment and wildlife, has been heeded to date. Government responsiveness to issues that citizens raise is critical to a functioning democracy. Bartra and Otero (2005), as well as Cortez Ruiz (2010), in describing the struggles of Mexico's Indigenous peoples for their rights and culture, have shown that when institutional routes to resolving political claims are blocked, a delinking from the government can occur, as seen in the autonomous Zapatista communities of Chiapas.

The Role of Organizers and Leaders

The social movement communities studied were rich in illustrations of organizers and leaders engaged in effective social justice work. Some, but not all, of their roles are determined by the location of the key person in the community in which they are working. For example, Marilyn Baptiste, the chief of the Xeni Gwet'in First Nation, is a member of the community, and Amy Crook, from the Centre for Science in Public Participation (CSP2), is an external support person. To distinguish the two locations from which people do this work, I will refer to those in primary roles who are members of the community as "leaders" and those who are external to the community as "organizers." Community leaders—like Chief Baptiste with the Xeni Gwet'in, Licha in her outreach work for Catholic Women for the Right to Decide, and COMPA building grassroots opposition to neo-liberalism in North America—are instrumental in roles such as promoting participatory democracy (Moyer, 2001). External organizers like Amy and CASART often play an intermediary role, such as providing consultation and technical assistance (Korazim-Korosy, Mizrahi, Katz, Karmon, Garcia, & Smith, 2007) and bridging different knowledges like Indigenous wisdom and science in British Columbia or artisan experience and government programs in Michoacán (Dobbie & Richards-Schuster, 2008). Several critical roles for leaders and organizers of collective struggles for social justice are described below. The first three—working in egalitarian partnerships, accompaniment, and learning from the people—are especially important for external organizers to keep in mind.

Figure 10.1 Egalitarian Relationships

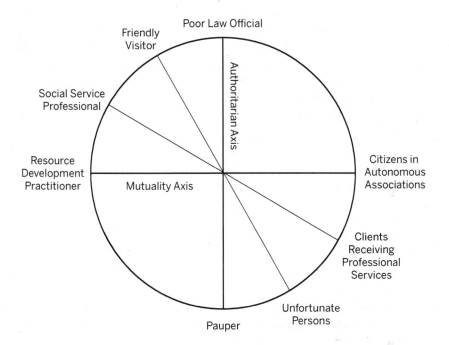

Source: Campfens (1994), p. 7.

Enid Cox (2001), in writing about empowerment in community practice, emphasizes the need for egalitarian relationships and working in partnership. Hubert Campfens (1997) provided a relevant diagram in an unpublished syllabus for community practica at Wilfrid Laurier University's Faculty of Social Work, which has been replicated in Figure 10.1. It depicts the shift from the authoritarian hierarchical relationship between the poor law official and the pauper in Elizabethan times to the current ideal of an egalitarian and mutually respectful relationship between a community practitioner in a resource development role and citizens in autonomous associations.

The horizontal relationship in Campfens's diagram was played out quite literally in Amy Crook's role in locating the resource people to provide technical expertise at the hearings of the environmental impact assessment panel at the request of the Xeni Gwet'in who are citizens in an autonomous association. The egalitarian relationship was also apparent in the work of the three women's resource centres and expressed very clearly by Lucille Harper, the director of the centre in Antigonish: "We recognize that women are the experts on their own lives; our job is to provide them with information so they can make informed decisions for themselves. We work with the women, not for them." Lakeman's (2012) writing about feminist anti-violence activism in Canada argues for this same type of equal partnership in work with women survivors:

> Nothing could be a greater disservice to a woman…[than to] reduce her to a service recipient, when really she's trying to be part of an international uprising (p. 94).… What she's really doing is calling for a truth-teller, calling for an ally, calling for public assistance on an action, calling for fellow travellers, calling for strategy discussion, calling to add numbers to hers.… She understands herself as being aided by the movement, not by some genius counsellor…but by an ordinary feminist whom she could be. (p. 95)

The role of accompaniment in social development and activism was introduced to English-speaking academics by Wilson and Whitmore (2000) out of their experience in Latin America as external resource developers. Accompaniment assumes an egalitarian partnership based on mutual trust, a recognition of the ownership of the change process by the host country/organization, a common analysis of the problem, and the practice of "engaged questioning, non-directive suggesting, and solidarity in the face of set-backs" (Clinton, cited in Wilson & Whitmore, 2000, p. 138). Conscious employment of this role was explicit in two of the Mexican examples. TADECO, in Guerrero, described their promotion of gender equality through discussion groups led by couples from the community. TADECO's role, the director said, is to accompany the couples in their leadership work and to provide resources such as films, poetry, and music with the new message of gender equality. The staff of MUSA, in their work with the women in the small-scale coffee-farm families in one of the Chiapas regions, spoke with enthusiasm about the members' requests for workshops to understand their rights as women: "For many it is a big change—to speak up, to be able to travel outside of their own community, etc. Little by little, the changes happen and the staff role is to walk with the women, to accompany them through the difficulties they encounter in the process." It is particularly interesting to see how the two staff, who are themselves daughters of small-scale coffee-farm families and thus indigenous members of the community, recognize that their reality as young, university-educated women working in town is now different from that of the core membership, and that they must step back and recognize the autonomy of the membership to decide on their own change processes.

The learner role is understood by all organizers to be part of an essential assessment process prior to implementation of a change strategy. However, in this and much other research about activist work, the organizer-as-learner stance emerges as an ongoing and more intense aspect of the mobilization process. As Trigg (2009) notes, "A collaborative model of leadership involves working as a team, affiliating and cooperating with others, and learning from those whom programs and initiatives intend to serve" (p. 7). TADECO is very explicit about maintaining this learner stance with the inclusion in their descriptive brochure of a creed that was written by Chinese rural educator James Yen in 1920 (my translation from the Spanish brochure):

We must go to the people
To live among the people
To learn from the people
To organize ourselves with the people
And to work with the people.
We begin with what the people know
And build with what the people have.
We teach by example and learn by doing.
We promote the people's own values
And not foreign ways.
We accomplish work that brings us closer to our goals
And don't waste our energy on easy and insignificant work.
We focus on the whole journey
And don't get lost in the details.
We enliven the strength and the will of the people to transform themselves
And we don't impose changes.
We provide tools for liberation
And not more charity.

Tere and Amado didn't mention Yen's creed, but they are certainly living it among the people in the marginalized neighbourhood in Guerrero, and learning about the people's difficulties by experiencing, along with them, the challenges of living with dirt floors, no electricity, and no running water. The Friends of the Nemaiah Valley, who acknowledge the Xeni Gwet'in as the strongest defenders they could hope to meet of the land and its wild inhabitants, said that FONV takes direction from the Xeni Gwet'in and the umbrella Chilcotin Six Nations groups before engaging in any of their major actions. Maria de los Angeles, from the marginalized neighbourhood in Veracruz, and Emelia, president of UNEAMICH in Michoacán, while being indigenous members of their communities, also said it is important to go to the people in order to understand the issues they face.

The remaining roles are equally important for both external organizers and internal leaders. Animator, teacher, researcher, and facilitator are roles that cluster together. Nepstad and Bob (2006) capture the essence of these functions in their description of the role of leaders in bringing about "cognitive liberation," a new consciousness that "an unjust situation must and can be changed" (p. 8). This is similar to Moyer's (2001) concept of creating participatory democracy by engaging, educating, and involving the citizenry in action to address critical issues. In this study, animation was epitomized by an organizer's imitation of a jumping circus dog to characterize the villagers' grateful acceptance of cakes from a corrupt politician to contrast how the CODIMUJ women's group could use International Women's Day as an occasion to demonstrate instead that they are critical thinkers who are capable of analyzing their situation. The ensuing laughter helped the women to recognize their energy and possibilities. The teaching role is evident in the creation of videos and radio broadcast scripts by the Oaxaca women's centre to help women realize their right to health care for safe pregnancy and childbirth. Licha, in her reproductive rights work, and COMPA, in promoting understanding of neo-liberalism, were developing teaching materials for their collaborators to use. A research role, especially when employing methods similar to the participatory action research method described by Fals-Borda (1995), is a very helpful role in organizing. TADECO's director described how the work in the community begins with a diagnostic phase involving the people in a reflection process. From this diagnosis/assessment about which the people concur, he said, develops the people's will to participate in the development of a solution. The facilitation role is one that foregrounds the decision and action of the community and backgrounds the enabling role of the leader or organizer. This is the role played by Tere and Amado, living and working in the marginalized Guerrero neighbourhood, who were adamant that they didn't consider themselves community leaders, but rather the "cultivators of leadership in others." Facilitation was also apparent in the way that Chief Marilyn Baptiste encouraged members of the Xeni Gwet'in in British Columbia, including the schoolchildren, to come to the environmental impact assessment hearings and tell the stories of their people—explaining their traditions and their understanding of the ways of the river and the wildlife.

Finn and Jacobson (2003) provide a fairly comprehensive listing of social justice worker roles while "accompanying the process": learner, teacher, collaborator, facilitator, animator, mediator, advocate, negotiator, researcher, and *bricoleur*. Most of these have been examined earlier, so only the remaining ones will be discussed now.

The advocate, mediator, and negotiator roles cluster together in social activism. In the examples studied, these roles were best illustrated in the work of the father and daughter sought out by the Guerrero ejidatarios who were struggling to protect themselves and their water from the consequences of the Canadian mining company activities. After the father became ill, his daughter represented the ejidatarios in meetings with the mining company and the government departments dealing with the environment, health, and justice, as well as seeking out the help of a non-governmental human rights organization when the threats against their lives and the implication of the state government became clear. These people were not formally trained as lawyers, nor were they employed by an organization to take on this advocacy and negotiating role. Rather, they were people with enough education to read and interpret the contracts offers by the mining company and with enough life experience outside of their small town to identify the pertinent government offices and eventually the non-government human rights organization to assist the ejidatarios in their negotiations with the mining company and their appeals to the relevant government offices. They did this work out of a commitment to social justice despite substantial risk to their own lives.

The final role in social justice work that Finn and Jacobson (2003) describe is that of a bricoleur. They reference Levi-Strauss, a French anthropologist, for the "handyman" analogy in the crafting of new meanings from the available cultural materials, and they relate this analogy to the social activist's need to "engage with the circumstances and resources at hand, be inventive, and expand the spaces for hope" (p. 282). The Kamloops Women's Resource Group Society in British Columbia has practised the creative bricoleur role in the face of funding cuts that ended their ability to provide drop-in services. They refocused their efforts to providing telephone referrals to other community resources, publishing books with the stories of local women of significance, holding events to raise awareness of women's issues such as the *Room Full of Missing Women* art exhibit, participating in initiatives of like-minded organizations such as local peace and justice walks, and seeking out future partnership possibilities.

Related to roles of organizers are important characteristics that Mondros and Wilson (1994) categorized as change vision attributes, technical skills, and interactional skills. Change vision attributes were implicit in earlier discussions of the contributions of committed individuals, as well as the influences of ideals and technical skills related to the strategies of mobilization that lie ahead. Thus, only the interactional attribute of resiliency that emerged in this study will be discussed here. Mondros and Wilson note that "the organizer is expected to be a high-energy person to survive in what is often an emotionally and physically exhausting job...to extend his or her energy to others...and not to be discouraged by members' passivity or low morale" (p. 27). When I discussed the demands of organizing with Amy Crook in relation to her work as an external adviser for communities dealing with the impacts of mining, she replied that she has learned to be patient with the interactional challenges since it is very common for communities to take out their angst on outsiders. She said she is "able to sit in the fire" (as if chanting in a meditation), which I viewed as remarkable resilience.

As a final note regarding the role of leaders and organizers, I return to the initial distinction between internal community leaders and external community organizers. Although the distinction is a useful starting point, it must now be clear to readers that the line between the two is very diffuse. In the end, it is not particularly useful to be concerned about whether the two staff at MUSA are leaders or organizers. Nor is it sensible to conclude regarding the couple facilitating social justice claims in the marginalized neighbourhood in Guerrero that Tere, since she is from a middle-class family in the state of Guanajuato and is trained as a professional social worker, is an external organizer, and that Amado, who was raised on a farm in the state of Guerrero and migrated to the city like many in the neighbourhood, is an internal leader. What is important to recognize is that the more external one is to the community in which one is playing a leadership or organizer role, the more critical is the need to heed the principles of egalitarian partnership, accompaniment, and learning from the people. Even those who are most clearly identifiable as internal leaders, like Chief Marilyn Baptiste, were very conscientious in talking with community members.

Aspects of Mobilization Strategy

TO ADDRESS THE TARGETED CONCERNS, people came together to engage in a variety of activities that Eschle and Maiguashca (2010) identify as collective action: protest, both disruptive and more conventional, along with "advocacy, service provision, knowledge production, popular education, and movement building" (p. 184). Central to the means of mobilizing and organizing for the collective good are the strategies for doing the work. A strategy is a plan of action to achieve the intended goals or alternative future within a particular context (Maney, Andrews, Kutz-Flamenbaum, Rohlinger, & Goodwin, 2012). The strategies that were valuable in the examples studied included consciousness-raising, clarifying objectives, education for members and the public, preparation for action, influencing change, and organizational strengthening. Many of the components of strategy occur in an iterative and overlapping fashion rather than in rigid chronology.

Consciousness-Raising

Paulo Freire's concept of learning through a process of conscientization involving praxis—the continuous cycle of action and reflection—was applied in many of the collectives studied. Freire's (1968/1984) own description of conscientization is provided below from an English translation that has left the word for "conscientization" or "consciousness-raising" in Portuguese. For our current understanding, I have changed the word "men" to "people" and removed the italics from other words in the original.

> Reflection upon situationality is reflection about the very condition of existence: critical thinking by means of which people discover each other to be 'in a situation'. Only as this situation ceases to present itself as a dense envel-

oping reality or a tormenting blind alley, and people can come to perceive it as an objective-problematic situation—only then can commitment exist. People emerge from their submersion and acquire the ability to intervene in reality as it is unveiled. Intervention in reality—historical awareness itself— thus represents a step forward from emergence, and results from the *conscientização* of the situation. *Conscientização* is the deepening of the awareness characterisitc of all emergence. (p. 100)

In the above paragraph, we can read "intervention" to mean "action." The cycle of praxis can be visualized as a circle beginning with the action of observation (see, hear, sense...), moving into a phase of reflection (analyze, think critically), followed by action (intervention), and then reflection (evaluation and celebration). The terms vary, especially with translation and, of course, the cyclical process moves forward as it brings about transformation; however, Figure 10.2 provides a basic schema.

Figure 10.2 Freire's Concept of Praxis

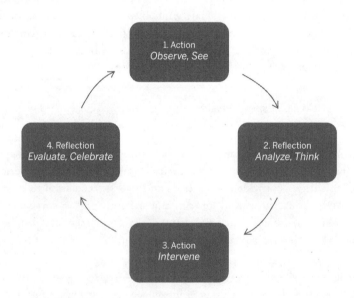

Source: Adapted from Freire (1968/1984).

Licha's description of the process used in the ecological organization in Tejalpa illustrates the use of the praxis process:

> The meetings followed a very specific method: see, think, act, celebrate/evaluate. *See:* People observed the contamination of the water, the smell of the factories, the loss of productive land. *Think:* The people reflected on the biblical messages about Creation and God's direction to care for the earth and all creatures. *Act:* They realized that they needed to join together to try to resolve the problem, so several CEBs with eight to ten people each joined across five parishes to form the Organización Ecológico Ixtelloatl. They carried out a three-part strategy: (1) disseminating information about their concerns; (2) demonstrating against factories without water-treatment systems and pressuring the authorities to require treatment; and (3) proposing community alternatives like recycling and composting. *Celebrate:* They celebrated the successes and evaluated them in terms of biblical messages and Christian thinking. They have since formed an ecological network at the state level.

Margo's work with a women's collective in Mexico City demonstrates this same process: "They took time to develop their consciousness about the earth. They reflected on what happens with the garbage, how their ancestors saw nature as composed of interconnected parts, and how we are affected if we don't have water." Although in these two examples, consciousness-raising was employed in environmental action, Ife (2010) considers it an important part of human rights work, and Lee (2001), as well as Gutiérrez, Parsons, and Cox (2003), sees it as central to the empowerment approach in social work.

Liberation theology is often used in concert with the cycle of praxis, particularly in the Christian Base Communities (CEBs), which were sparked by the Church (Kane, 2012). This is evident in Licha's description above where the evaluation criteria for the reflection sessions after their action were drawn from the biblical Creation story. Similarly, examples of liberation theology were abundant in the CODIMUJ sessions in Chiapas and in the health promotion case examples throughout Mexico, which the Guerrero priest linked to Christ's practice of healing.

On the other hand, not all uses of the cycle of praxis involved liberation theology. Margo's example above tied the reflection to an Indigenous worldview. And not all uses of reflection are a deliberate application of the cycle of praxis.

Marilyn Baptiste, chief of the Xeni Gwet'in in British Columbia, quite apart from the praxis methodology, intentionally increased her own consciousness of Indigenous teachings by seeking guidance from the elders and heeding the voices of ancestors now gone (for example, what they had to say about the earlier run-of-the-river projects to generate electricity). Similarly, TADECO, in the couple discussion groups in Guerrero, asked the participants to reflect on their roles in society and consider the validity of the inequality in the gender roles—liberation theology wasn't described as part of the conversation. All of the women's centres, as part of the women's movement, have embraced the notion of consciousness-raising, but didn't explicitly connect it to Freire or liberation theology. Social movement and organizing theory, likewise, have content about the value of reflection and evaluation apart from discussions of praxis and liberation theology. Maney et al. (2012), writing about strategies for change, recommend a follow-up to action of "revisiting and assessing the effectiveness of strategic choices once implemented" (p. xx), and Mondros and Wilson (1994), writing about community organizing, emphasize the importance of evaluating outcomes.

Clarifying Objectives

Out of a consciousness-raising process, or at least a period of reflection about the context and its problems in light of collective principles, a social movement group will begin to clarify its objectives and build a common vision. This was certainly true of the WEE Society in Nova Scotia, which met with 1,540 women at kitchen tables, community centres, and in church basements across the province over the course of forty days. What they learned from those listening sessions has formed the basis of their work ever since in creating accessible employment programs that enhance women's capacity. Brecher, Costello, and Smith (2002) describe this as the construction of an emerging belief system that "becomes a guide for efforts to transform" (p. 25).

Maney et al. (2012) describe "clarifying goals" as the initial step in strategy development. Agustina, referring to her work in Morelos, affirmed the importance of having goals and objectives clear in one's mind: "to say, for example, 'in the next three years this community must be able to continue on its own' and to never forget that they must take the leadership in order to carry on." A similar recognition of the significance of clear goals was evident in the statement by the director of the British Columbia women's centre that members need specific projects to support, and that a project like a women's wellness centre operated in partnership with another organization might be both compelling and feasible in the current funding environment. This is in accord with assertions by Choudry et al. (2012) regarding the significance of finding sustaining objectives that will limit opposition's gains.

Education for Members

Education for members of the collectives is discussed here prior to examining public education. Some of the learning within the social movement communities is part of the reflection process described in the above section on consciousness-raising. Hence, in the ongoing cycle of praxis, once the objectives of the group are clear, the next step of gathering resources for learning how to go about the collective work begins. After each opportunity to observe new material, to understand it, try out new knowledge, and evaluate the results, the opportunity for another journey through the cycle presents itself. As Chovanec, Lange, and Ellis (2009) state in their chapter about social movement learning, "learning and action are dialectical and iterative processes" (p. 191). Lee (2001) includes "education for critical thinking" as part of the development process in empowerment in which collectivities come together for mutual aid and frequently move forward to take action for broader social change. This confidence in the members' abilities to think critically about injustice and to plan their response in the face of powerful opponents was demonstrated in many of the examples and was explicit in comments already quoted from people in the marginalized neighbourhood in Veracruz and from the organizer of the CODIMUJ group in the Chiapas village.

Kane (2001, 2012) has contributed greatly to the literature about popular education, which he defines as education for the people (the majority poor) for the purpose of social change. He affirms Freire's concept that "the movement is the school," and emphasizes the need to "start from people's own experiences" (Kane, 2012, p. 77). This pedagogical principle echoes the line from Yen's credo "we begin with what the people know." It was exemplified beautifully in Margo's suggestion to the Mexico City collective, after they had clarified their objective of working with medicinal plants, that they each bring to the next meeting a plant they already know. Kane's sentence continues with the advice to "ensure dialogue between 'expert' and 'grassroots' knowledge and enable people to become subjects of change, not followers of leaders" (p. 77). Margo's work carried on in this same manner as the members together searched the countryside for more plants they knew and then consulted scientific studies to learn more about the properties of those plants. Amy Crook, in acting as a bridge between science and the Xeni Gwet'in's traditional knowledge about water-flow patterns is another excellent illustration of this principle. It is noteworthy that both Margo and Amy position themselves as co-learners with the community members in a manner that respects the members' autonomy as "subjects of change."

Other health collectives found similar ways to educate themselves about natural medicine and traditional healing methods. The leader in the Veracruz neighbourhood said "we learned a lot about natural health care from the Indigenous people." The group in Morelos undertook extensive and long-term training through a church-related centre, which included learning from a Chinese practitioner and through a university program, which included learning from Indigenous elders and curanderos. The members of the pottery collectives learned in similar ways. The Indigenous women potters needed to recover the knowledge of their mothers and grandmothers in order to re-establish the production of traditional pottery. In like manner, the potter-physician in the Michoacán association went to a community elder to learn a pre-Hispanic lead-free method of giving a shine to the traditional pottery, and is passing on this knowledge to local youth. In all cases, the knowledge development occurred "in community" and was derived from the experience of people and not just from academics—additional recommendations from Kane (2012).

Many of the collectives were composed of women, and often particular attention was paid to member education related to gender issues. Piza Lopez and March (1991), in one of the first critical examinations of women's economic enterprises, found that "The more successful economic projects...include elements of consciousness-raising. Building gender awareness should be an integral part of any income-generating project" (p. 1). The Women's Economic Equality (WEE) Society in Nova Scotia is intentional about including gender awareness in their employment programs. Their publication, *Tea You Could Trot a Mouse On: The Elements of Community-Based Economic Development*, which is accessible in its popular education format and in its availability on their website, illustrates this with an early section on "women and CED." The women carpet weavers co-operative in Oaxaca brought in external resource people to help them learn about managing a collective enterprise and to foster discussion about gender issues such as self-esteem, women's rights, and spousal violence. The feminist organization, Mujeres para el Diálogo, as has already been mentioned, had provided workshops and publications to a remarkable number of the women's groups in this study. Similarly, the national office of Catholic Women for the Right to Decide (CDD) provided training opportunities for the state-level leaders on women's rights and feminist theology. As Hoogvelt (2001) notes, women who came together for reasons related to their families' daily survival often encountered women from feminist groups and found their "consciousness was raised in societies characterized by centuries of male domination" (p. 254).

A train-the-trainer approach was used in several of the programs in order to provide educational opportunities to members. In Ita-Teku, the women's program within the state-level coffee co-operative in Oaxaca, an agricultural engineer provides monthly training at their greenhouse and nursery centre about cultivation of different plants for the technical representatives of each region. The regional representatives then provide this same training to the women in their own communities. The agricultural engineer praised this "campesina a campesina" (farmwoman to farmwoman) method because "it is much easier for the women in the communities to learn from one of their own community members who can explain the cultivation processes in their own indigenous language." MUSA, the regional coffee-producer co-operative women's program in Chiapas, also uses the train-the-trainer method to learn the various specialty businesses that particular collectives have chosen. For example, in the sewing project, two women left their communities for the training and returned to provide sewing workshops for other women in their towns. The MUSA staff said the training model makes it possible for women with child-care responsibilities to learn the skills without needing to leave their communities. Although not for income-generating purposes, the leadership of CODIMUJ and CDD, similarly, provide learning opportunities to the regional representatives, who, in turn, share this learning in their local communities. Fabricant (2002) describes how these processes "facilitate ever greater circles of social network and membership relationship...[through which people] can come to new understandings of a shared political and economic circumstance and the need for solidarity and social action" (p. 15).

Education for the Public

Education for the public about critical issues is important in changing societal attitudes and building solidarity for social movements (Dobbie & Richards-Schuster, 2008; Wilson, Calhoun, & Whitmore, 2011). Attention must be paid to the presentation of educational material and the *framing* of issues, ensuring that the content is accessible and resonates with the experiences and values of the particular audiences in order to "communicate views…connect to potential members…[and] shape beliefs of others" (Caniglia & Carmin, 2005, p. 205).

The great variety of educational media used in the projects studied was helpful in targeting the messages for different audiences (Jasper, 2004). Licha, for example, spoke of the ecological organization providing information to residents and holding demonstrations in the campaign to end contamination of the water in the industrial valley in Morelos, and she described CDD holding gatherings, workshops, and training sessions to build support for women's reproductive rights. Across all of the collectives, the various materials and media for public education included flyers, newsletters, mailings, mainstream media, Internet, events, speakers, popular theatre, exhibits, videos, demonstrations, and publications.

Simple "one-pagers" with explanatory visuals were used to communicate small amounts of information, such as the flyers distributed by the environmental group that Estela worked with in Morelos to show how to separate household refuse. CASART produced brochures for each of the trademarked products so that the artisans in Michoacán could give them to customers. Similarly, TADECO in Guerrero had a striking poster promoting their youth program that listed twenty rights to which young people are entitled. Newsletters allow for communication of more detailed information. Updates regarding the mining proposal for Fish Lake in British Columbia and efforts to stop it were provided in a newsletter compiled by Friends of the Nemaiah Valley, and Marilyn Baptiste, chief of the Xeni Gwet'in, coordinated production of a more local newsletter to counter misinformation about the proposed mine that business people in Williams Lake were disseminating. In keeping with their good-humoured approach, the various gaggles of the Raging Grannies publicize their endeavours in a newsletter entitled the *Granny Grapevine*. Mailings are heeded more by politicians than Internet communications and were used very effectively by the Nova Scotia women's centre in their Valentine's Day campaign, which included a fact sheet on women's poverty and related public policy with the hot-pink cards.

Generation of media coverage is one of the six important strategic hurdles for social movement organizations to clear, according to McAdam (1996). National and international recognition of the reproductive rights campaign fostered by CDD in Mexico garnered them a great deal of free media coverage that explained their position to the public. In British Columbia, Chief Marilyn Baptiste and Past Chief Roger William secured interviews with *The Globe and Mail*, which has provided a substantial amount of coverage of the Fish Lake mining proposal, and Friends of the Nemaiah Valley president, David Williams, was able to obtain an interview on a nationwide CBC radio program, as well as other radio programs in British Columbia. In the Guerrero conflict over mining on ejido land, when threats against the organizers began, the community sought out a mining resistance organization that arranged a press conference to "shine a light" on the particular community and its struggle as "a form of protection." These positive examples of mainstream media coverage, unfortunately, are not the norm for social movement activists.

Mainstream media, particularly those owned by private enterprise, as Carroll and Ratner (2010) note, "are unlikely to lend credence to counter-hegemonic struggles" (p. 16), so many use or create alternative media distributed via the Internet. The Zapatistas may have been the first social movement to make use of the Internet to publish their communiqués, which helped them to build an international network in support of their actions (Gilbreth & Otero, 2001; Lievrouw, 2011). Most of the social movement organizations in this study make use of the Internet to provide information for members of the public. All of the women's resource centres and the WEE Society have particularly effective websites; however, it is the Friends of the Nemaiah Valley (FONV) that has made the most extraordinary use of the Internet in the "Protect Fish Lake" website they created. As well as the useful content, the website provides access to the film *Blue Gold*, produced by Sue Smitten; it supported an online petition and hosted an online music competition. In addition, FONV invites interested people to provide their email addresses to be added to the listserv in order to receive electronic copies of the newsletter and other notices and updates. Lievrouw (2011) observes that activists using alternative new media in this manner are able to challenge the dominant portrayal of issues and share new information and a more critical perspective with the public. The Internet has also increased the possibilities for collective action beyond national boundaries (Buechler, 2011). Thus networks like COMPA—the Convergence of People's Movements in the Americas—and the umbrella Hemispheric Social Alliance were able to bring together opposition across the hemisphere to fight the proposed Free Trade Area of the Americas.

Public events were another means of reaching the broader community to share the organizations' concerns about important matters and relevant knowledge. Friends of the Nemaiah Valley held several events at the University of Victoria, which, along with their collaborative relationship with one of the professors, stimulated students' interest in the Fish Lake mining proposal such that some students presented at the environmental impact hearings. Several of the women's organizations used the International Women's Day (IWD) opportunity to stage events to keep feminist issues in the public eye. Taking advantage of opportunities like IWD was employed well by the British Columbia women's centre, which hosted the *Room Full of Missing Women* art exhibit and participated in other organizations' initiatives like a seniors' event and Canada Day celebrations. The women's centre in Oaxaca displayed an ongoing commitment to public education through open events in their regular Wednesday-evening speakers series. Each month a particular focus is chosen and I observed their conference room fill up with a large proportion of university students when a researcher spoke about her findings related to women's participation in the political life of Oaxaca towns.

Popular education, as described for members of social movement communities by Kane (2012), is also effective for education among the general public because of its intentional inclusivity. Ife (2010) mentions aspects of popular education in his description of principles for practising human rights (and, in particular, cultural rights), in which he emphasizes a reflexive approach in dialogical, egalitarian relationships. Again, boundaries blur between and within typologies, but I would suggest that most of the public education in the examples from the research that fall in the remaining categories of arts, videos, exhibits, publications, and demonstrations contain substantial doses of popular education.

The use of arts included Tere and Amado's inclusion of traditional drumming, painting, and poetry in their work with youth, instilling pride in their Indigenous heritage and providing opportunities for self-expression. TADECO also used the arts to reach the general public by selling films and music related to local culture and protests. Choudry, Hanley, and Shragge (2012) commend the contribution of the arts to organizing, and feature a chapter on music and one on poetry and literature. Popular theatre, introduced originally by Augusto Boal (1973/1985), a colleague of Paulo Freire in Brazil, has some commonalities with the surprise and witty criticism of the Raging Grannies' performances and the Xeni Gwet'in youth presentations at the environmental impact hearings, as well as radio program scripts developed by the Oaxaca women's centre for the rural communities without access to their videos. Videos, similarly, can provide educational information that is culturally contextualized and accessible for people without skills or time for reading. The twenty-minute videos produced by the Oaxaca women's centre were an excellent example of this. One video promoting prenatal care described a woman in a rural town whose husband didn't want her to attend a prenatal clinic because he assumed the examinations would be done by male physicians; when she became ill with toxemia late in the pregnancy and needed to be taken to hospital, the roads crew agreed to take her in the town's only truck when they finished their day's work; unfortunately, that wasn't soon enough and the woman died—too common an outcome in rural Oaxaca. The *Blue Gold* video about the traditional uses of Fish Lake and the surrounding land was made in a participatory manner with the Xeni Gwet'in people, who are featured in the film. My own experience facilitating the development of a group of single mothers on social assistance (Mothers Making Change) in Ontario in the 1980s included supporting their work with the local cable television company in producing a video they called *Mother Hubbard's Got Nothing on Us*. The process of identifying their common concerns, telling their own stories, gathering related data, and presenting it was a heartening activity for the group, and the result was a compelling documentary for audiences. Steigman and Pictou (2010) similarly attest to the empowering potential of participatory video.

Exhibits or museums are another educational venue that pique the public's interest and allow them to reflect on new information. The Luna Creciente collective member assisting the weavers co-operative in Chiapas sought out planned artisan exhibitions, as well as opportunities to arrange exhibits throughout Mexico and the United States, where she could travel with a few of the weavers so they could sell products on behalf of the co-operative and talk about the situation of Indigenous women in Chiapas. The Just Us! Coffee Roasters Co-op in Nova Scotia has a museum at their roastery, as well as a store and café, that provide customers, who may have stopped with the intention of having something to eat or of buying fairly traded items, to learn about coffee production and the benefits of fair trade. In Chiapas, the state-level coffee co-operative operates a café with a coffee museum in San Cristóbal that displays the history of exploitation of coffee producers on small family farms, which it does in a very visual way that doesn't assume all visitors have reading skills in Spanish.

Publications do assume reading abilities; however, they provide members of the public with opportunities to learn more in their own time. The Casa de las Artesanías (CASART) in Michoacán has a gift shop in their building along with their offices, artisans workshops, and a museum. The gift shop carried several books, including a very comprehensive one with a chapter on each region of the state that provided descriptions and photographs of the specialty artesanía and its history in the particular region. The Tejalpa health and well-being project in Morelos has a display of small publications on natural and traditional approaches to health, including one written by Estela, the project leader. There are other examples, but only one other will be highlighted here. The women's resource centre in British Columbia has focused intentionally on "recording women's herstory," and they featured local activist women in their first publication, *Not Just a Tea Party*. They were completing a second called *The Never Ending Story*. This is the kind of "writing local history" that Ife (2010, p. 177) suggests in his description of effective popular education that contributes to gains in community's cultural rights.

Public education also happens through demonstrations in the messages displayed and the news coverage provided. The demonstrations described in the study varied in intensity and longevity. The mildest form of demonstration was the British Columbia women's society's participation in a peace walk initiated by another group. The most intense was the march protesting the agreements proposed at the WTO meeting in Cancun, which culminated in presenting white flowers to the guards. The most long-lasting was the vigil at the entrance to the garbage dump in the humble neighbourhood in Veracruz, which took place around the clock for nine years until the government finally agreed to provide a proper landfill site for the municipality.

Arundhati Roy (2003), in her presentation at the World Social Forum, affirmed the importance of education for the public through these varied means to challenge the neo-liberal consensus. She instructs us to continue this strategy of "confronting empire":

> To deprive it of oxygen. To shame it. To mock it. With our art, our music, our literature, our stubbornness, our joy, our brilliance, our sheer relentlessness— and our ability to tell our own stories. Stories that are different from the ones we're brainwashed to believe. (p. 246)

Preparation for Action

In preparation for making change, social movement organizations continue to reach out to others, carry out research and analysis, develop credibility, and ensure a clear strategy. Although outreach to others was occurring in a general way during the public education process, in the preparation for action phase, the outreach is more targeted. Here it includes recruiting specific people, inviting more participants, reaching out to potential members, courting allies, and building the movement.

Attracting new recruits is another of the strategic hurdles identified by McAdam (1996). Castelloe and Prokopy (2001) suggest making incentives explicit and involvement enjoyable, addressing the most pressing needs, and removing barriers by providing transportation, for example. These ideas were evident in Licha's recruitment of seven specific volunteers to carry out the reproductive rights campaign in the state of Morelos, who then were able to participate in the gatherings, workshops, and training provided by the national office of CDD. Inviting additional participants occurs after a core group with a clear objective is in place. Once the Mexico City group had selected production of natural medicine as their focus, they invited other women to join them; once they had completed a growing season and prepared the medicines, they sought people to work with them in the marketing area. Similarly, the potters in the Chiapas village recovered the traditional skills and built a rustic store by the highway to sell their pottery and, when they saw that there was sufficient demand for more of their pale-grey pottery, they persuaded more village women to join their co-operative and increased it to fifty members. As Tinker (2000) noted, in relation to community development programs run by women, a democratic space is often created where members "form ties with each other and develop as individuals" (p. 237) while working for the betterment of the community. Organizers and leaders, at this stage, validate members' contributions, encourage critical reflection on common issues, and promote excitement for a better future (Finn & Jacobson, 2003; Goodwin & Jasper, 2009).

Outreach to potential members and supporters is extended through communicating the identity of the collective, its beliefs and practices—its image (Caniglia & Carmin, 2005). The British Columbia women's centre did this in their approach to faculty at Thompson Rivers University, and the Nova Scotia women's centre, in like manner, did this by promoting their dual focus on needed services and social change. The Friends of the Nemaiah Valley (FONV) introduced their concerns about the proposed mine at Fish Lake to the university community in Victoria, British Columbia. A common vision builds as allies and sympathizers are sought among the public, credible experts, and power holders (Brecher, Costello, & Smith, 2002; Swank, 2006). The Xeni Gwet'in, together with FONV, were exceptionally adept at bringing in people and organizations they hoped could help them. They obtained the technical expertise from environmental consultants; public support through the promotional efforts of David Suzuki, Mining Watch, and the Council of Canadians; as well as the political weight of the Union of British Columbia Indian Chiefs and the National Assembly of First Nations. The environmental impact assessment panel, in addition to being impressed by the mixture of science and Indigenous wisdom in the Xeni Gwet'in presentations, must have been moved by the presentations of the students, including their poetry and drama, the appeal to empathize with the dying wildlife, and the unflinching speech by a five-year-old.

Social movements strengthen as they transmit their vision and enthusiasm so that more people develop a commitment and they "build a growing base of support for an equitable society" (Kuyek, 2011, p. 13). The British Columbia women's centre intends to extend its message to the larger community through events like the *Roomful of Missing Women* art exhibit, which attracted like-minded people who wanted to be part of a collective opposing violence against women. They reach out to fathers who will participate in the "Walk for Justice" because they want safety for their daughters, and to men who will wear T-shirts with the message "My strength is not for hurting," making the movement for women's equality more inclusive. When defeats occur, resilient social movement communities interpret them in the context of a longer struggle in which they will be victorious. This was evident in the remarks of John McKay, whose bill to make Canadian extractive industries operating in developing countries respect human and environmental rights was narrowly defeated in the Canadian legislature, as well as in the reactions of organizations like KAIROS and Mining Watch, which advocated for this same bill. Together they urged supporters to see the result of the vote as only a temporary delay while a movement strong enough to defeat the powerful mining lobby grows. Stolle-McAllister (2005), writing about building social movements, ascribes a great deal of the Zapatistas' success to their ability to communicate with, in addition to their base in the Mayan communities of

Chiapas, "much wider audiences and…to insert their demands into larger debates about democracy, human rights and sustainable development" (p. 27). These positions are consistent with that of Joan Kuyek (2011), who affirms that if we increase and "broaden the movement we can reclaim our political, environmental, social and cultural life" (p. 172).

Research and analysis are essential components of preparation for social action. Eschle and Maiguashca (2010) include "knowledge production" as one of the six types of political practice in collective action, and Castelloe, Watson, and White (2002) identify research as one of the ten steps in participatory change. Furthermore, Choudry, Hanley, and Shragge (2012) assert that research and theory "can and do emerge from engagement in action and organizing contexts, rather than as ideas developed elsewhere by movement elites" (p. 12). They concur with Wilson, Calhoun, and Whitmore (2011) that successful activism requires analysis of both structural factors (broader societal inequalities and power relations) and conjunctural moments (the forces at play and opportunities present at a specific time). Both an assessment of such opportunities and the preparation to take advantage of them are required (Choudry, Hanley, & Shragge, 2012). This type of research and analysis was practised by the Women's Economic Equality (WEE) Society, which prepared itself well for offering employment programs to women by holding forty days of listening sessions to understand women's realities and barriers to employment. When they heard that there were skill shortages in Nova Scotia, they identified this as an opportunity and took advantage of it by finding out about the specific shortages and making relevant training available for unemployed and underemployed women.

Research done in an empowering way can make good use of Freire's methods—discovering the generative themes, understanding the oppression experienced, and discovering what help is needed (Lee, 2001). This was exemplified in the manner in which the Just Us! Coffee Roasters Co-op was working with the UCIRI coffee producers' co-operative in Oaxaca to explore with UCIRI its possible interest in ecotourism. There was recognition of the inequality inherent in the economic means of Oaxacan farmers and North American tourists and of the differences in the Indigenous and mainstream culture views of nature. Just Us! is honouring the community's right to determine what "just tourism" means to them—understanding that fair prices are a foundational part of this, but perhaps not everything.

The women's centres in Nova Scotia demonstrated a similar strengths-based approach in their research project on social assistance. They listened in interviews and focus groups to women across the province living on social assistance, and as a final step involved some of the women from the focus groups in prioritizing the recommendations and describing them to senior staff from the Department of Social Services. This is consistent with Saleebey's (2001) suggestions for engaging community strengths as well as fostering agency and autonomy by "seeking out the heroic elements in the lives of the oppressed...[and] giving voice to the voiceless" (p. 31). McKnight and Kretzmann's (2005) framework for doing community assessment by focusing on assets is a research method that fits with the strengths-based approach. An emphasis on community assets and internal resources was evident in the way the Centre for Science in Public Participation (CSP2) worked with the Xeni Gwet'in to do their research for submission to the environmental impact assessment panel examining the mine proposed for Fish Lake. CSP2 recognized the importance of the historical knowledge that the Xeni Gwet'in elders had of the water levels and how they change, which, in turn, provided valuable data for their scientific impact study.

One last point regarding research and analysis that is relevant here is the importance, identified by Piza Lopez and March (1991), for organizations promoting women's community economic development of using gender-focused research techniques to apprise women's situation. The women's centre in Oaxaca was very conscientious in this regard. Several of their board members are social scientists and their research commonly documents women's reality—for example, women's participation in the public life of the Oaxaca municipalities and the needs of women in prison in the state.

In preparation for social action, attention to the credibility of the organization is merited. Wilson, Calhoun, and Whitmore (2011) found credibility of the organization to be another factor contributing to success in Canadian activism. The women's centre in Oaxaca has found that their credibility with the press gains them access to the broader public and therefore the opportunity to increase public sensitivity to women's issues. The Raging Grannies, similarly, do their research about issues very diligently before they compose their songs to get their message across to the public.

A final aspect of preparation for collective action is the development of a clear, detailed strategy. Although we have examined the overall aspects of strategy for mobilization, including consciousness-raising, clarifying objectives, etc., more specific choices among various tactics must be made prior to taking action. Maney et al. (2012) suggest envisioning sequences of action and possible reactions, resolving choices, and determining roles. The ecological organization that came together to address industrial contamination in Morelos developed such a strategy. Theirs was well defined and conceptualized in three phases: (1) to inform other community members about the problem; (2) to demonstrate against the factories creating the problem and pressure government to require treatment of industrial discharge; and (3) to begin community recycling and composting programs.

Influencing Change

Influencing change is at the heart of social mobilization. It encompasses three of the six types of collective action identified by Eschle and Maiguashca (2010): protest (both conventional and disruptive), advocacy, and service provision. To examine these modes of collective action, it is useful to arrange them from the least to the most confrontational—from service provision and other alternatives or resistance to oppressive systems, through advocacy, and, finally, to protest. This aligns with Warren's (1975) classic typology of purposive change in community organization practice in which he differentiates collaborative, campaign, and contest strategies. Warren's collaborative approach is appropriate in situations where people come to agreement through discussion as happens in decisions by like-minded people to provide a needed service or organize a co-operative to sell their products and generate needed income. Warren suggests that campaign strategies are needed when agreement is still likely through discussion, but a great deal of persuasion or advocacy is necessary to win agreement from a third party. When agreement cannot be achieved through discussion, Warren identifies contest (protest) strategies as necessary, and these contest strategies can be subdivided into those that are not intended to harm the opponent and those that are. Hence, one can envision beginning to address an issue using a collaborative strategy and, if the agreement of power holders blocks resolution of the issue, moving to a campaign or advocacy strategy; if agreement is not obtained through a campaign or advocacy strategy, it becomes necessary to move to a contest or protest strategy. In employing contest or protest strategies, people seeking social justice premised on the value of human dignity and human rights principles will use only non-violent means of protests. Harm may be done to the opponents' reputation in order to resolve an issue that is impeding the well-being of many people; however, decisions to intentionally harm opponents, as perhaps in a "necessary" revolution or "just" war, are beyond the scope of the community organizing and social mobilizing work considered here. This value-anchored bounding of actions has been described by Buechler (2000) as "prefigurative politics," in which "the movement organized its activities in a manner that prefigured the broader cultural values and social relations that it was seeking in a transformed society" (p. 204). Aside from these ethical boundaries, the variations and blending of the social change activities happen within a form of creative dance with outside forces as best described by Tilly (2002):

> Creative interaction appears most visibly in such activities as jazz and soccer. In these cases, participants work within rough agreements on procedures and outcomes; arbiters set limits on performances; individual dexterity, knowledge, and disciplined preparation generally yield superior play; yet the rigid equivalent of military drill destroys the enterprise. (p. 211)

Collaborative projects engaged in collective resistance to the individualizing market focus of the dominant political-economic model and to the exclusionary practices of patriarchy were evident in numerous examples within this study. Communities were constructing alternatives to neo-liberal economics by developing co-operatives to generate income. Similarly, they were creating alternatives to exclusionary market and cultural practices by providing needed services through health promotion collectives and spaces to attend to women's well-being and equality. Carroll and Ratner (2010) concur that dissent does not necessarily originate from class conflict; instead, community members may "find common ground in an ethical and political project that unifies oppositional cultures around a democratic socialist alternative to capital's injustices and ecological calamities" (p. 20).

Community economic development projects are consistent with the activities that Oxhorn (1995) incorporated in his "low threshold" or broad definition of "what is political" (p. 306)—those that are alternatives to the market-oriented model favoured by the state. Such CED projects include all of the income-generating collectives: the coffee-producing co-operatives in Mexico and the complementary Just Us! Coffee Roasters Co-op in Canada; the numerous artesanía producing co-operatives in both countries and the tortilla-making collective in Veracruz; as well as the WEE Society's work to prepare women for equitable employment opportunities in Nova Scotia and the Oaxaca women centre's university entrance scholarships for young women with excellent grades and a record of work with women.

Collaborative approaches, in addition to economic co-operation activities, include collective services provision. Health services and anti-violence programs provided by social movement organizations with a feminist orientation and an understanding of power relations are included by Choudry, Hanley, and Shragge (2012) in their illustrations of alternative practices that challenge dominant ones. Alternative health care and preparation of traditional medicines were exemplified in this research by the health promotion collectives in the Guerrero parish, Mexico City, and Cuernavaca, Morelos, as well as by the health and wellness programs of the Tejalpa centre in Morelos and the women's group in the marginalized neighbourhood of Veracruz. Such a program focusing on women's health was being explored by the women's organization in the British Columbia city. Spaces dedicated to women's well-being and equality were also numerous in the study. Clearly, the women's centres in Oaxaca, Nova Scotia, and British Columbia existed to ensure that women received needed services and to work together for women's equality. CODIMUJ in Chiapas did much the same through the regular meetings in the communities that attended to women's right to dignity, and provided group support for women who were being abused to insist with their partners on their right to live free of violence, as well as help to leave if the abuse didn't stop. Eschle and Maiguashca (2010) describe this concrete help in women's daily lives, provided in a manner that seeks "to empower them to determine their own lives," as "principled pragmatism" (p. 185), a distinctive mode of service provision within collective action.

A final category of constructing alternatives to oppressive systems through collaborative strategies is the cluster of collective efforts for land, housing, utilities, education, and ecologically balanced environments. This study offered many examples of these, especially the work of the Guerrero neighbourhood settlers and community founders working together "like ants" to take over the empty land, clear away the brambles with machetes, dig a shallow well with picks, and widen the entrance to the community with shovels. Alternatives like these to oppressive systems, Choudry, Hanley, and Shragge (2012) note, must also include agitation for a better future. This the Guerrero community did in its direct actions to gain the right to occupy the land and to secure the water, electricity, and elementary school. Friedmann's (1992) dual focus for achieving empowerment in alternative development similarly asserts that, although the starting point is the immediate needs of the locality, the community must carry on to "seek to transform social into political power" (p. viii).

Advocacy or campaign strategies, the second of Warren's (1975) types of purposive change, are necessary when problem resolution is blocked by lack of agreement, usually on the part of power holders. They often result in the changes to practices, policies, or laws that Wilson, Calhoun, and Whitmore (2011) identified among the outcomes that Canadian activists in their study described as success. Advocacy since the advent of neo-liberalism has become more difficult. In Canada, organizations engaged in advocacy risk losing their government funding, as well as their charitable status, which jeopardizes their non-governmental funding through donations. The women's centre in Nova Scotia has found that "talk of social advocacy must now be recast in softer terms like community development." However, staff members remain committed to advocacy, and their Valentine's Day postcard campaign promoting policy changes to address women's poverty was well taken up. The British Columbia centre had foregone charitable status in its first twenty-five years in order to have the freedom to engage in advocacy. However, as noted previously, the cuts in government funding meant they needed to consider means of increasing donations, including seeking charitable status. One member emphasized, though, that "Charitable status can be very limiting. If one takes a structural view of the causes of many issues facing women (like poverty), it is clear that advocacy is necessary to challenge these. An open democracy requires advocacy groups." These cautions about advocacy currently are consistent with those in Mulay and Siddiqui's (2012) description of their feminist activism in Montreal, Canada, where they did their lobbying behind the scenes and more open political action was done only "as part of a larger movement" (p. 116).

Advocacy in the Mexican cases was also difficult in the present context. The Catholic women's campaign for reproductive rights was difficult under the regressive regimes of Pope Benedict XVI and Mexico's right-wing PAN Party. The Oaxaca women's centre continued its long-term practice of publishing the positions of political candidates on women's issues and inviting newly elected officials to workshops on gender equality; however, the governments were no longer sending very high-level representatives. Layton et al. (2010), when writing about advocacy to reduce maternal mortality in Mexico, found a phased manner of working in the restrictive circumstances to be effective as "each success brought the struggle to a new level, revealing the limitation of each advance and making plain the next challenge" (p. 104).

The use of legal measures as a means of advocacy was practised in a few of the case examples. Finn and Jacobson (2003) list both legislative and litigation avenues. The limitations of the legislative route with the Harper government in power in Canada became clearer to me during my 2010 experience promoting Bill C-300. Our local MPs, despite some expressions of concern about the civil and environmental rights abuses related to the Canadian mining company's activities in Guerrero, like all other members of the Conservative Party, voted against the bill.

The Chilcotin Six Nations (which encompass the Xeni Gwet'in) have used court rulings that constitute a third avenue, but are they sufficient without litigation? The Chilcotin Six Nations obtained a court ruling that stated they met the test for rights to 100 percent of their claimed land. The Friends of the Nemaiah Valley found it unbelievable that, although the Chilcotin won the rights in court, a mining company can stake a claim and have a proposal that destroys a fish-bearing lake be given consideration. The FONV member concluded:

> To establish the rights is not enough—a community must enforce them. This can be done, for example, by suing the government. But, of course, this is difficult because of the cost: The Xeni Gwet'in people don't have a lot of money and the government and the mining companies do.

Although litigation may not be affordable for an individual community, strategic litigation may be a feasible tactic for a large advocacy organization or network. In 2013, a coalition of human rights and mining injustice solidarity organizations used this practice effectively to set a legal precedent that allows claims against Canadian mining companies for offences committed by their subsidiaries in foreign countries to be tried in Canada (Marotte, 2013). The coalition is backing the claims of Guatemalan Mayans who protested evictions by the HudBay-owned mine on their land over which one man was killed, another was shot and disabled, and eleven women were gang-raped—all thirteen of whom were members of their Mayan community. This strategic litigation is a particularly astute approach since foreign-country communities affected by Canadian mining companies do not always have recourse to effective government legislation, policy, and enforcement in their own countries. The ejido in Guerrero, Mexico, had taken their concerns about arsenic contamination resulting from mining activities to the state's justice, environment, and health departments—all to no avail. The outcome of the HudBay case will be important for many other foreign communities dealing with rights abuses by Canadian-owned mining enterprises.

Contest or protest strategies are the third of Warren's (1975) types of purposive change, which he suggests are appropriate when there is no likelihood of reaching agreement through discussion. Desmarais (2007), in describing the international eco-agricultural movement, states that "mobilization and public protest remain the most important strategies that critical social movements use" (p. 24). Examples were found in this study of a variety of forms of non-violent protest ranging from peaceful demonstrations, through vigils, to blockades.

Demonstrations were used to mark international celebrations like International Women's Day and to draw attention to violations like the contamination of the water supply by factories in the Morelos industrial basin. They included the peace walk that the British Columbia women's centre participated in, as well as the Raging Grannies' surprise performances and the initial land occupation in the humble Guerrero neighbourhood.

In the last two examples, cultural stereotypes based on age and gender were used to the group's advantage. The Grannies took to the stage at a pre-election all-candidates meeting hosted by Nova Scotia university students even though extra security had been arranged. One of the students attempted to direct one of the Grannies off the stage by gently pushing her. The Granny dramatized the moment, shrieking out something to the effect of "How dare you push me, sonny!" which left the inexperienced chair quite confounded about what to do. This gave the Grannies sufficient opportunity to sing a few stinging political songs and exit on their own terms. In the Guerrero community's early struggle for ownership of their land, Cástula had been jailed for two hours until the students' protests persuaded the authorities to let her go: "Fed-up old ladies we were and I went forward without fear," she said. "'Don't be jerks,' I told the police when they grabbed me. 'Don't forget me,' I said. That's how it went." Both the Grannies in Nova Scotia and Cástula in Guerrero were able to use the common stereotype of "meek, frail, old ladies" and the social conventions of "respecting one's elders" and "protecting the weak" to their advantage in a highly comical way. The Granny I interviewed described their modus operandi as "laughing your way to social justice"—congruent with the message attributed to Emma Goldman that "If I can't dance, I don't want to be part of your revolution." Clearly, humour can be a highly beneficial aspect of protest.

Vigils are a more intense form of protest. The women from the marginalized neighbourhood in Veracruz maintained a continuous vigil at the entrance to the dump near their homes to stop the dumping of garbage, which led to contamination of their food. The following quotes from community members describe their action:

> The flies were horrible and the smell was intolerable too. So we organized ourselves, holding vigils as watch guards, to stop the dumping of garbage in our neighbourhood.... We organized and struggled, doing watch guard duty.... One night there were only about six of us and several of our teenage sons (more boys than mothers, in fact). The police chided us that we were only a group of six women and a bunch of kids, but we insisted that we represented a community of thirty who needed to take turns to allow the others to rest.... And bit by bit, over the course of nine years, we were successful.

Protest in its more disruptive, yet non-violent, mode may take the shape of blockades and demonstrations that unsettle the forces of hegemony (Carroll & Ratner, 2010; Gramsci, 1929-1935/1971). The guards at the 2003 WTO meeting in Cancun must have been very unsettled indeed by the women speaking many different languages who brought down the perimeter fence and then handed them white flowers symbolizing peace.

Blockades are part of the story of both the Canadian and Mexican communities in this study who were fighting against mining companies' contamination of their water. The Xeni Gwet'in people and the broader Chilcotin Nation first stopped incursions on their land during the gold rush in the Chilcotin War of 1864. In 1992, after a court ruling was ignored by a logging company, the Chilcotin used a blockade at Henry's Crossing and again in 1997, when another logging company attempted to enter against the wishes of the First Nations people, the road was blockaded—both times successfully stopping the planned infringement. With this Chilcotin history of willingness to stop attempts to take resources from their land, it is not surprising that the comment by one of the elders—that if necessary to stop the mine, she would be there on the road with her shotguns—was taken seriously by the media (Stueck & Curry, 2010). An insider, however, told me in a subsequent telephone conversation that the elder had only been kidding, and this rang true to me since I had been in their home where a flying beetle was chased outside rather than swatted, and caught fish were not eaten until the next day in order to allow their spirits to leave.

The Guerrero ejido, in 2008, after attempting to negotiate with the mining company and reach out to the state authorities with no success, established a blockade at the entrance to the mine to prevent the trucks and mining equipment from entering. Families took turns at the blockade. But, as detailed in Part II, this resulted in threats against the father and daughter who were assisting the ejido; a shooting in 2009 of one of the protesting ejidatarios, who had to go into hiding when he was able to leave the hospital; and, a few weeks later, arrests without warrants of three men from the same family. This experience was consistent with the explanation provided by the director of TADECO for the disappearance of another activist and good friend—the government has "criminalized the social struggle." As Cortez Ruiz's (2010) analysis of the trajectory of the Zapatista movement points out, there are serious risks in using confrontational protest in a context like Mexico, where repressive state reaction is very possible. Organizers have a responsibility to ensure that participants are aware of those risks and that people are making informed decisions about their participation.

Strengthening the Organization

The final aspect of mobilization strategy to be addressed is organizational strengthening. Brecher, Costello, and Smith (2002) describe building the common vision and strengthening the organization as a key phase in developing social movements. Similarly, "community-building" is one of the three tasks that Carroll and Ratner (2010) identify as essential in order to counter hegemonic force; as well, sustaining the morale and commitment of current adherents is another of the six strategic hurdles that McAdam (1996) says must be cleared for movement organizations to prompt social change. During the final afternoon of the two-day CODIMUJ workshop for regional and zone representatives in the San Cristóbal diocese of Chiapas, participants were asked to address two important questions. The first concerned their objectives—and I will return to it in the next paragraph—but the second question asking what they needed to do to achieve these yielded the following responses: "Dialogue," "look for agreement," "recover our strength," and "create unity"—all activities that relate to strengthening their organizations.

The continental coordinator of COMPA revealed a clear understanding of the importance of this and identified consolidating the network as her first priority. The four key components of empowerment practice identified by Lee (2001), in addition to consciousness-raising and taking action for change, include strengthening capabilities and problem-solving skills, as well as building the group, collectivity, and community. The organizer, who had been a facilitator of the activities in the Veracruz town with the tortilla-making collective, cautions that she believes her role was to help the groups become strong and stable, but that "some of the earlier facilitators and advisers took on leadership roles in which they created a dependency and left the groups weaker when they departed." UNEAMICH—the statewide union of Michoacán artisans, which was an initiative of the state under Cuauhtémoc Cárdenas's governorship—seemed to be working relatively well for both the artisans and CASART. However, its close relations with the state make it vulnerable to the problems of corporatism described in Part I. Fisher and Karger (1997) also emphasize the importance of strong autonomous grassroots organizations:

Local networks serve as the basis of broad social movements. This requires patience, time, leadership and a committed practice belief system. Broader political or social change must be built upon a foundation of painstaking, incremental work that fosters social networks, recreates organizations, and readies people for a time of greater progressive opportunity. (p. 20)

Themes related to these, which emerged from the data in this study, include building commitment to specific common principles, training for managing the collective, emphasis on respect for the grassroots members, uniting the community, and links to related social movement communities. These themes align very closely with the success factors related to the functioning of the activists' groups, according to participants in Wilson, Calhoun, and Whitmore's (2011) Canadian study.

Building dedication to the principles and goals at the core of these social movement organizations and communities is important for retaining the commitment and enthusiasm of members (Kuyek, 2011; McAdam, 1996). The CODIMUJ representatives, in the workshop session described earlier, gave the following responses to the question about their objectives: "We want equality," "to be free," "to have a life with dignity," "a new society." "We need to be able to practise our autonomy." "We want health services," "good education," "to be able to make and sell our products," and "to be the government." I asked two of the nuns who were working with CODIMUJ communities what they thought was most important in facilitating the organization of women's groups with the potential for social mobilization that was described earlier in the workshop. One said that she thought the reflection meetings every fifteen days, using the liberation theology method, were key to building strong organizations of committed women. A more Indigenous worldview is apparent in Margo's group who work with natural medicines, but nevertheless, similar attention was paid to building commitment to core principles, and she emphasized that "it takes time." Layton et al. (2010), in describing the work of the groups engaged in activities to reduce maternal mortality in Mexico, point out that it was the shared commitment that held the coalition together. Cheryl Hyde (1994), in writing about commitment to social change in the feminist movement, was most eloquent:

> To commit oneself to a cause, feminist or otherwise, is to craft a meaning-ful and purposeful life in concert with others who share a vision for a better society.... Social change or "cause" commitment encompasses three basic principles: active participation in and labor for the social movement; risk or sacrifice on personal and professional levels; and, an often high degree of bonding or group solidarity among participants. (p. 47)

Training for managing collectives was highlighted by Hugman (2010) in his identification of five essential features in international social development or community economic development (CED): "focusing on capacity building through attention to human resources and social as well as economic capital" (p. 65). Amy recognized the importance of capacity building in her work with the Xeni Gwet'in—acting as a mentor by helping the community's mining coordinator understand how to engage and negotiate with the government. Piza Lopez and March (1991), in their pioneering report on women's community economic development, also pointed out that training is essential, both in leadership and organizational administration, as well as in the production and marketing area. MUSA, very early in its life, received assistance from a Spanish woman, supported by an NGO, to provide leadership for its development, as noted earlier. She was with them for four years, and her primary role was to help the two current staff develop the necessary skills to take over her leadership. These two staff, in turn, are delighted that the women in the local communities want literacy training in reading and arithmetic in order to be successful with their micro-enterprises such as running the mill. Women from the carpet-weaving collective in Oaxaca brought in resource people to address their learning needs, and it was an Indigenous woman from the neighbouring town whose suggestions they appreciated the most. Similarly, the women's pottery collective in Chiapas obtained some of its initial inspiration from an Indigenous woman from a nearby village who talked to them about the need for changes in women's situation. They found it very helpful to have discussions about what is possible with a woman from very similar circumstances and cultural traditions. This is consistent with the findings in my earlier research comparing women's employment initiatives in Canada and Chile in which instructors with the same economic and cultural background best understood the learners' challenges and embodied the potential of overcoming them (Snyder, 2000).

Attention to the grassroots membership and local communities, as well as respect for their autonomy, was emphasized by the social movement organizations in this study. Former Chiapas bishop, Samuel Ruiz, reflected this perspective in his comment that the priests helped the oldest and largest coffee co-operative in the area to succeed, "but the indigenous people are in complete control" (Menocal & Ruiz, 1998, p. 86). Executive members of CEPCO, the coffee producers' association of Oaxaca, demonstrated their commitment to the grassroots in their response to my question about how they address concerns noted in their annual report about some regional representatives not getting the state-level information to the members and regular meetings of the memberships not being held in some regions:

> As members of the board of directors we attend the regional assemblies, but in these meetings we must respect the autonomy of the regional organization. We are there as guests, not as authorities—the base (grassroots) is the authority. We do not impose our wishes on them. We can offer our ideas about these problems, but we remind them that the solution must come from them.

They then drew my attention to the list of principles in the report and pointed out that autonomy and democracy are the first two on the list of four principles (plurality and transparency are the other two) and emphasized their importance. A final example is provided in the conscious attention paid to autonomy by the MUSA staff, who were described earlier in the discussion of training. As noted in Part II, each of the women's programs at the local community level in Unión de la Selva's region of Chiapas has its own coordinator. These coordinators receive support from the MUSA staff, but increasingly they are taking more responsibility for leadership in their own communities. I asked the coordinators what they thought was most critical in the organizing and development work they do, and they said "the most important thing is to understand what the women need and want (by asking them) and to respect the decisions that they make."

Uniting the community is essential to building a strong social movement organization. Schugurensky (2013) contends that "an ongoing process of community building, of healthier relations with other community members and with nature" (p. xii) is, along with improving governance, critical to deepening democracy. Tere, referring to her initial discussions with the amate-paper painters in the marginalized Guerrero neighbourhood, called this "the common, slow beginning work of unifying people in the community to work toward common purposes." Several of the social movement communities had the additional challenge of needing to unite heterogeneous groups. Dobbie and Richards-Schuster (2008) maintain that solidarity among people united across differences enhances likelihood of success in social movements. This principle of plurality was most evident in the CEPCO organization, where I asked if producers belonged to various political parties or if the members of the organization favoured a particular party. The president replied that "members belong to various political parties, but we are all the colour of coffee; it is the commitment to plurality that allows us to unify."

Another matter relating to unity that emerged in this study was the concern about division in the communities. Freire (1968/1984) contrasted community unity for liberation with power holders' reaction of division: "It is in the interest of the oppressor to weaken the oppressed still further, to isolate them, to create and deepen rifts among them" (p. 137). This strategy was evident in the Chiapas communities where government policies and military presence had polarized communities (Gilbreth & Otero, 2001). These rifts were problematic for the CODIMUJ women's groups in those communities. The Luna Creciente organizer was attempting, along with two visiting nuns, to help the Chiapas weavers collective address any relationship problems in the collective by talking about their concerns and bringing them to the attention of the two guardians of the organization. The divide-and-conquer strategy was also used by the mining company operating in Guerrero. Two ejidos whose water was contaminated with arsenic from the mining process had formed a coalition to attempt to resolve the matter; however, the company "bought" the leader of one of the ejidos, who accepted a deal for less than half of what the community had requested, thereby splitting the coalition. In contrast, the Xeni Gwet'in people were firmly united. Earlier processes like making the Declaration of the Nemaiah Aboriginal Wilderness Preserve in 1989 had accomplishing this unification, according to Past Chief Roger William. Nor had the promise of jobs caused the Xeni Gwet'in to break ranks—they greatly doubted that the number of jobs predicted would even materialize. The Xeni Gwet'in community possesses the collective identity that Kutz-Flamenbaum (2012) argues "provides a shared sense of purpose and unifies a group of individuals in ways that make mass action possible" (p. 290).

Linking to other social movement communities is the final component of the strengthening organizations topic. Several academics describe developing relations with allies and forming coalitions as an important step in social movement building for social justice (Bishop, 2002; Brecher, Costello, & Smith, 2002; Lundy, 2004). Antrobus (2004) describes the globalized women's movement as originating in local women's struggles for safety, livelihood, and community well-being, as mentioned earlier, then moving into networking, connecting with other women's groups regionally on similar issues and with global organizations on larger structural issues. All three of the women's centres in this study are engaged in collaborative activities with other women's organizations: in their own communities, such as the British Columbia group's connections with the local sexual assault counselling centre, the university status of women committee, and the Elizabeth Fry Society; provincially, as in the Nova Scotia coalition of women's organizations who promoted the Valentine's Day postcard campaign; and nationally, as well as internationally, in the work on women's sexual and reproductive rights that included the efforts of both the Oaxaca women's centre and the Morelos representative for Catholic Women for the Right to Decide.

Linkages to national and international non-governmental organizations and the existence of international norms were the other critical factors that Khagram (2002) identified in the successful domestic resistance to the Narmada Valley dam proposal in India (in addition to the democratic context mentioned earlier). The Xeni Gwet'in, along with the Friends of the Nemaiah Valley, were adept in connecting with many like-minded people and organizations: legal and technical specialists; NGOs like RAVEN, the Council of Canadians, and Mining Watch; as well as broader Indigenous organizations. The ejido struggling against the mining company in Guerrero had connected with the Mexican Network of People Affected by Mining (REMA), a mining resistance support organization in Mexico, and a human rights organization in Guerrero; in addition, they were being supported by the Green Party from Texas and the Texas Environmental Justice Advocacy Service. They were also looking for help from Canadians since over 70 percent of the mining concessions in Mexico are held by Canadian companies. Kuyek (2011) strongly concurs with the need for this linkage beyond national borders:

> If we work with communities in the Global South, almost all their leaders will beg us to work in Canada, to change the behaviour of the "developed" countries that are disorganizing them and pillaging their resources.... In their view, it is the power structures in Europe and North America that need to change. (p. 163)

TADECO, in its work on human rights issues, is a member of the state and national human rights networks and often works with other organizations on large projects, one of which included a United Nations committee on human rights. Josephine Grey (2012), the coordinator of Low Income Families Together (LIFT) and Canada's representative in COMPA (Convergence of People's Movements in the Americas) believes this international bridge-building is important partly due to repression, which can happen at a national level. Grey was interviewed by CBC on the 6:00 p.m. news upon her return from presenting at a meeting of the United Nations committee dealing with the Covenant on Economic, Social and Cultural Rights. However, CBC officials didn't allow the interview to be played a second time—she was told there had been interference—nor did LIFT receive any government funding after that. Linkages and political affinities are now being forged across particular identities, as well as across borders, united by a common critique of globalized neo-liberalism (Eschle & Maiguashca, 2010; Giroux, 2008; Olesen, 2011). ∎

ELEVEN

CHALLENGES, CELEBRATIONS, AND CONCEPTUALIZATIONS

A FINAL CLUSTER of themes and theories that emerged from the case studies relates to the challenges that the organizations faced in their social mobilization processes, the outcomes of the struggles, and overall conceptualizations for effective practice in bringing about greater justice.

Challenges Faced in the Social Mobilization Process

THE CHALLENGES EXPERIENCED by the Canadian and Mexican communities in their social mobilization work included repression, the culture of non-participation, the impact of poverty on participation, problems from the Church, problematic government programs, and divisions in the communities. Lack of financing, other than its connection to problematic government programs, was discussed earlier in the resources and challenges section of Chapter 9.

Repression was experienced to varying degrees in the different communities. Tarrow (1998) identified institutional responses from power holders as a common reaction following the repertoires of action and cycles of protest carried out as a social movement spreads. Protests at meetings of the international financial institutions have often been met with direct repression. The WTO meeting in Cancan was no exception—prior to the dramatic presentation of flowers, women climbed through holes in the perimeter fence and the guards beat them back with batons. Forced disappearances of activists in the social struggle is a grave concern of TADECO staff members who have lost close colleagues and participated on a committee that documented twelve hundred forced disappearances in Guerrero between 2005 and 2009. Watt and Zepeda (2012), writing about narco-related violence, concur with the TADECO director that the military have targeted protesters "under the pretext of eradicating drug trafficking" (p. 206). The heavy military presence in Chiapas coincides with the location of the Zapatista communities, Watt and Zepeda note, and not with data on drug involvement. This level of militarization caused many of the group leaders at the CODIMUJ workshop to identify with Mary, the mother of the disciple John, in a reading about her experience of repression under the Roman Empire. Layton et al. (2010) concur that repression in Mexico through militarization and narco-trafficking is "weakening the prospects for citizen engagement" (p. 102). Certainly, the violent arrest without warrants of three of the men involved in the protest against mining in the Guerrero ejido must have contributed to the eventual capitulation by the majority of the ejidatarios to the mining company's proposed agreement regarding use of their land to access the mine.

Mexico's historic pattern of clientelism—rewarding communities for their political compliance with small gifts—was noted in Chapter 3. It was a substantial factor in the creation of a culture of non-participation in which "people are not used to being expected to participate and are slow to do so without an external incentive" (Zúñiga Zárate & Garza Treviño, 2007, p. 116). The practice of clientelism was clear in the nun's story at the CODIMUJ women's group meeting in the rural Chiapas town: a very corrupt politician had visited the town handing out cakes and the people applauded when he spoke. TADECO staff spoke about needing to struggle against the current in organizing people to work for solutions because "the paternalistic government processes in Mexico have created a great sense of dependence in the people—a belief that the government will address all the problems." The COMPA coordinator confirmed this as well, saying that social mobilization is a challenge in Mexico because there is a culture of non-participation arising from the many years of corruption and people's conclusion that involvement in politics is bad.

The impact of poverty on participation in the social movement organizations was found to be more complicated than most of the literature suggests. Carroll and Ratner (2010) observed difficult challenges for the groups they studied in British Columbia, "given the desperate neediness of their constituents" (p. 14). This was the case for the women's centre in British Columbia, where one of the board members commented on the unrealistic expectation of funders that the work be done by volunteers: "Many people don't understand what women's centres do—although many women become volunteers after contact with the centre, they are often in crisis when they first come in and are dealing with urgent immediate needs."

In Mexico, "the urgent immediate needs" often continue for longer because of less public financial assistance. Sara, one of the amate-paper painters, told me that she wasn't able to attend school until age nine, and then only for three years because there wasn't enough money (although public education is free, the families still need to provide for uniforms, notebooks, and a small registration fee). The director of the women's centre in Oaxaca said that the poorest women are unable to benefit from participation in many of their programs. She told me that women who are preoccupied with getting food for the family's next meal are unable to attend educational programs. Similarly, she said, women who attend such programs and learn about the importance of good nutrition during pregnancy can't implement their learning if they can't afford more nutritious food. One of the CODIMUJ leaders working in the city of San Cristóbal mentioned their comparable experience that many women in the city are fully occupied with their individual economic survival activities and, therefore, it has been more difficult to organize collective income-generating projects than in the rural communities of Chiapas, where extended family and community ties exist. Piven and Cloward (1977), in their analysis of poor people's movements in the United States, "maintained that political influence by the poor is mobilized, not organized...[and that if the poor] were asked to contribute to an organization on a continuing basis, [Piven and Cloward] did not think they would, for organizers had no continuing incentives to offer" (p. 284). This is consistent with my earlier findings that in Chile, where public financial assistance programs like those in Mexico did not meet survival needs, the poorest of the poor were unable to participate in employment preparation programs, whereas in Canada they could (Snyder, 2000).

The impact of poverty on participation in the broader civil society organizations studied herein, however, is more consistent with Thompson and Tapscott's (2010) contention that "the material conditions of the very marginalized can act both as an incentive and a disincentive to mobilization" (p. 20). In the collective that Margo led in Mexico City, during the long process of learning about the natural medicines and how to prepare them, "some left because they wanted to earn money rapidly." Even for people who are employed, Smith, Stenning, and Willis (2008) state: "formal organized protests and resistance are very difficult to achieve given the precarious nature of their working existence" (p. 4). The amate-paper painters in the Guerrero neighbourhood were in this kind of precarious situation: they were reluctant to work collectively in a form of resistance without the merchant, since they were afraid that they might not be able to sell the paintings; although the pay was very low (Cdn. 33 cents per hour), at least it was guaranteed. This may also have been the case for the Guerrero ejidatarios. I don't know what amount they settled on with the mining company for use of their land to access the below-ground minerals in 2010, but one hopes it is substantially more than the Cdn. $18 per family that they received for the first three years of exploration. Given the tremendous pressure that assurances of a small amount of money must place on people with very little, perhaps the greater surprise is that they do mobilize when there is no guarantee of improved incomes or well-being. But this study and others do show that people, including poor people, do organize to form income-generating projects; to obtain better health, housing, and environments; and to work toward greater dignity and equality for women. For many of them, as noted earlier, their mobilization was done out of necessity.

There were problems related to the Church that social movement communities in Mexico brought forward. It has already been mentioned that the Catholic Church hierarchy rejected the principles of liberation theology by the 1980s and replaced the bishops who had promoted it with conservative ones. This meant the work of the Christian Base Communities (CEBs) was no longer supported by the Church leaders. Pope Benedict XVI (2005–2013) brought more conservative dogma to the Catholic Church, which meant a retrenchment in women's rights, according to the feminist activists interviewed. In particular, the Church hierarchy has opposed the work of Catholic Women for the Right to Decide regarding women's sexual and reproductive rights. Licha said this has been one of CDD's biggest challenges because very traditional people take the Church's position seriously. Another problem for Catholic workers and communities inspired by liberation theology has been the missionary work of charismatic, evangelical churches in the poor communities. These churches are attracting members to a perspective that doesn't have a commitment to social change for the benefit of the poor.

Government programs and policies were problematic for numerous groups in their collective efforts. Particular issues identified related to programs and policy dealing with mining, gender equity, support for producers and for families, and impact on communities. In both Canada and Mexico, government policies related to mining had opened up opportunities for the mining industry with little consideration given to the consequences for the people or the environment. Canada has removed protection from all but a small proportion of its water bodies in a conglomerate piece of legislation that allowed for very little public debate. The state and federal governments in Mexico now welcome foreign mining interests and provide a hasty environmental review process.

Government policies in both countries demonstrate a lack of commitment to gender equality. Dobrowolsky (2014) has documented the contracting of funding for women's programs in Canada: "as in 1995, when the CACSW [Canadian Advisory Council on the Status of Women] and the [Secretary of State's] Women's Program were collapsed into SWC [Status of Women Canada]" (p. 159), which was dealt a budget blow of $5 million in 2006 with funding for advocacy prohibited. Both of the Canadian women's centres suffered from these drastic cuts. The Antigonish women's centre director, in particular, spoke of the redirection "from opposition to service provision" noted by Hanley and Shragge (2007, p. 63). The women's centre in Oaxaca experienced similar decreases in funding from the Mexican government, and the coordinator doubted that the president's attention to addressing both "chicos y chicas" (young men and young women) carries over into real attention to creating equality for the young women. Licha in describing the regression in women rights in Mexico, placed the conservative PAN Party, which was in power from 2000 to 2012, in equal place with the conservative Catholic Church hierarchy for this achievement.

Criticisms of government programs and policies were abundant in Mexico. As Thompson and Tapscott (2010) note, in the global South the oppressed are unable to realize their rights through formal channels with the government and, therefore, social movements "form part of a broader process of holding the state accountable for the welfare of all its citizens" (p. 27). The coffee producers' co-operatives found that, although the government had created a special fund for the stabilization of prices, nothing was forthcoming and the process was bogged down and moving at a turtle's pace. Some artisans in Michoacán were very disappointed that after constituting themselves as civil associations as CASART had encouraged them to do, other government programs mandated to promote enterprises and industrial development had not been willing to provide them with the necessary guarantees to allow them to access credit without unreasonable interest rates or impossible collateral requirements. The Oportunidades program, described in Chapter 3, was the program that met with the greatest amount of criticism. TADECO's political committee described the Oportunidades cash benefits as a type of palliative that does nothing to resolve the issues at the root of poverty. At the CODIMUJ workshop, the Oportunidades program was mentioned in reports from breakout groups several times and PROCAMPO was mentioned as well. Women expressed anger at what they called pitiful programs when what are needed are fair prices for their products. One region reported that such government programs have weakened the women's collectives in the communities:

> Oportunidades offers allowances for attending their talks; other programs provide a pig or lamb. These are just little scraps that hungry people can't turn down, but they don't help long term. They take the women's time away from the CODIMUJ groups' activities and they divide the women.

In fact, this is exactly what happened in the community that the two visiting nuns described to the San Cristóbal weavers collective facilitated by Luna Creciente. The community that the nuns described has a health clinic operated by a women's collective. The collective had experienced some earlier tensions because of the military presence and the resultant resentment on the part of some women toward the Zapatista members and supporters in the community. Most recently, government programs like Oportunidades have drawn away several of the clinic volunteers, which has created a serious rift in the community and jeopardized the viability of the clinic.

Divisions in the communities that created challenges in the social mobilization activities came not only from government programs and the churches but also from political differences. The nun working with the women's group in the rural Chiapas village considering their options for International Women's Day spoke of divisions in the village. She explained that there is such a high level of animosity between supporters of the PRI and supporters of the PRD that it hasn't been possible to organize any income-generation projects there. In another municipality in Chiapas, the PRD had been elected and the

Zapatista supporters had refused to participate on the municipal committees for water, education, health, and roads. In retaliation, the PRD municipal government suspended the supply of water to the Zapatista communities. A final example pertains to Williams Lake in British Columbia, which is the city nearest to the Nemaiah Valley and the place where the Xeni Gwet'in youth live to complete their senior secondary school education. Some people in Williams Lake have supported the Xeni Gwet'in in their struggle to have the federal government turn down the proposal for mining at Fish Lake, in particular, the local chapter of the Council of Canadians. However, the majority of the residents are pro-mining—most vociferously the members of the Chamber of Commerce. Supporters of the Xeni Gwet'in have received retributions in the form of racism and ostracism—youth being ridiculed in school and shops being boycotted. In this case, the mobilization of the Xeni Gwet'in was not impeded because their own community was very united, but the price that opposing the mining exacted was higher because of division in the nearest city.

Outcomes, Celebration, and Historical Review

SUCCESSFUL OUTCOMES OF THE STRUGGLES carried out by the communities in this study were abundant. They include influencing state action and policy, as well as changing public attitudes in the direction of greater priority to human rights, dignity, and the natural environment. They also include establishing alternatives to the neo-liberal economic model and providing services, programs, and products that met basic needs and enhanced people's well-being.

The Xeni Gwet'in of British Columbia and their supporters experienced the successful outcome of their actions to persuade the environmental impact assessment panel that Taseko's proposed mine at Fish Lake would likely have significant adverse effects on the environment, wildlife, and First Nations' traditional use of the land (Canada, CEAA, 2010a). And, with the panel review results behind them, they influenced the Canadian federal cabinet in the fall of 2010 to reject the mining company's proposal. This was not the end of their struggle—the mining company submitted a follow-up proposal, which, by February 2014, was rejected again and the mining company indicated it will reapply again (CBC, 2014).

The various income-generating projects had created viable alternatives to the individualistic free-market model. Desmarais (2007) describes these achievements in the global eco-agricultural small-scale farming movement:

> Indeed, peasants and farmers are using three traditional weapons of the weak—organization, co-operation, and community—to redefine "development" and build an alternative model of agriculture based on principles of social justice, ecological sustainability, and respect for peasant cultures and peasant economies. This includes building viable alternatives ranging from small agricultural co-operatives, local seed banks, and fair trade ventures to reclaiming traditional farming practices. It also means linking these efforts beyond the local by working at the national, regional, and international levels. (p. 200)

These types of alternatives are epitomized in the Union de la Selva and CEPCO coffee producers' co-operatives along with the Just Us! co-operative, which provides the international solidarity for fair trade ventures and the participants in the protest at the WTO meeting in Cancun. Other co-operatives and income-generating projects have had similar benefits. The Cheticamp Artisans Cooperative has been operating since 1964, eliminating the loss of excessive profits to traders. The potters' collective in the Chiapas village has brought vital income into their households and, in addition, contributed to the women's image of themselves as capable people with rights and provided a space to cultivate their political work for change.

Health promotion collectives were generating a small amount of income for most of the participants, but, in addition, they were providing benefits to the community members who could now access affordable health care. As well, the leader of the health and well-being project in Morelos noted that the natural therapies help women who are oppressed in their relationships and economically "to recover their power and demand changes." The health centre collective in the Veracruz neighbourhood, as well as providing direct care, has successful dealt with the environmental and health issues related to the garbage and constructed improved housing for a number of the families.

Gender issues were being addressed in a variety of ways in the organizations studied. Htun and Weldon (2012) affirm the importance of autonomous organizing in civil society, which, according to the results of their multi-country study of thirty years of public policy regarding violence against women, had greater influence on policy than women's representation in Parliament or economic factors. In various communities and in a documentary provided by the Oaxaca women's centre, I heard that little by little things are changing and women are respected more. A national coalition that included the women's centre in Oaxaca was effective in getting increased government attention and federal funding allocated to maternal mortality prevention (Layton et al. 2010). The social assistance reform project done collaboratively by women's centres in Nova Scotia had considerable impact on senior government officials. The Women's Economic Equality (WEE) Society has operated exciting and accessible programs to help women with employment barriers obtain employ in many areas, including in non-traditional trades and the high-technology field. The materials and gatherings organized by CDD in Mexico were opening the minds of women raised in a very patriarchal culture and, similarly, events coordinated by the women's centre in British Columbia were bringing fathers and husbands on board as allies for women's right to safety and to be treated with respect.

Projects working more broadly for justice and human rights reported gratifying outcomes as well. The Raging Grannies gaggle in Nova Scotia was typically able to complete its poignant choruses since the police were reluctant to confront seemingly harmless women who might be their mothers. In the Guerrero neighbourhood much had been accomplished, although sometimes slowly. The facilitators were particularly happy when they introduced me to a girl whose parents are not literate; however, she is now in *preparatoria*—the final school years before university.

Of course, not all outcomes for the communities studied were positive. The governments' cuts to funding for women's centres in both countries revealed ongoing patriarchal attitudes that impacted service provision negatively. In British Columbia, the elected member of the provincial government who had made the derogatory remark about women sitting around drinking coffee also referred to social workers as "poverty pimps." The BC women's centre had to give up its drop-in availability and reduce its staffing to ten hours per week.

The outcome of the struggles against Canadian mining's toll on the environmental, health, and human rights in Guerrero is particularly unsatisfactory. The Canadian government's failure to pass legislation to sanction corporations infringing on rights in other countries is a shameful change from half a century ago when Canada was a leading promoter of international human rights and development. The Guerrero ejido was not able to carry on its fight for an end to the contamination of its water and a comparison with the success (so far) of the Xeni Gwet'in in British Columbia, Canada, highlights some of the important factors. Democracy in Canada, although flawed, is relatively strong and the justice system ensures that laws are enforced. In Mexico, democracy and justice have been obstructed by corruption at very high levels. The current increased militarization and drug-related crime, in a context where the state has a history of using repression against protesters, creates an environment in which the armed forces and police can be called upon by governments in Mexico to resolve "other problems," and the pretext of "drug involvement" can be used to explain forced disappearances. The Xeni Gwet'in and the broader Chilcotin Six Nations have a history of struggle and victory, whereas Mexican Indigenous peoples and campesinos have a history of struggle, victory, and repeated oppression. The Xeni Gwet'in people have very effective external supports in the broader First Nations organizations, as well as in expert and advocacy groups who are not subjected to fear. The Guerrero ejido's representatives were threatened and isolated and leaders in the Mexican Network of People Affected by Mining (REMA) had been killed. The Xeni Gwet'in's internal leadership was highly communicative and participatory, whereas several of the Guerrero ejido leaders were frightened away or jailed. The Xeni Gwet'in people had been strongly united through past struggles and victories and were not vulnerable to economic incentives, while the Guerrero ejido had less hope of victory and the offers by the mining company created division in the community because of their less secure economic status.

Despite the ongoing struggles in Mexico, people in the social movement communities often refer to the fact that much of their oppression dates over five hundred years to the Spanish Conquest and patriarchy goes back even further. They recognize the long history, the many battles, and don't expect full victory in their own lifetime. However, they use an expression with a fierce determination and a sense of community and hopefulness in the face of setbacks: La lucha sigue! [The struggle continues!]

Celebration and doing historical review were part of the cycle of social mobilization work in many of the communities and organizations studied. Ife (2010), in his writing about human rights work, describes the importance of balancing negative content with positive without losing the sense of urgency and including culturally appropriate celebratory components like barbecues and music. As noted earlier in the description of Freire's cycle of praxis, celebration is the fourth and final step in the conscientization process before beginning a new round, and it was used in many of the groups influenced by liberation theology as well as others. Licha's example was provided of the application of the cycle of praxis concept in the work of the coalition of CEBs in the Morelos industrial valley, and how after each action they evaluated them and celebrated the successes. The CODIMUJ two-day workshop took place ten years after the Zapatista uprising in Chiapas, and a half-day was devoted to reviewing what had happened each year with attention to the importance of the movement events and the role of the women in them—both of which the women present acknowledged were significant. In the Guerrero neighbourhood studied, I observed Tere and Amado using introductions as an opportunity for celebration of the people's history. Tere explained that a family we visited was one of the first who settled in the neighbourhood and that the man, in fact, was the builder of the original parts of her house. Amado began a meeting with the community founders by asking if his assumptions were correct about when each of the people present had arrived in the community, including the nineteen-year-old, who was one of the first babies born in the community. CASART used celebration in its work with the artisans by holding a large annual competition concurrent with a week-long fair during the Mexican Easter vacation week. The artisans themselves frequently spoke of the long family tradition of doing the work—some of these go back to pre-Hispanic times. Among the Xeni Gwet'in in British Columbia there was great respect for the ideas of the elders and ancestors. Chief Marilyn Baptiste used these as her base and then sought new knowledge from consultants and the Internet that were compatible with these core beliefs. The women's centre in British Columbia, after losing funding for their drop-in services, chose to celebrate local women's history through their Untold Stories project.

Overall Conceptualizations for Bringing about Greater Justice

SOME BROADER CONCEPTUALIZATIONS emerge from a holistic consideration of the efforts to bring about greater justice. These are presented in the suggestions that the activists themselves put forward, as well as my commendations of the praxis spiral in planning and phasing the work, and of a paradigm for visioning and constructing a congruent practice.

Recommendations from Activists

Some of the activists' suggestions that haven't already been mentioned in the earlier discussions of the social mobilization work are noteworthy. They include personal reflections on doing the work, the focus on the people's interests, and integrity in one's practice.

The first recommendations are from two activists regarding their personal perspectives on doing the organizing or mobilizing. Interestingly, both use the cycle of praxis in conceptualizing their own process. Maria de los Angeles, the leader of the programs in the marginalized neighbourhood on the outskirts of the town in Veracruz, listed four steps:

1. See the reality of the community. Learn, by spending time with the people, what their necessities are.
2. Become clear about your own motivation through self-reflection: Do you have strong convictions that work with the poor is your vocation?
3. Help the people to learn that it is necessary to work together—organize. They will have to struggle for many things—for themselves personally and for the community.
4. If you are clear that this is what you want to do, you have to learn to live this life—to be open to new ideas and not be afraid of the work, the hours, and the sacrifice.

Estela, leader of the Tejalpa health and well-being program in Morelos, also offered her recommendation for success in this organizing work. She said it is important to work from one's own experience and to observe the realities in the community. Next, one reflects on the findings and analyzes them since from this analysis, one can develop concepts and theories. Then one acts on these theories and tests them in the reality of the community. Estela noted that the approach comes from Paulo Freire's method of praxis, but adds the feminist perspective.

Several of the recommendations emphasize the focus on the people and their needs. Agustina, whose work began in the CEBs and now encompasses many facets of mobilization in Morelos, makes the same point as Maria de los Angeles about personal clarity and goes on to stress the observation component of the cycle of praxis:

To do this work it is important to discover what you love and to become conscious of your convictions—you must discover what is meaningful to you in order to enjoy your work. Then, as you begin, you must also learn to be very observant in order to understand the people in their entirety and in their context in order to be helpful—you have to have the capacity to listen and to learn from the people what is needed.

Margo, in doing her work with the health promotion collective in Mexico City, similarly underscored that "the focus must be on what the women are interested in—it will require a long-term commitment on their part." These recommendations echo learnings reported in other literature: the advantage of an accompaniment approach (Calhoun, Wilson, & Whitmore, 2011) and the importance of tenacity and personal sustainability (Calhoun et al., 2011; Ricketts, 2012). Castelloe, Watson, and White (2002) also affirm the significance of focusing on the people and truly hearing them: "It comes from the people…draw out people's wisdom…ask questions…listen" (pp. 26-27).

A final recommendation comes from Agustina: "also there must be coherence and consistency between what you say and do because the people can see if you really mean what you say." This resonates with Desmarais's (2007) point that a social movement organization advocating "inclusion and democracy must champion these in its own processes" (p. 191). In other words, it is very important for social movement leaders and organizers to have a practice in which our day-to-day methods and overall objectives are congruent with the ideals and theories that motivate and guide our work.

The Praxis Spiral in Planning and Phasing the Work

The overall way of going about the social mobilization and community organizing work is very usefully conceptualized through Freire's continuous cycle of praxis shown in Figure 10.2. Although the notion of praxis was employed effectively at the micro-practice level as an aspect of mobilization strategy (consciousness-raising through reflection after observation and prior to action), it is also valuable for conceptualizing a project holistically.

This holistic perspective uses the continuous cycle of praxis in planning and phasing the overall project. It was evident in Licha's description of the process of addressing the ecological concerns in the industrial basin of Morelos, and it was central to the recommendations for practitioners from Maria de los Angeles in Veracruz and from Estela and Agustina in Morelos recounted earlier. The first step of action, focusing primarily on observation, includes going to the people, engaging with the people, learning from the people, and working with the people to gather data related to the issues of concern. The second step—one of reflection—involves engaging in a critical thinking process, analyzing the data, clarifying objectives, agreeing on a strategy, and preparing for an action. If during this reflection process it becomes clear that additional information is needed, the next action step may be a return to further observation and data gathering at the first step. If the outcome of the work in the reflection phase indicates the people are prepared, the process moves forward to the third step—one of action—the actual intervention to influence change. The fourth step—one of reflection—evaluates the action taken and celebrates the work accomplished. The outcome of the evaluation frequently reveals that further work is needed and the cycle begins again with the first step of action—observing and gathering further data. The process carries on in a spiral that moves forward, influencing change in a positive manner and reflecting critically on what is needed next.

Many writers applaud the consciousness-raising process and others the importance of evaluation, as was noted in Chapter 10. The holistic perspective of applying praxis to conceptualize the planning and phasing of the overall project aligns most closely with the "process of political learning" that Choudry, Hanley, and Shragge (2012) describe as "analysis and learning about their power through action" (p. 10) in the radical organizing they encourage.

A Paradigm for Congruent Practice

The notion of paradigm, introduced by Kuhn (1962/1996) and applied to social science by Mullaly (1997), provides a valuable way of conceptualizing our ideals, theories, objectives, and practices as the essential components of a cognitive framework in our work for justice. Of course we all live with contradictions despite wanting to live principled lives. But the concept of a paradigm, in which the four components align in an internally consistent manner, provides a model we can use to examine the alignment of our own values, beliefs, objectives, and practice.

Mullaly (1997) presented four contrasting politico-philosophical paradigms: neo-conservatism, liberalism, social democracy, and Marxism. For each of these he identified the ideology (social, economic, and political beliefs), the theory

Figure 11.1 Paradigm for a Congruent Practice

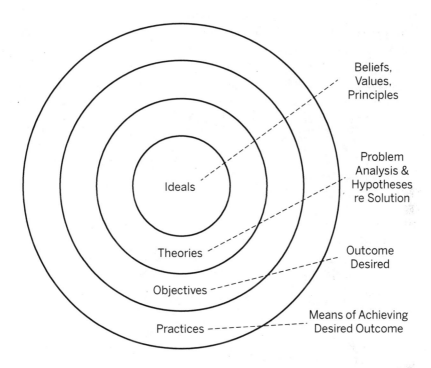

Source: Adapted from Mullaly (1997), p. 19.

(analysis and explanation of social problems), the objective (ideal type of welfare state), and the nature and form of social work practice (pp. 19, 102–103). My adaptations of Mullaly's conceptualization (Figure 11.1) are to use it as a practice paradigm, to add theories regarding potential solutions to social problems to the explanation of problems, and to label as "objectives" the component that Mullaly was using to focus on the ideal type of welfare state or view of social welfare.

This paradigmatic way of conceptualizing practice provided a logical manner for organizing the conclusions regarding existing theory in the academic literature that was affirmed in the data from this research project. In their stories of social mobilization and community organizing for social, economic, and environmental justice, the communities studied provided valuable information about their ideals and motivations; their theories or beliefs about what was wrong and what could remediate it; their objectives or desired outcome (development of a local service, social policy change, or winning against an opponent); and the practice-level means of achieving it. In addition, I believe that this conceptualization of an internally consistent practice paradigm is a useful tool for community organizers and leaders, as well as social movement communities, to evaluate the congruence of their ideals, theories, objectives, and practice methods. ∎

CONCLUSION

THE ANALYSIS OF THESE CASE STUDIES demonstrates the usefulness of an interdisciplinary approach in understanding social mobilization and illustrates many important theories. The theories affirmed are summarized here using the framework of the practice paradigm presented in the last chapter. As well, some ideas for further exploration are put forward.

The Interdisciplinary Approach

THEORIES FROM A VARIETY OF DISCIPLINES do have much to offer practitioners involved in social mobilization work. Whether they are community organizing specialists in the social work discipline, community economic development practitioners, church workers with a strong social justice perspective, feminists, community health promoters, environmentalists, human rights activists, or others involved in social movements, an interdisciplinary approach in seeking and integrating applicable knowledge will be fruitful. This is especially true in circumstances where people with expertise from a variety of disciplines are working together in a social mobilization effort such as the numerous contributors to the Xeni Gwet'in fight against the mine proposed in their part of British Columbia.

In the analysis of the findings from this research project, highly relevant theory was drawn from a number of disciplines in the social sciences and humanities. At the grand theory level, the political-philosophical thought of Gramsci provided a useful framework. Mid-level theory on models of community organizing and types of purposive change were drawn from the social work and sociology disciplines. Practice-level theory contributions came from a wide range of fields and were the principle focus of the research.

Sociology offered valuable theory on social movements, particularly the recent work that recognizes the synthesis of thinking about resource mobilization, political processes, and social construction. Social constructionism was especially useful with its ideas about framing grievances, collective identities, and new social movements emanating from oppression related to race, gender, and other identity characteristics beyond class. The contribution of social work theory, especially that pertaining to community organizing, was abundant with inclusion of theory from the related fields of community economic development and international social development. There is also a useful synthesis of ideas from sociology and social work in movement-related theory attending to the agency or efficacy of participants, as well as in theory for anti-oppression and empowerment practice.

Other disciplines provided valuable theory as well. Political science contributed to understanding state and civil society relations in Mexico, and social psychology added knowledge about motivating influences in social movement activity. Management science offered theories about organizational structures, leadership, and decision making. Educational science contributed Freire's pedagogy and more recent ideas about popular education and, lastly, religious studies provided an understanding of liberation theology.

The Ideals, Theory, Objectives, and Practice Methods

THE KEY THEORIES from the multiple disciplines that were affirmed in this research can be usefully organized according to ideals, grand theory, objectives, and practice methods. These four categories are the elemental components of the practice paradigm that I presented in Chapter 11. Considered together, they provide a rich theoretical basis set in a logical framework for organizing one's social justice work and carrying out principled and effective practice.

The Ideals

The ideals of the social movement communities studied were described in the second section of Chapter 8 and were characterized as the core values, principles, and beliefs that underpinned the social mobilization activities. Values of social justice and democracy, beliefs in the dignity of all human beings, and principles of collective responsibility for each other, as well as respect for the earth and all living things, were ideals identified by the communities and their leaders. Even a belief in the need to work together in order to survive, although not a lofty principle, is a fundamental ideal and one that was central to many of the social movement activities in Mexico. Cheryl Hyde (1994), as noted earlier, identified commitment to a cause rooted in such ideals as crafting a "meaningful and purposeful life in concert with others who share a vision for a better society" (p. 47).

Within the multiple disciplines tapped here, particularly those with an applied focus, there are specific approaches that are congruent with these ideals. The critical approach in social work, building on critical theory that emerged from the Frankfurt School, recognizes the importance of practice grounded in the above ideals and committed to transforming society toward the realization of them (Campbell & Baikie, 2012). Ife's (2010) approach to human rights practice "from below" focuses on work with communities toward these ideals in a manner that respects the communities' own perspectives regarding them. Friedmann's (1992) empowerment approach to alternative development, like Mullaly's (1997, 2007) structural social work and Shragge's (2003) community economic development, requires that in addition to addressing immediate survival needs, practitioners assist social movement communities in promoting social transformation toward egalitarian ideals. Similarly, liberation theology upholds a social mission working toward dignity for all and an end to oppression that involves community members in collective action to bring about such transformation to social justice (Boff & Boff, 1986).

Theory

At the level of grand theory, perspectives emerged related to the social movement actors' views of the problems inherent in their contextual reality and what would be necessary to remediate them. In the first part of Chapter 8, the specific challenges of the communities studied were described. The economic consequences of the neo-liberal model were paramount with the Mexican farm families feeling abandoned by a government that allowed the entry of US grains with decreasing tariff protections and that abruptly ended the role of the state in marketing the coffee crop. In both Canada and Mexico, protection of the environment had become secondary to revenue from mining, and governments were constraining political activity in various ways. Power imbalances within the socio-cultural context were described that maintained oppression based on class, gender, and race. In all the communities studied, people had come together out of a belief that they could accomplish more by working collectively than through individual efforts.

These perspectives are consistent with the theory developed by Antonio Gramsci (1929–1935/1971) while imprisoned under Mussolini in Italy. Gramsci identified a preponderance of power, which he termed hegemony, held by market and state forces that perpetuate a dominant, but false, ideology. This power, Gramsci held, could best be challenged through the dissent of civil society contesting the legitimacy of that power. Sociologists Carroll and Ratner (2010) contemporize Gramsci's theory, relating it to the current dominance of neo-liberal, market-centred economics supported by powerful elites connected to the state. They have contributed to the body of knowledge on social movement building with findings from their research in British Columbia. Historian Jeremy Brecher, along with his activist and journalist co-authors Costello and Smith (2002), bring Gramsci's concepts into the vernacular by using the metaphor of Jonathan Swift's Lilliputians tying up Gulliver to illustrate the power of social movements, which when composed of large numbers of weaker people, can overcome the powerful.

Objectives

Given the above ideals and theoretical understandings of the problem and its redress, what then is to be done? Objectives range from local resistance and lived alternatives to the neo-liberal model; through advocacy to bring about more just, egalitarian, and sustainable state policies; to direct actions to disrupt unjust activities of the powerful. Here mid-range theories are useful to conceptualize the range of possibilities and two classic contributions continue to bear the test of time, proving their usefulness again in the analysis of this research data. Jack Rothman (2001), a social work academic, developed the three models of community organizing in the 1970s as noted earlier. He has acknowledged the blending of models in actual practice; however, the three principle models provide the anchors that make the blends intelligible. Roland Warren (1975), a sociologist, contributed his typology of strategies for intentional social change, providing a parallel practice theory. The components of the two theories align very well, as shown in Table C.1. Locality development projects use collaborative strategies in work with like-minded people who are able to reach consensus in their decisions. Work in social planning and social policy advocacy involves campaign strategies to persuade others who have a different opinion about a social issue. Thirdly, social action using contest or protest strategies is necessary to win against opponents who cannot be convinced through discussion.

Among the social movement communities studied, there were clear examples of the three models and strategy types, as well as examples of blended or phased models. Collaborative, locality development models were exemplified in the projects aimed at meeting basic needs, frequently as a means of resistance or as an alternative to the dominant neo-liberal or patriarchal pattern. These included projects addressing the needs of the members' own communities such as the co-operatives formed by the coffee producers and the artisans. They also included projects carried out in solidarity with others to establish needed services such as WEE's employment programs and the Just Us! Coffee Roasters Co-op.

Table C.1

Models of Community Organizing and Corresponding Types of Change

Degree of Agreement	Consensus	Difference	Dissensus
Rothman's Models of Community Organizing	Locality Development	Planning and Policy	Social Action
Warren's Types of Purposive Change	Collaborative	Campaign	Contest

Policy advocacy projects with campaign strategies were evident in singularly purposed examples like the Raging Grannies and Catholic Women for the Right to Decide (CDD), as well as in combination or blended models. The women's centres practised a blend of campaign strategies in the policy advocacy for women's equality and collaborative strategies in the development of essential services. The Xeni Gwet'in people were engaged in a campaign strategy that advocated the rejection of the mining proposal; however, they were ready to employ contest strategies like the blockades they had used in the past if persuasion was unsuccessful.

Contest strategies were evident in the social action protests at the WTO meeting in Cancun and in the demonstrations against the expansion of free trade agreements that COMPA mobilized. The Guerrero ejido used social action's contest strategy in their blockade of the entrance to the mine on their land, but only after campaign strategies with the mining company and the government departments had failed.

Several of the activists and communities began their collective work using collaborative strategies to create local alternatives to the neo-liberal schemes in order to meet their own immediate needs. However, from their local successes and their deepened critique of broader social structures they became involved in larger social movement activities. For example, people who participated in the CEBs became involved with ecological movements, women's rights, and protests against free trade. These findings lend credence to Choudry, Hanley, and Shragge's (2012) contention that local organizing can contribute to the creation of a broader pressure for social change.

Practice Methods

Given the ideals related to social justice and other core principles, clarity regarding useful theories and fitting objectives, how then should this social mobilization work be done? The analysis of material from the social movement communities studied yielded a great deal of evidence for valuable practice-level theory. Some of the practice-level theory related to the important role of leaders and organizers, as well as to aspects of strategy.

Important role of organizers Egalitarian relations between the community members and the leaders or community organizers providing guidance or consultation were very important in the social movement communities studied.

Amy Crook's role as a consultant with the Xeni Gwet'in, the three women's centres in their services and advocacy for women, Maria de los Angeles in Veracruz, as well as Tere and Amado in Guerrero who didn't accept a formal title to acknowledge their leadership role, plus many others, believed the egalitarian relationship was essential to the outcomes of their work. Campfens's diagram, along with literature emphasizing a strengths perspective (Saleebey, 2001) and an empowerment approach (Gutiérrez, Parsons, & Cox, 2003; Lee, 2001), provide concepts and practice theory about relations between practitioners and community members that respect the wisdom of the community members and foster their increasing capabilities in the ways that were commended in this study's case examples.

Accompaniment of community members who themselves determine their own next steps is an important role and stance of organizers that was mentioned in several of the case studies. TADECO with the various communities it serves in Guerrero, and MUSA with the women's collectives in the regional-level coffee producers' co-operative in Chiapas, were most explicit about this. Wilson and Whitmore introduced this important aspect of practice theory to English-speaking social development workers in 2000 and have elaborated on it in subsequent publications. Related to the role of accompaniment is the importance of positioning oneself as a co-learner the way Amy Crook did in British Columbia and Margo did with the health promoters in Mexico City. In doing so, these organizers conveyed their respect for the community's autonomy and normalized the need of all to continue learning. Mary Trigg's (2009) contribution documents the important learner role as well.

It has long been recognized in the field of community organization that those experiencing a problem must participate in and be in control of the change they seek. Participation was described by Campfens (1997) as the *sine qua non* of community development in his international collection in which he especially hailed the formation of "self-managing organizations of the poor and excluded" (p. 461). Similarly, it is a core principle in Castelloe, Watson, and White's (2002) formulation of participatory change. The examples in this study affirm this understanding and demonstrate the importance of participation in maintaining the sustained efforts necessary to achieve long-term change. The committed participation of the women's nine-year vigil at the entrance to the garbage dump in the state of Veracruz is most poignant; however, it is present in every example. Clearly, sustained efforts are necessary to achieve structural change given that power and resources are not easily relinquished (Brecher, Costello, & Smith, 2002). Furthermore, barriers to participation in these activities for those experiencing oppression and lacking power and resources can be enormous (Snyder, 2000, 2004).

The important roles for social justice work described by Finn and Jacobson (2003) were observed in the functions of effective leaders and organizers in this study: learner, teacher, collaborator, facilitator, animator, mediator, advocate, negotiator, researcher, and bricoleur. Nepstad and Bob's (2006) description of the critical role of leaders in bringing about "cognitive liberation" and Moyer's (2001) identification of principle functions for social movement organizers corroborate the comprehensiveness of Finn and Jacobson's list.

Essential elements of social mobilizing strategy   As detailed in Chapter 10, several elements of strategy surfaced as important in the social mobilizing activities of the communities studied: consciousness-raising, clarifying objectives, education for members and for the public, preparation for action, influencing change, and organizational strengthening. These elements align unequivocally with three of McAdam's (1996) six strategic hurdles that movements must clear to effect change, and they are fully compatible with the remaining three.

Consciousness-raising was often an explicit element of the reflection process that the social movement communities studied were engaging in. It was most evident in the groups rooted in liberation theology, but was also present in many other examples. This is consistent with Choudry, Hanley, and Shragge's (2012) recommendation of a process of learning through action, followed by analysis for effective radical organizing. Maney et al. (2012) similarly suggest reflection after action in order to evaluate particular strategies.

Clarifying objectives was emphasized as an important strategy by several of the activists in order to have a project that members could move forward in and to ensure that members could keep a focus on the desired outcome in choosing their actions. Again, the work of Choudry et al. (2012) was affirmed, specifically regarding the significance of finding the sustaining objectives.

Attention was paid to education for members in many of the social movement communities. In all of the health promotion collectives, the health promoters had to learn about the curative properties of various plants in order to be helpful. The co-operatives engaged in learning in order to improve the quality of their produce or artesanía, often employing train-the-trainer approaches. Principles of adult education and methods of popular education as articulated by Kane (2012) and others were frequently engaged with much success. Leaders and organizers started with what the people already knew and asked the members what they needed to know next. The learning processes were carried out in ways that were understandable even to those without high levels of literacy and that were enjoyable for participants.

Education for the public was important in many of the communities in order to challenge dominant perspectives in society and to gain support for the social movement. A tremendous variety of educational media were used by the different groups: flyers to demonstrate recycling; brochures describing trademarked artesanía; posters declaring rights; newsletters to keep people updated about resistance to the mining proposal at Fish Lake; a postcard campaign to elected representatives; generation of media coverage through award presentations, interviews, press conferences, and communiqués; websites; videos (especially when available online); electronic listservs for updates; public events such as a speakers series, International Women's Day celebrations, and an art exhibit on missing women; reviving traditional arts; popular theatre, including the quick and witty performances by the Raging Grannies; publications; and demonstrations. Theory related to these public education objectives and media were affirmed: Caniglia and Carmin (2005), as well as Jasper (2004) regarding the framing and accessibility of content; McAdam (1996) about the importance of media coverage and Carroll and Ratner (2010) about awareness of mainstream media hostility to much social movement activity; Kane (2012) in relation to the effectiveness of popular education methods; Choudry, Hanley, and Shragge (2012) regarding the contribution of the arts; and Ife (2010) about writing local history.

The study revealed the social movement communities engaging in a cluster of activities related to preparation for action, including focused outreach, research, developing credibility, and ensuring strategic clarity, which again was consistent with relevant theory. The focused outreach included recruiting additional participants after a group had clarified its purpose as many of the health promotion and artisan collectives did. The literature confirmed this approach is useful in building collective identity and excitement about working together (Caniglia & Carmin, 2005; Goodwin & Jasper, 2009). Outreach was also a critical strategy in finding allies (Brecher, Costello, & Smith, 2002) as the Xeni Gwet'in did, and in building a growing base of support (Kuyek, 2011) as the British Columbia women's centre did in its public events. Research and analysis were done by the several of the communities prior to action. The

WEE Society, Just Us! Coffee Roasters Co-op, TADECO, and the Nova Scotia women's centres all engaged in research and analysis to prepare themselves for the action step. Their effective use of research and analysis prior to action substantiates the considerable literature that argues the importance of structural and conjunctural analysis in determining the courses and timing of action (Wilson, Calhoun, & Whitmore, 2011) and the empowerment potential inherent in carrying out the research in a participatory way (Lee, 2001; Saleebey, 2001). Lastly, preparation for action was enhanced in movement communities who also refined their strategies at the micro-detail level. This was observed in the three-phased strategy developed by the ecological organization that tackled the problem of contamination in Morelos, adding further credence to the suggestion from Maney et al. (2012) to envision sequences of actions and possible reactions.

The preparation for action strategies of the communities studied embodied three of the types of collective action that Eschle and Maiguashca (2010) identified: protest, advocacy, and service provision. These parallel Warren's contest, campaign, and collaborative strategies, which accompany Rothman's models of community organizing, described earlier as comprising the project objectives of the social movement communities. Specific examples of these will not be reiterated here. However, it is important to note that campaign and contest strategies were being confronted with increased repression in the current context. In Canada, government funding, as well as charitable status, which enhances civil society contributions, are no longer compatible with advocacy. In Mexico, contest strategies had resulted in the disappearances of many social activists, including the imprisonment of three of the ejidatarios protesting the activities of the mining company. This latter reality was consistent with Cortez Ruiz's (2010) conclusions about the limitations of protest in repressive states. Leaders finding themselves in complex circumstances such as these recognized that no straightforward, evidence-based solutions existed; they would need to "make the path by walking," to use an idea from a poem by Antonio Machado (1912/1964). This is consistent with a central concept in Snowden and Boone's (2007) Cynefin framework that Calhoun, Wilson, and Whitmore (2011) also observed in their study of Canadian activism.

The final element of mobilization strategy that became apparent in this study was the strengthening of the social movement organization itself. Again, the case examples affirmed a great deal of existing theory. The overall importance of building strong autonomous organizations has been emphasized by Brecher, Costello, and Smith (2002), Carroll and Ratner (2010), McAdam (1996), and Fisher and Karger (1997). The subthemes that emerged in this study as a means of strengthening the organization were consistent with the success factors noted in Wilson, Calhoun, and Whitmore's (2011) latest research. The multiple case illustrations of aspects of strengthening the organization were detailed in Chapter 10 so, as with the theme of influencing change, they will not be reiterated here. Building commitment to specific common principles has been highlighted by Kuyek (2011), McAdam (1996), Layton et al. (2010), and Hyde (1994). Hugman (2010), Piza Lopez and March (1991), and Snyder (2000) have described important features of training for managing the collectives. Attending to and respecting the grassroots membership and local communities has been stressed by Menocal and Ruiz (1998). The importance of uniting the community while acknowledging diversity has been pointed out by Schugurensky (2013), Dobbie and Richards-Schuster (2008), and Kutz-Flamenbaum (2012). Establishing linkages, the last aspect of strengthening organizations, has been emphasized by Bishop (2002) and by Brecher, Costello, and Smith (2002) in relation to other social movement communities, and by Khagram (2002) and Olesen (2011) in relation to national and international NGOs.

Thoughts for Further Research

QUESTIONS REMAIN that are food for thought in further research. The questions relate to three areas: the motivations and framing of options; distinct forms of structuring, funding, and educating in Mexico; and the possibilities in contexts of poverty and repression.

Motivations and Framing of Options

Several of the communities studied said their organizing was done out of necessity and, in the cases of the coffee farmers, the neighbourhood in the state of Veracruz with food contamination because of flies from the garbage dump, and the neighbourhood in the state of Guerrero without running water or electricity, the community members said they engaged in collective action for their survival. As was noted in Chapter 8 in relation to these communities, I doubted Thompson and Tapscott's (2010) suggestion that, in desperate situations outside the contexts where much social movement research has been done, theories about the conscious framing of options and sophisticated selections of strategies may not apply. In this study, all four of the Mexican communities where survival needs motivated their action were very deliberative and intentional in their examination of options and selection of strategies. As one of the CODIMUJ leaders described, in traditional communities within Mexico, there is a practice of continuing discussion until an agreement is reached that everyone can accept. The praxis methods of reflection and critical thinking were being used in all four of these communities due to the influence of liberation theology. And, lastly, the strategies that they selected had been successful over a significant period of time. Hence this data does not substantiate Thompson and Tapscott's concerns about limited applicability of framing theories; rather, it suggests the possibility of veracity of these theories in contexts outside of their origin.

Further study is also needed about fear as a motivating influence for social mobilization. A women's group in Chiapas was considering protesting the "menacing presence" of a military checkpoint since it was known that soldiers had raped other Indigenous women. TADECO staff were also motivated by fear to participate in a committee of "friends of the disappeared" since one of their close friends and a partner in "the social struggle" was among the hundreds missing. Recognizing my own fear of repercussions in Mexico (miniscule as that likelihood was) if I directly confronted the Canadian mining company with videotaped testimony from the Guerrero ejidatarios motivated me to become involved in advocating for legal means of requiring Canadian mining corporations to respect human and environmental rights when operating outside of Canada. Although there seemed to be little in the social movement literature about fear as a motivator, it is possible that political science with its coverage of experiences under repressive regimes may have knowledge to contribute in this area.

Distinct Forms of Structuring, Funding, and Educating

In the case examples, there were distinct manners of structuring and funding the organizations that were observed in Mexico but not in Canada. As well, a particular form of education for members was lauded that is seldom mentioned in the social movement literature.

The level of informality noted in some of the social movement communities studied was a phenomenon that was seen only in Mexico. The most poignant example of this was the collective in the Veracruz neighbourhood that tackled the garbage problem and went on to develop a community health centre using natural healing methods. They had been operating informally for twenty years without registering the organization, developing a board of directors, or recognizing the leader with an official decision or title. Although civil society organizations in Canada often arise as a result of informal discussions among like-minded people, they usually register as non-profit and charitable organizations very early in their development in order to receive funding and to issue receipts to donors for income-tax reductions. Most Canadian health practitioners would also want some formal protection in case of lawsuits. In Mexico there is less likelihood of individual donations or lawsuits; however, formal registration of organizations and trademarks was becoming a more common consideration. Further study would be useful to determine if less formal structures would benefit some fledgling projects in Canada, and if encouraging donor contributions and protections against litigation would be beneficial in Mexico.

Unique aspects in the structures of boards of governors and roles within executives were also observed. The structure of the board of directors of the women's centre in Oaxaca was one that I have never seen elsewhere. As described earlier, the organization does not have a membership who elect a board; rather, a twelve-member board has been structured to include women who as a group possess the various types of expertise that the centre requires to accomplish its objectives. When one of the members needs to resign from her responsibilities, the board searches for another woman to take that position, based on the expertise that is currently needed. The Tejalpa health and environmental project has a leadership team of six that similarly was not elected by a membership but rather included committed women who were willing to rotate through the three executive roles. Most of the organizations' executives consisted of a president, treasurer, and secretary; however, unique positions of guardian were identified in Chiapas, in the textile workers collective, and in the regional-level coffee co-operative whose responsibility was to foster well-functioning relationships within their collective. Organizational theory emphasizes the principle in designing structures that "form follows function." As Daft (2007) states, "for organizations to be effective, there must be a goodness of fit between the structure and the conditions in their external environment" (p. 27). Further study would be useful to document the creative structures that have been designed in various parts of the world and the contexts in which they are particularly effective. Clearly, any social justice workers coming into a community from elsewhere must refrain from suggesting only organization structures with which they are familiar from their own external context.

Self-funded organizing was also particular to the Mexican social movement communities studied, aside from all of the co-operatives. The Luna Creciente collective in Chiapas creates its own income from its café, bookstore, and artesanía sales, which supports their organizing work with various artisan co-operatives. TADECO in Guerrero operates an Internet café out of their own offices with such related services as printing and copying, as well as selling music and films in the city square to finance its community development work. Similar, but less formalized, were the contributions of committed individuals and couples who provided significant organizing leadership to communities without typical expectations of financial remuneration: Maria de los Angeles, as well as Tere and Amado in Mexico; and the coordinator of the British Columbia women's centre (recently), as well as Jeff and Debra Moore (earlier) in Canada. Other than Kuyek's (2011) writing about some activists freeing themselves from the need for full-time work, very little literature seems to exist about creative ways to fund social justice work. Yet it would be valuable for more practitioners to know about these options.

A particular form of education for members appears to be important in social mobilization. Two Indigenous women's collectives—pottery artisans in Chiapas and carpet weavers in Oaxaca—expressed their appreciation for opportunities to learn from Indigenous women living in nearby villages. As I noted earlier, this same finding emerged in my earlier research about women's employment initiatives in Chile and Canada. Women found that instructors from similar circumstances and cultures understood their challenges and personified the possibility of succeeding in making changes. Farmer (1997), in writing about women's career development, noted that it is important for learners to be able to identify with role models. This is a topic that merits further study in relation to social mobilization.

Despite Poverty and Repression

The final theme that emerged in this research as requiring further study is the question of whether serious challenges to social mobilization like repression and poverty cause communities to relent, or whether these challenges strengthen their resolve to carry on. Tarrow (1998) has noted that repression is a common institutional response to the actions and protests of social movements. At the Cancun protest, after guards beat down women stepping through the perimeter fence, the women courageously moved forward to present the guards with flowers and sat down in their astonishing display of peaceful protest. In Guerrero, where twelve hundred disappearances were documented between 2005 and 2009, including many active in social mobilization, staff of TADECO and similar organizations were emboldened to form a committee of friends and family of the disappeared to decry the "criminalization of the social struggle." Yet in the Guerrero ejido that was demanding the mining company cease contamination of their water before renewing the agreement granting access through their land to the mine, the outcome was different. Through threats, shootings, arrests without warrants of resisters and their family members, and more threats, the community became divided and the majority succumbed to the mining company's offer. Further research is needed to understand, in the frequent repression that follows protest, what leads to divisions in social movement communities and what galvanizes them.

As noted in Chapter 10, the impact of poverty on participation in social mobilization was complicated also. Much literature and many examples from this study attest to the fact that people fully engaged in meeting their immediate survival needs do not have the time or energy to take on another task. Similarly, Piven and Cloward (1977), in their pioneering work on poor people's movements, maintained that the poor could be mobilized for short-term actions, but not organized for ongoing participation. However, this study did find poor people organizing along with others to generate income; to address health, housing, and environmental issues; and to fight for dignity and equality, often out of necessity. This lends credence to Thompson and Tapscott's (2010) theory that poverty can be both an incentive and a disincentive to social mobilization. This, then, is another important matter for further study.

My Hopes and Beliefs

THE DESCRIPTION of the struggles and accomplishments of the social movement communities and their leaders/organizers have provided useful illustrations for practitioners. The communities studied have demonstrated the ability of people working collectively to address basic needs; to work for changes in social values and policy in order to bring about greater justice and equality; and to contest the dominant forces of neo-liberalism, patriarchy, and racism underlying many of the problems of the poor, women, and Indigenous peoples in Canada and Mexico.

The discussion of the pertinent literature in the presentation of the findings confirms the value of an interdisciplinary approach and enriches practitioners' understandings of theory in a manner that can enhance the effectiveness of their justice work. The practice paradigm will serve as a useful tool for practitioners in assessing the congruence of their ideals, theories, objectives, and practices. In addition, I believe that this research and analysis makes a contribution to the body of knowledge about social mobilization and community organizing through its offering of empirical evidence that affirms a great deal of existing theory and proposes some new thoughts and questions for further study.

Certainly, we can all draw inspiration from the stories of the organizers and the organizations in their struggles for justice—their commitment, their creativity, and their accomplishments in seeking transformation toward a more just and sustainable world. ∎

Appendix
The Case Studies

Appendix 1a

The Income-Generation Projects

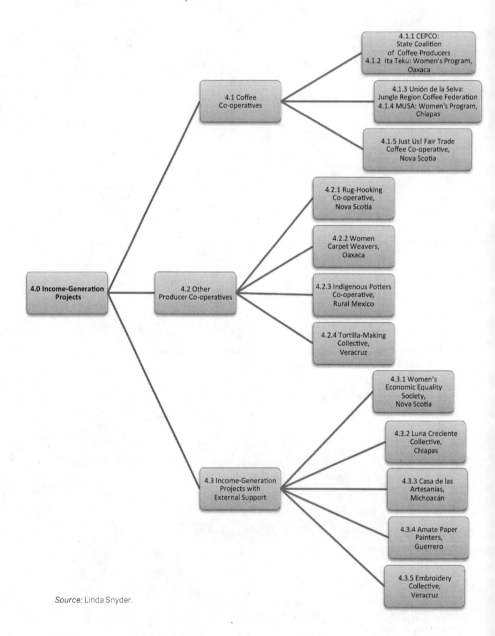

Source: Linda Snyder.

Appendix 1b

The Health, Housing, and Environment Projects

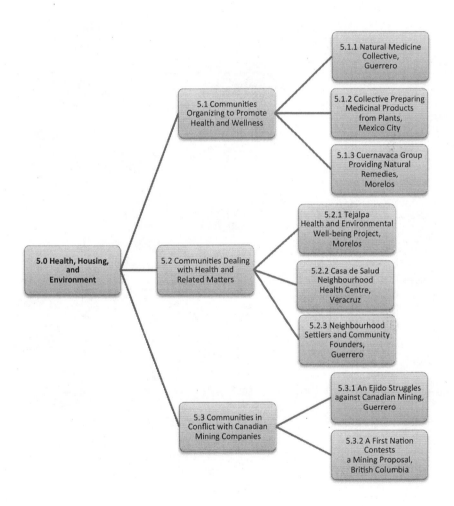

Source: Linda Snyder.

Appendix 1c

Women's Resources and Advocacy

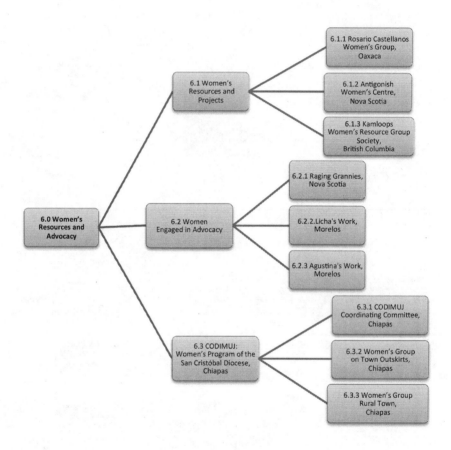

Source: Linda Snyder.

Appendix 1d

Grassroots Support Organizations and Independent Community Organizers

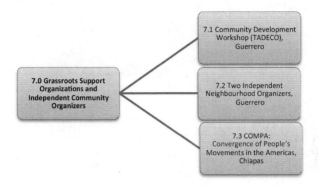

Source: Linda Snyder.

References

Acuña Rodarte, Olivia. (2003). Toward an equitable, inclusive, and sustainable agriculture: Mexico's basic grains producers unite. In Timothy Wise, Hilda Salazar, & Laura Carlsen (Eds.), *Confronting globalization: Economic integration and popular resistance in Mexico* (pp. 149–170). Bloomfield, CT: Kumarian.

Altimirano-Jiménez, Isabel. (2013). *Indigenous encounters with neoliberalism: Place, women, and the environment in Canada and Mexico*. Vancouver: UBC Press.

Alvaredo, Facundo, Atkinson, Tony, Piketty, Thomas, & Saez, Emmanuel. (2013). *The world top incomes database*. Retrieved from http://www.wid.world/

Amin, Samir. (1990). *Delinking: Towards a polycentric world*. London: Zed Books.

Amnesty International. (2007, August). *Mexico: Human rights at risk in La Parota Dam Project.* Retrieved from http://www.amnesty.org/en/documents/AMR41/029/2007/en/

Amnesty International. (2007, November). *Mexico: Release of Magdalena Garcia Duran: A glimmer of hope for all Atenco detainees?* Retrieved from https://www.amnesty.org/en/press-releases/2007/11/mexico-release-magdalena-garcc3ad-duran-glimmer-hope-all-atenco-detainees-2/

Amnesty International Canada. (2013, May 29). *Invasive surveillance of human rights defender Cindy Blackstock.* Retrieved from http://www.amnesty.ca/news/news-updates/invasive-surveillance-of-human-rights-defender-cindy-blackstock

Antrobus, Peggy. (2004). *The global women's movement*. Dhaka, Bangladesh: University Press.

Aranda Bezaury, Josefina. (2003). Peasant farmers in the global economy: The State Coalition of Coffee Producers of Oaxaca. In Timothy Wise, Hilda Salazar, & Laura Carlsen (Eds.), *Confronting globalization: Economic integration and popular resistance in Mexico* (pp. 149–170). Bloomfield, CT: Kumarian.

Ashcroft, Bill, Griffiths, Gareth, & Tiffin, Helen. (2000). *Post-colonial studies: The key concepts*. London: Routledge.

Associated Press. (2012, July 9). *Mexico election results to face court challenges*. Retrieved from http://www.cbc.ca/news/world/mexico-election-results-to-face-court-challenges-1.1189373

Bacon, David. (2008). Equality and human rights, instead of displacement and criminalization. In Global Exchange (Ed.), *The right to stay home: Alternatives to mass displacement and forced migration in North America* (pp. 25–31). San Francisco: Global Exchange. Retrieved from http://www.scribd.com/doc/10161450/Final-Web-Report

Bajak, Frank. (2009, November 2). Indian political awakening stirs Latin America. *Native Times*. Retrieved from http://www.nativetimes.com/index.php/news/international/2585-indian-political-awakening-stirs-latin-america

Ballón, Eduardo. (1990). Movimientos sociales: Itinerario de transformaciones y lecturas. In Eduardo Ballón (Ed.), *Movimientos sociales: Elementos para una reflectura*. Lima: DESCO.

Barkin, David. (2006). Building a future for rural Mexico. *Latin American Perspectives, 33*(2), 132–140.

Barrick, Frances. (2012, September 20). Layoffs, group homes to close as family and children's services fights $2.5M shortfall. *Waterloo Region Record*. Retrieved from http://www.therecord.com/news-story/2613976-layoffs-group-homes-to-close-as-family-and-children-s-services-fights-2-5m-shortfall/

Bartra, Armando (2004). Rebellious cornfields: Towards food and labour self-sufficiency. In G. Otero (Ed.), *Mexico in transition: Neoliberalism, the state and civil society* (pp. 18–36). Black Point, NS: Fernwood.

Bartra, Armando, & Otero, Gerardo. (2005). Indian peasant movements in Mexico: The struggle for land, autonomy and democracy. In Sam Moyo & Paris Yeros (Eds.), *Reclaiming the land: The resurgence of rural movements in Africa, Asia and Latin America* (pp. 383–407). London: Zed Books.

Bernard, Ron. (2003, August 22). *Welcome to the land of the Algonquins*. Address at the Summer Retreat organized by the Centre for Social Justice held at Camp Arowhon, ON.

Bevington, Douglas, & Dixon, Chris. (2005). Movement-relevant theory: Rethinking social movement scholarship and activism. *Social Movement Studies, 4*(3), 185–208.

Bishop, Anne. (2002). *Becoming an ally: Breaking the cycle of oppression in people* (2nd ed.). Halifax: Fernwood.

Blaze Carlson, Kathryn. (2014, June 27). Court ruling reshapes resource sector nationwide. *Globe and Mail*, A4.

Bloomberg Billionaires. (2014, January 3). *Today's ranking of the world's richest people*. Retrieved from http://www.bloomberg.com/billionaires/2014-01-03/cya

Boal, Augusto. (1973/1985). *Theatre of the oppressed* [translation]. New York: Theatre Communications Group.

Boff, Leonardo, & Boff, Clodovis. (1986). *Introducing liberation theology*. Maryknoll, NY: Orbis.

Boglio Martínez, Rafael. (2008). Grassroots support organizations and transformative practices. *Journal of Community Practice, 16*(3), 339–358.

Bouchard, Gérard. (2008). *The making of the nations and cultures of the world* (pp. 261–275a). Montreal & Kingston: McGill-Queen's University Press.

Bowden, Charles. (2010, April 14). Charles Bowden on "Murder city: Ciudad Juárez and the global economy's new killing fields." *Democracy Now*. Retrieved from http://www.democracynow.org/2010/4/14/charles_bowden_murder_city_ciudad_jurez

Brandt, Nicola, & Paillacar, Rodrigo. (2011). Fiscal reform for a stronger and cleaner Mexican economy. *OECD Economics Department Working Papers*, No. 904. Paris: OECD. Retrieved from http://www.oecd-ilibrary.org/economics/fiscal-reform-for-a-stronger-fairer-and-cleaner-mexican-economy_5kg271q4vm34-en

Brecher, Jeremy, Costello, Tim, & Smith, Brendan. (2002). *Globalization from below: The power of solidarity*. Cambridge, MA: South End Press.

Brennan, Jordan. (2012, November). *A shrinking universe: How concentrated corporate power is shaping income inequality in Canada*. Ottawa: Canadian Centre for Policy Alternatives. Retrieved from https://www.policyalternatives.ca/publications/reports/shrinking-universe

Bricker, Kristin. (2011). *Military justice and impunity in Mexico's drug war*. Waterloo, ON: Centre for International Governance Innovation. Retrieved from https://www.cigionline.org/sites/default/files/ssr_issue_no3_1.pdf

British Broadcasting Corporation (BBC). (2011, July 24). *Mass arrests in Mexico human trafficking raids*. Retrieved from http://www.bbc.com/news/world-latin-america-14271112

Bucardo, Jesus, Brouwer, Kimberly, & Strathdee, Steffanie. (2005). Historical trends in the production and consumption of illicit drugs in Mexico. *Drug and Alcohol Dependence, 79*(3), 281–293. Retrieved from http://www.ncbi.nlm.nih.gov/pmc/articles/PMC2196212/

Buechler, Steven. (2000). *Social movements in advanced capitalism: The political economy and cultural construction of social activism*. New York: Oxford University Press.

Buechler, Steven. (2011). *Understanding social movements: Theories from the classical area to the present*. Boulder, CO: Paradigm.

Burton, Fred. (2007). Mexico: The price of peace in the cartel wars. *Stratfor Global Intelligence*. Retrieved from https://www.stratfor.com/mexico_price_peace_cartel_wars

Calhoun, Avery, Wilson, Maureen, & Whitmore, Elizabeth. (2011). Activism that works: Emergent themes. In Elizabeth Whitmore, Maureen Wilson, & Avery Calhoun (Eds.), *Activism that works* (pp. 133–152). Halifax: Fernwood.

Campbell, Carolyn, & Baikie, Gail. (2012). Beginning at the beginning: An exploration of critical social work. *Critical Social Work, 13*(1), 67–81.

Campfens, Hubert. (1997). Comparisons and conclusions: An international framework for practice in the twenty-first century. In Hubert Campfens (Ed.), *Across the world: Community development* (pp. 439–469). Toronto: University of Toronto Press.

Canada. (2013). *Canada's system of government.* Retrieved from http://www.parl.gc.ca/MarleauMontpetit/DocumentViewer.aspx?Sec=Ch01&Seq=2

Canada, Elections Canada. (2011). *Distribution of seats by political affiliation and sex—Table 7.* Retrieved from http://www.elections.ca/scripts/ovr2011/default.html

Canada, Employment & Social Development. (2014). *Current and forthcoming minimum hourly wage rates for experienced adult workers in Canada.* Retrieved from http://srv116.services.gc.ca/dimt-wid/sm-mw/rpt1.aspx?lang=eng

Canada, Environment Canada: Canadian Environmental Assessment Agency (CEAA). (2010a). *Report of the federal review panel: Prosperity Gold-Copper Mine Project—Taseko Mines Ltd. British Columbia.* Retrieved from http://ceaa-acee.gc.ca/050/documents/46911/46911E.pdf

Canada, Environment Canada: Canadian Environmental Assessment Agency (CEAA). (2010b). *News release: Government of Canada announces decisions on Mount Milligan and Prosperity gold-copper mines.* Retrieved from http://ceaa-acee.gc.ca/050/document-eng.cfm?document=46186

Canada, Health Canada. (2012). *Diseases and health conditions from website on First Nations & Inuit Health.* Retrieved from http://www.hc-sc.gc.ca/fniah-spnia/diseases-maladies/index-eng.php

Canada, Indigenous and Northern Affairs Canada. (2013). *Matrimonial real property on reserves.* Retrieved from http://www.aadnc-aandc.gc.ca/eng/1100100032553/1100100032557

Canada, Royal Commission on Aboriginal Peoples. (1996). *Report of the Royal Commission on Aboriginal People.* Ottawa: Minister of Supply and Services.

Canada, Statistics Canada. (2011). *Women in Canada: A gender-based statistical report.* Retrieved from http://www.statcan.gc.ca/pub/89-503-x/89-503-x2010001-eng.htm

Canada, Statistics Canada. (2012). *Low income measures: What is the LIM?* Retrieved from http://statcan.gc.ca/pub/75f0002m/2012002/lim-mfr-eng.htm

Canada, Statistics Canada. (2013a). *Latest indicators.* Retrieved from http://www.statcan.gc.ca/start-debut-eng.html

Canada, Statistics Canada. (2013b). *CANSIM Table 202-0701: Market, total and after-tax income, by economic family type and income quintiles.* Retrieved from http://www5.statcan.gc.ca/cansim/pick-choisir?lang=eng&searchTypeByValue=1&id=2020701

Canada, Statistics Canada. (2013c). *2011 National household survey: Income of Canadians.* Retrieved from http://www.statcan.gc.ca/daily-quotidien/130911/dq130911a-eng.htm

Canada, Statistics Canada. (2013d). *National household survey, 2011: Data tables: Selected demographic, sociocultural, education and labour characteristics.* Retrieved from http://www12 .statcan.gc.ca/nhs-enm/2011/dp-pd/dt-td/Index-eng.cfm

Canada, Statistics Canada. (2013e). *2011 National household survey: Data tables: Selected economic family and persons not in economic family characteristics.* Retrieved from http://www12 .statcan.gc.ca/nhs-enm/2011/dp-pd/dt-td/Index-eng.cfm

Canada, Statistics Canada. (2013f). *Aboriginal peoples in Canada: First Nations people, Métis and Inuit.* Retrieved from http://www12.statcan.gc.ca/nhs-enm/2011/as-sa/99-011-x/99 -011-x2011001-eng.cfm

Canada, Statistics Canada. (2013g). *National household survey, 2011: Data tables: Labour force status, highest certificate, diploma or degree, Indigenous identity.* Retrieved from http://www12 .statcan.gc.ca/nhs-enm/2011/dp-pd/dt-td/Index-eng.cfm

Canadian Association of Social Workers. (2005). *Code of ethics.* Ottawa: Author.

Canadian Broadcasting Corporation (CBC). (2014, February 26). *Taseko New Prosperity Mine at Fish Lake rejected again.* Retrieved from http://www.cbc.ca/news/canada/ british-columbia/taseko-new-prosperity-mine-at-fish-lake-rejected-again-1.2553002

Canadian Feminist Alliance for International Action & Canadian Labour Congress. (2010). *Reality check: Women in Canada and the Beijing Declaration and Platform for Action fifteen years on.* Retrieved from http://ywcacanada.ca/data/research_docs/00000114.pdf

Canadian Institute of Wellbeing. (2012). *How are Canadians really doing?* Retrieved from https://uwaterloo.ca/canadian-index-wellbeing/sites/ca.canadian-index-wellbeing/ files/uploads/files/CIW2012-HowAreCanadiansReallyDoing-23Oct2012_0.pdf

Canadian Labour Congress. (2013a). *Youth unemployment, quality of jobs a big concern.* Retrieved from http://canadianlabour.ca/news/newsarchive/youth-unemployment-quality-jobs -big-concern-georgetti-comments-august-job-numbers

Canadian Labour Congress. (2013b). *CLC criticizes freeze on EI premiums.* Retrieved from http:// canadianlabour.ca/news/news-archive/clc-criticizes-freeze-ei-premiums-georgetti -says-it%E2%80%99s-being-done-backs-unemployed

Canadian Research Institute for the Advancement of Women. (2010). *Factsheet: Women and restructuring in Canada.* Retrieved from http://www.criaw-icref.ca/sites/criaw/files/ Women_and_Restructuring_Factsheet_June_2010.pdf

Canadiana. (2004). *Canada in the making.* Retrieved from https://web.archive.org/web/ 20150214065615/http://www.canadiana.ca/citm/index_e.html

Caniglia Schaefer, Beth, & Carmin, JoAnn. (2005). Scholarship on social movement organizations: Classic views and emerging trends. *Mobilization, 10*(2), 201–212.

Carroll, William, & Ratner, Robert S. (2010). Social movements and counter-hegemony: Lessons from the field. *New Proposals, 4*(1), 7–22.

Carter-Whitney, Maureen, & Duncan, Justin. (2008). *Balancing needs, minimizing conflict: A proposal for a mining modernization act.* Retrieved from http://www.ecojustice.ca/wp-content/uploads/2014/11/Balancing-Needs-Minimizing-Conflict-2008.pdf

Castelloe, Paul, & Prokopy, Joshua. (2001). Recruiting participants for community practice interventions: Merging community practice theory and social movement theory. *Journal of Community Practice, 9*(2), 31–48.

Castelloe, Paul, Watson, Thomas, & White, Craig. (2002). Participatory change: An integrative approach to community practice. *Journal of Community Practice, 10*(4), 7–31.

Centre for Science in Public Participation (CSP2). (2016). *What we do.* Retrieved from http://csp2.org/what-we-do

Centro de Estudios de la Región Cuicateca [Centre for Studies of the Cuicatec Region]. (2010, April 28). *Asesinan a coordinadora de REMA, Bety Cariño.* Retrieved from http://centroestudiosregioncuicateca.blogspot.ca/2010/04/asesinan-coordinadora-de-rema-betty.html

Centro de Investigaciones Económicas y Políticas de Acción Comunitaria [Centre for Economic and Political Research on Community Action] (CIEPAC). (2004, April 12). *Informe de la delegación de observación de derechos humanos a las comunidades…de Zinacantán.* Retrieved from http://chiapas.laneta.org/urgencia/040412zinacantan.htm

Cernea, Michael. (1993). Culture and organization: The social sustainability of induced development. *Sustainable Development, 1*(2), 18–29.

Chapman, Debra. (2012). *The struggle for Mexico: State corporatism and popular opposition.* Jefferson, NC: McFarland.

Chávez Carapia, Julia del Carmen. (2013). En aumento, los hogares con jefatura femenina. *Boletín UNAM-dgcs-288.* Retrieved from http://www.dgcs.unam.mx/boletin/bdboletin/2013_288.html

Choudry, Aziz. (2007). *Global web of bilateral accords and international resistance movements.* Retrieved from http://bilaterals.org/multimedia/audio/Across%20the%20Board/Global+web+of+bilateral+trade+accords+and+international+resistance+movements+%28December+2007%29.mp3.php

Choudry, Aziz, Hanley, Jill, & Shragge, Eric. (2012). Thinking ahead. In Ariz Choudry, Jill Hanley, & Eric Shragge (Eds.), *Organize: Building from the local for global justice* (pp. 1–22). Oakland, CA: PM.

Chovanec, Donna, Lange, Elizabeth, & Ellis, Lee. (2009). Social movement learning: A catalyst for action. In Marie Hammond-Callaghan & Matthew Hayday (Eds.), *Mobilizations, protests, and engagements: Canadian perspectives on social movements* (pp. 186–202). Halifax: Fernwood.

Cockcroft, James. (2010). *Mexico's revolution: Then and now.* New York: Monthly Review Press.

Cohen, Jeffrey. (2004). Community, economy and social change in Oaxaca, Mexico: Rural life and cooperative logic in the global economy. In Gerardo Otero (Ed.), *Mexico in transition: Neoliberalism, the state and civil society* (pp. 154–168). Black Point, NS: Fernwood.

Comisión Sexta del EZLN [Sixth Commission of the EZLN]. (2013). *Enlace Zapatista: La otra campaña.* Retrieved from http://enlacezapatista.ezln.org.mx/category/la-otra-campana/

Conference Board of Canada. (2013). *Unemployment rate.* Retrieved from http://www.conferenceboard.ca/hcp/details/economy/unemployement-rate.aspx

Conn, Melanie. (2006). Why women? In Eric Shragge & Michael Toye (Eds.), *Community economic development: Building for social change* (pp. 125–137). Sydney, NS: Cape Breton University Press.

Conrad, Margaret. (2012). *A concise history of Canada.* New York: Cambridge University Press.

Convergencia de Movimientos de los Pueblos de las Américas (COMPA). (2011). *Asambleas.* Retrieved from http://lacompa.org/

Corcoran, Terence. (2011, May 25). *Dow scores NAFTA challenge victory over famous herbicide.* Retrieved from http://business.financialpost.com/fp-comment/quebec-backs-down-on-24-d-says-it-is-not-harmful-to-humans

Cortez Ruiz, Carlos. (2010). The struggle toward rights and communitarian citizenship: The Zapatista movement in Mexico. In Lisa Thompson & Chris Tapscott (Eds.), *Citizenship and social movements: Perspectives from the global south* (pp. 160–183). London: Zed Books.

Council of Canadians. (2012). *News: Water protections lost under Harper's C-38 and C-45.* Retrieved from http://canadians.org/node/9033

Council of Canadians. (2013a). *North American Free Trade Agreement.* Retrieved from http://canadians.org/nafta

Council of Canadians. (2013b, January 28). *Newsletter.* Ottawa: Author.

Council of Canadians. (2016). *Schedule 2.* Retrieved from http://canadians.org/schedule2

Cox, Enid Opal. (2001). Community practice issues in the 21st century: Questions and challenges for empowerment-oriented practitioners. *Journal of Community Practice, 9*(1), 37–55.

Crowe, Kelly. (2014, September 2). Grassy Narrows: Why is Japan studying the mercury poisoning when Canada isn't? *CBC News.* Retrieved from http://www.cbc.ca/news/health/grassy-narrows-why-is-japan-still-studying-the-mercury-poisoning-when-canada-isn-t-1.2752360

Daft, Richard L. (2007). *Organization theory and design* (9th ed.). Mason, OH: Thomson South-Western.

Daly, Herman, & Cobb, John, Jr. (1989). *For the common good: Redirecting the economy toward community, the environment, and a sustainable future.* Boston: Beacon.

Desmarais, Annette Aurélie. (2007). *La Vía Campesina: Globalization and the power of peasants.* Halifax: Fernwood.

Dhillon, Sunny. (2014, August 7). First Nations leaders are outraged ahead of the BC salmon run. *Globe and Mail,* A9.

Diamond, Larry, & Morlino, Leonardo. (2005). *Assessing the quality of democracy.* Baltimore: Johns Hopkins University Press.

Díaz, Cecilia. (1997). *Planificacíon participativa.* San Jose, Costa Rica: Alforja.

Dobbie, David, & Richards-Schuster, Katie. (2008). Building solidarity through difference: A practice model for critical multicultural organizing. *Journal of Community Practice, 16*(3), 317–337.

Dobrowolsky, Alexandra. (2014). The women's movement in flux: Feminism and framing, passion, and politics. In Miriam Smith (Ed.), *Group politics and social movements in Canada* (2nd ed.) (pp. 151–177). North York, ON: University of Toronto Press.

Dominelli, Lena. (2002). *Anti-oppressive social work theory and practice.* New York: Palgrave Macmillan.

Donkin, Karissa. (2013, April 7). *RBC defends their plan to replace 45 Canadians, outsource their jobs.* Retrieved from http://www.thestar.com/news/gta/2013/04/07/rbc_defends_plan _to_lay_off_45_canadians_outsource_their_jobs.html

Dougherty, Sean, & Escobar, Octavio. (2013). The determinants of informality in Mexico's states. *OECD Economics Department Working Papers,* No. 1043. Retrieved from http:// www.oecd-ilibrary.org/economics/the-determinants-of-informality-in-mexico -s-states_5k483jrvnjq2-en

Drolet, Julie, & Heinonen, Tuula. (2012). Gender: Concepts and controversies. In Tuula Heinonen & Julie Drolet (Eds.), *International social development: Social work experiences and perspectives* (pp. 75–97). Black Point, NS: Fernwood.

Dufour, Pascale, & Traisnel, Christophe. (2014). Nationalism and protest: The sovereignty movement in Quebec. In Miriam Smith (Ed.), *Group politics and social movements in Canada* (2nd ed.) (pp. 255–280). North York, ON: University of Toronto Press.

Durand, Cliff. (2010). The exhaustion of neoliberalism in Mexico. In Richard Westra (Ed.), *Confronting global neoliberalism: Third world resistance and development strategies* (pp. 235–243). Atlanta, GA: Clarity.

Dyer, Gwynne. (2003, September 17). World Trade Organization: New gang in town—The one-sided reign of the rich is over. *The Record,* A19. Retrieved from http://gwynnedyer .com/tag/wto/

Earthworks & Mining Watch. (2012). *Troubled waters: How mine waste dumping is poisoning our oceans, rivers, and lakes.* Retrieved from https://www.earthworksaction.org/files/ publications/Troubled-Waters_FINAL.pdf

Economist Intelligence Unit. (2013). *Democracy index 2012*. Retrieved from http://pages.eiu
.com/rs/eiu2/images/Democracy-Index-2012.pdf

Engler, Mark. (2013, July/August). Obama's "free trade" voyages are another big mistake. *New Internationalist, 464*, 33.

Engler, Yves. (2009). *The black book of Canadian foreign policy*. Black Point, NS: Fernwood.

Engler, Yves. (2012). *The ugly Canadian—Stephen Harper's foreign policy*. Black Point, NS: Fernwood.

Enlazando Alternativas. (n.d.). Bety Carino with UN Special Rapporteur on Human Rights Defenders. Retrieved from http://www.enlazandoalternativas.org/spip.php?article802

Escalante Gonzalbo, Pablo. (2004). El México antiguo. In Pablo Escalante, Bernado García, Luis Jauregui, Josefina Zoraida, Elisa Speckman, Javier Garciadiego, & Luis Aboites (Eds.), *Nueva historia mínima de México* (pp. 11–57). Mexico City: El Colegio de México.

Eschle, Catherine, & Maiguashca, Bice. (2010). *Making feminist sense of the global justice movement*. Lanham, MD: Rowman & Littlefield.

Esping-Andersen, Gøsta. (1990). *The three worlds of welfare capitalism*. Princeton, NJ: Princeton University Press.

Ester, Comandante. (2001, March 8). *Words of Commandante Ester at Milpa Alta*. Retrieved from http://www.criscenzo.com/jaguarsun/chiapas/chiapas119.html

Estrada Ochoa, Adriana. (2006). Canadian mining operations in Mexico: An initial overview. In Liisa North, Timothy Clark, & Viviana Patroni (Eds.), *Community rights and corporate responsibility* (pp. 143–159). Toronto: Between the Lines.

Fabricant, Michael. (2002). Agency based community building in low income neighborhoods: A praxis framework. *Journal of community practice, 10*(2), 1–22.

Fair Trade Advocacy Office. (2006). *Business unusual: Successes and challenges of fair trade*. Brussels: FTAO.

Fairtrade International. (2011). *History of fairtrade*. Retrieved from http://www.fairtrade.net/about-fairtrade/history-of-fairtrade.html

Fals-Borda, Orlando. (1995). *Research for social justice: Some north-south convergences*. Plenary address at the southern sociological meeting, Atlanta, GA. Retrieved from http://comm-org.wisc.edu/si/falsborda.htm

Farmer, Helen. (1997). Career counseling for the next decade and the twenty-first century. In Helen Farmer & Associates (Eds.), *Diversity and women's career development* (pp. 271–292). Thousand Oaks, CA: Sage.

Findlay, Andrew. (2009, August 27). Mining firm promises a new lake, but Native leader says that's the Creator's job. *Vancouver Free Press*. Retrieved from http://www.straight.com/article-249305/fight-looms-over-fish-lake

Finn, Janet, & Jacobson, Maxine. (2003). *Just practice: A social justice approach to social work*. Peosta, IA: Eddie Bowers.

First Nations, Métis, and Inuit GBA. (2009). *Our voices: Health status.* Retrieved from http://www.aboriginalgba.ca/

Fisher, Robert, & Karger, Howard. (1997). *Social work and community in a private world.* White Plains, NY: Longman.

Flavelle, Dana. (2010, October 8). *Loblaw makes gains with Ontario deal.* Retrieved from http://www.thestar.com/business/2010/10/08/loblaw_makes_gains_with_ontario_deal.html

Fong, Petti. (2010, November 3). Gordon Campbell resigns as BC premier. *The Star.* Retrieved from http://www.thestar.com/news/canada/2010/11/03/gordon_campbell_resigns_as_bc _premier.html

Food Banks Canada. (2013). *About hunger in Canada.* Retrieved from http://www .foodbankscanada.ca/Learn-About-Hunger/About-Hunger-in-Canada.aspx

Forbes. (2013). *The world's billionaires* (Lists). Retrieved from http://www.forbes.com/

Frank, Andre Gunder. (1975). *On capitalist underdevelopment.* Oxford: Oxford University Press.

Frechette, Christine, & Studnicki-Gizbert, Daviken. (2010). Mining: High stakes for Canada-Mexico relations. *Focal Point, 9*(1). Retrieved from http://www.focal.ca/en/publications/ focalpoint/220-february-2010-christine-frechette-and-daviken-studnicki-gizbert-en

Freire, Paulo. (1968/1984). *Pedagogy of the oppressed.* New York: Continuum.

Frideres, James. (2011). *First nations in the twenty-first century.* Oxford: Oxford University Press.

Friedmann, John. (1992). *Empowerment: The politics of alternative development.* Cambridge, MA: Blackwell Publishers.

Gabriel, Dana. (2014, May 21). Trilateral defense ministers meeting continues to build North American security framework. *Be your own leader.* Retrieved from http://beyourownleader .blogspot.ca/search?updated-min=2014-01-01T00:00:00-08:00&updated-max=2015 -01-01T00:00:00-08:00&max-results=3

Gamble, Andrew. (1994). *The free economy and the strong state: The politics of Thatcherism.* Basingstoke, UK: Macmillan Education.

García Martínez, Bernardo. (2004). La época colonial hasta 1760. In Pablo Escalante, Bernado García, Luis Jauregui, Josefina Zoraida, Elisa Speckman, Javier Garciadiego, & Luis Aboites, *Nueva historia mínima de México* (pp. 58–112). México City: El Colegio de México.

Giardini, Hernán (2011, November 4). No más sangre. *Contracultural.* Retrieved from http:// revistacontracultural.blogspot.ca/2011/11/no-mas-sangre-estamos-hasta-la-madre .html

Gilbreth, Chris, & Otero, Gerardo. (2001). Democratization in Mexico: The Zapatista uprising and civil society. *Latin American Perspectives, 28*(4), 7–29.

Giroux, Henry. (2008). *Against the terror of neoliberalism: Politics beyond the age of greed.* Boulder, CO: Paradigm Publishers.

González, Laura. (2006). Women and globalization in Mexico. In Jane Bayes, Patricia Begné, Laura Gonzalez, Lois Harder, Mary Hawkesworth, & Laura Macdonald (Eds.), *Women, democracy, and globalization in North America* (pp. 107–129). New York: Palgrave.

Goodwin, Jeff, & Jasper, James. (2009). *The social movements reader: Cases and concepts* (2nd ed.). West Sussex, UK: Wiley-Blackwell.

Grabb, Edward. (1999). Concentration of ownership and economic controls in Canada: Patterns and trends in the 1990s. In James Curtis, Edward Grabb, & Neil Guppy (Eds.), *Social inequality in Canada: Patterns, problems, policies* (3rd ed.) (pp. 4–12). Scarborough, ON: Prentice-Hall.

Grabb, Edward, & Hwang, Monica. (2009). Corporate concentration, foreign ownership, and state involvement in the Canadian economy. In Edward Grabb & Neil Guppy (Eds.), *Social inequality in Canada: Patterns, problems, policies* (5th ed.) (pp. 19–28). Toronto: Pearson Education Canada.

Graham, John, Swift, Karen, & Delaney, Roger. (2003). *Canadian social policy* (2nd ed.). Toronto: Prentice-Hall.

Gramsci, Antonio. (1929–1935/1971). *Selections from the prison notebooks of Antonio Gramsci.* New York: International Publishers.

Grayson, George. (2010). *Mexico: Narco-violence and a failed state?* New Brunswick, NJ: Transaction Publishers.

Green, Duncan. (2008). *From poverty to power.* Oxford: Oxfam Publishing.

Grey, Josephine. (2012). Against poverty: Josephine Grey on poor people's struggles for human rights. In Scott Neigh (Ed.), *Resisting the state: Canadian history through the stories of activists* (pp. 157–187). Black Point, NS: Fernwood.

Grillo, Ioan. (2011). *El narco: Inside Mexico's criminal insurgency.* New York: Bloomsbury Press.

Grillo, Ioan. (2012, November 1). Hit Mexico's cartels with legalization. *New York Times.* Retrieved from http://www.nytimes.com/2012/11/02/opinion/hit-mexicos-cartels-with -legalization.html?_r=1

Guidi, Ruxandra. (2007, July/August). Death over dams. *Orion Magazine.* Retrieved from https://orionmagazine.org/article/death-over-dams/

Gutiérrez, Lorraine, Parsons, Ruth, & Cox, Enid. (2003). *Empowerment in social work practice.* Belmont, CA: Wadsworth/Thomson.

Ha, Tu Thanh. (2009). *Payback comes knocking for Mexico's "boss of bosses."* Retrieved from http://www.theglobeandmail.com/news/world/payback-comes-knocking-for-mexicos -boss-of-bosses/article1366017/

Hall, Gilette, & Patrinos, Harry (Eds.). (2012). *Indigenous peoples, poverty, and development.* Cambridge: Cambridge University Press.

Hammond, John. (2003). Another world is possible: Report from Porto Alegre. *Latin American Perspectives, 30*(3), 3–11.

Hammond-Callaghan, Marie, & Hayday, Matthew. (2008). Introduction. In Marie Hammond-Callaghan & Matthew Hayday (Eds.), *Mobilizations, protests, and engagements: Canadian perspectives on social movements* (pp. 11–16). Halifax: Fernwood.

Hamnett, Brian. (1999). *A concise history of Mexico.* New York: Cambridge University Press.

Hampson, Fen Osler. (2013). *A world awash in crime.* Waterloo, ON: Centre for International Governance Innovation. Retrieved from https://www.cigionline.org/articles/2013/01/world-awash-crime

Hanley, Jill, & Shragge, Eric. (2007). Radical social work traditions in Canada: Examining the Quebec community movement. In Michael Lavalette & Iain Ferguson (Eds.), *International social work and the radical tradition* (pp. 51–72). Birmingham, UK: Venture Press.

Harper, Stephen. (2008, June 11). Prime Minister Stephen Harper offers full apology on behalf of Canadians for the Indian residential schools system. Retrieved from http://www.aadnc-aandc.gc.ca/eng/1100100015644/1100100015649

Hartley, Jackie, Joffe, Paul, & Preston, Jennifer. (2010a). From development to implementation: An ongoing journey. In Jackie Hartley, Paul Joffe, & Jennifer Preston (Eds.), *Realizing the UN Declaration on the Rights of Indigenous People* (pp. 12–16). Saskatoon, SK: Purich Publishing.

Hartley, Jackie, Joffe, Paul, & Preston, Jennifer. (2010b). Hopes and challenges on the road ahead. In Jackie Hartley, Paul Joffe, & Jennifer Preston (Eds.), *Realizing the UN Declaration on the Rights of Indigenous People* (pp. 189–194). Saskatoon, SK: Purich Publishing.

Hasham, Alyshah. (2013, September 12). *G20 assault trial: Guilty verdict for officer who hit Adam Nobody.* Retrieved from http://www.thestar.com/news/gta/2013/09/12/g20_assault_trial_guilty_verdict_for_officer_who_hit_adam_nobody.html

Hayden, Tom. (2002). *The Zapatista reader.* New York: Nation Books.

Hernández Castillo, Rosalva Aída. (2006). The Indigenous movement in Mexico: Between electoral politics and local resistance. *Latin American Perspectives, 33*(2), 115–131.

Hoogvelt, Ankie. (2001). *Globalization and the postcolonial world: The new political economy of development.* Baltimore, MD: Johns Hopkins University Press.

Houtart, François, & Polet, François (Eds.). (2001). *The other Davos: The globalization of resistance to the world economic system.* London: Zed Books.

Htun, Mala, & Weldon, S. Laurel. (2012). The civic origins of progressive policy change: Combatting violence against women in global perspective, 1975–2005. *American Political Science Review, 106*(3), 548–569.

Hugman, Richard. (2010). *Understanding international social work: A critical analysis.* Houndmills, UK: Palgrave.

Human Rights Watch. (2013, February 20). *Mexico's disappeared.* Retrieved from https://www
.hrw.org/news/2013/02/20/mexico-crisis-enforced-disappearances

Hyde, Cheryl. (1989). A feminist model for macro-practice: Promises and problems. In
Yeheskel Hasenfeld (Ed.), *Administrative leadership in the social services: The next challenge*
(pp. 145–181). New York: Haworth.

Hyde, Cheryl. (1994). Commitment to social change: Voices from the feminist movement.
Journal of Community Practice, 1(2), 45–64.

Ife, Jim. (2010). *Human rights from below: Achieving rights through community development.* Cambridge: Cambridge University Press.

Insight Crime. (2012). *Mexico.* Retrieved from http://www.insightcrime.org/mexico-organi
zed-crime-news/mexico

Institute for Research on Public Policy (2003). *First Nations Governance Act: A legacy of loss.*
Retrieved from http://policyoptions.irpp.org/issues/big-ideas/the-first-nations-governance
-act-a-legacy-of-loss/

Inter-American Court of Human Rights. (2011). *Case of Rosendo Cantú et al v. Mexico: Judgement
of May 15, 2011.* Retrieved from http://corteidh.or.cr/docs/casos/articulos/seriec_225_
ing.pdf

Internal Displacement Monitoring Centre. (2011, November 5). *Mexico: Displacement due to
criminal and communal violence.* Retrieved from http://www.internal-displacement.org/
americas/mexico/2011/mexico-displacement-due-to-criminal-and-communal-vio
lence/

International Association of Schools of Social Work (IASSW) & International Federation of
Social Workers (IFSW). (2014). *Global definition of the social work profession.* Retrieved from
http://www.iassw-aiets.org/global-definition-of-social-work-review-of-the-global
-definition/

Jasper, James. (2004). A strategic approach to collective action: Looking for agency in social
movement choices. *Mobilization, 9*(1), 1–16.

Jolom Mayaetik [Mayan Weavers]. (n.d.). Website. Retrieved from http://cooperativajolom
.blogspot.ca/

Jordan, Pav, Berman, David, & Erman, Boyd. (2013, April 19). *Pension funds dig in heels on
Barrick Gold bonus for co-chairman.* Retrieved from http://www.theglobeandmail.com/
report-on-business/industry-news/energy-and-resources/pension-funds-dig-in-heels
-on-barrick-gold-bonus-for-co-chairman/article11410541/

Kamel, Rachael, & Hoffman, Anya. (1999). *The maquiladora reader.* Philadelphia, PA:
American Friends Service Committee.

Kamloops Women's Resource Group Society (KWRGS). (n.d.). *Herstory.* Retrieved from
http://www.kwrgs.ca/herstory

Kane, Liam. (2001). *Popular education and social change in Latin America*. London: Latin American Bureau.

Kane, Liam. (2012). Forty years of popular education in Latin America: Lessons for social movements today. In Budd Hall, Darlene Clover, Jim Crowther, & Eurig Scandrett (Eds.), *Learning and education for a better world: The role of social movements* (pp. 69-84). Rotterdam, Netherlands: Sense Publisher.

Kelly, Katharine, & Caputo, Tullio. (2011). *Community: A contemporary analysis of policies, programs, and practices*. Toronto: University of Toronto Press.

Kelly, Mary. (1992). Free trade: The politics of toxic waste. *Report on the Americas, 26*(2), 4-7. New York: North American Congress on Latin America (NACLA).

Kesler, Linc. (2009). *Aboriginal identity and terminology*. Vancouver: UBC First Nations Studies Program. Retrieved from http://indigenousfoundations.arts.ubc.ca/?id=9494

Keynes, John Maynard. (1936/2007). *The general theory of employment, interest and money*. Basingstoke, UK: Palgrave Macmillan.

Khagram, Sanjeev. (2002). Restructuring the global politics of development: The case of India's Narmada Valley Dams. In Sanjeev Khagram, James Riker, & Kathryn Sikkink (Eds.), *Restructuring world politics: Transnational social movements, networks, and norms* (vol. 14, pp. 206-230). Minneapolis: University of Minnesota Press.

Klein, Naomi. (2011). Foreword: G20 trials and the war on activism. In Tom Malleson & David Wachsmuth (Eds.), *Whose streets: The Toronto G20 and the challenges of the summit protest* (pp. xi-xviii). Toronto: Between the Lines.

Korazim-Korosy, Yossi, Mizrahi, Terry, Katz, Chana, Karmon, Amnon, Garcia, Martha Lucia, & Smith, Marcia Bayne. (2007). Towards interdisciplinary community collaboration and development: Knowledge and experience from Israel and the USA. *Journal of Community Practice, 15*(1), 13-44.

Kovic, Christine. (2003a). The struggle for liberation and reconciliation in Chiapas, Mexico: Las Abejas and the path of nonviolent resistance. *Latin American Perspectives, 30*(3), 58-79.

Kovic, Christine. (2003b). Demanding their dignity as daughters of God: Catholic women and human rights. In Christine Eber & Christine Kovic (Eds.), *Women of Chiapas: Making history in times of struggle and hope*. New York: Routledge.

Kuhn, Thomas S. (1962/1996). *The structure of scientific revolutions* (3rd ed.). Chicago: University of Chicago Press.

Kutz-Flamenbaum, Rachel. (2012). Conclusion: Conceptualizing strategy in an interactive processional model. In Gregory Maney, Rachel Kutz-Flamenbaum, Deana Rohlinger, & Jeff Goodwin (Eds.), *Strategies for social change* (pp. 285-299). Minneapolis: University of Minnesota Press.

Kuyek, Joan. (2011). *Community organizing: A holistic approach*. Black Point, NS: Fernwood.

Ladner, Kiera. (2014). Aysaka'paykinit: Contesting the rope around the nations' neck. In Miriam Smith (Ed.), *Group politics and social movements in Canada* (2nd ed.) (pp. 227-253). North York, ON: University of Toronto Press.

Lakeman, Lee. (2012). Feminist anti-violence activism in Woodstock and Vancouver. In Scott Neigh (Ed.), *Gender & sexuality: Canadian history through the stories of activists* (pp. 69-96). Black Point, NS: Fernwood.

Layton, Michael, Campillo Carrete, Beatriz, Ablanedo Terrazas, Ireri, & Sánchez Rodríguez, Ana María. (2010). Reducing maternal mortality in Mexico: Building vertical alliances for change. In John Gaventa & Rosemary McGee (Eds.), *Citizen action and national policy reform* (pp. 89-108). London: Zed Books.

Lee, Judith. (2001). Empowerment method: The how-to. In *The empowerment approach to social work practice: Building the beloved community* (2nd ed.) (pp. 56-93). New York: Columbia University Press.

Leonard, Peter. (1997). *Postmodern welfare: Reconstructing an emancipatory project*. London: Sage.

Libertinus. (2006, October 28). *Indymedia volunteer Brad Will killed in attack by paramilitaries in Oaxaca*. Retrieved from https://www.indymedia.org/en/2006/10/849305.shtml

Lievrouw, Leah. (2011). *Alternative and activist new media. Young women's activism for social change* (pp. 1-18). Cambridge: Polity Press.

Lockhart, James. (1969). Encomienda and hacienda: The evolution of the great estate in the Spanish Indies. *The Hispanic American Historical Review, 49*(3), 411-429.

Lotz, Jim. (1997). The beginning of community development in English-speaking Canada. In Brian Wharf & Michael Clague (Eds.), *Community organizing: Canadian experiences* (pp. 1-14). Toronto: Oxford University Press.

Lotz, Jim, & Welton, Michael. (1997). *Father Jimmy: Life and times of Jimmy Tompkins*. Wreck Cove, NS: Breton Books.

Lowrey-Evans, Berklee. (2012). *Hasta la victoria: La Parota Dam cancelled*. Retrieved from http://www.internationalrivers.org/blogs/244/hasta-la-victoria-la-parota-dam-cancelled

Luccisano, Lucy. (2006). The Mexican Oportunidades program: Questioning the linking of security to conditional social investments for mothers and children. *Canadian Journal of Latin American & Caribbean Studies, 31*(62), 53-86.

Lundy, Colleen. (2004). *Social work and social justice*. Peterborough, ON: Broadview Press.

Macdonald, David. (2011). *Corporate income taxes, profit, and employment performance of Canada's largest companies*. Ottawa: Canadian Centre for Policy Alternatives.

Macdonald, David, & Wilson, Daniel. (2003). *Poverty or prosperity: Indigenous children in Canada*. Ottawa: Canadian Centre for Policy Alternatives.

Machado, Antonio. (1912/1964). Caminante, no hay camino. From "Proverbios y cantares" in *Campos de Castilla*. Salamanca: Anaya.

Mackenzie, Hugh. (2014). *All in a day's work: CEO pay in Canada*. Ottawa: Canadian Centre for Policy Alternatives.

Mackinley, Horacio, & Otero, Gerardo (2004). State corporatism and peasant organizations: Towards new institutional arrangements. In Gerardo Otero (Ed.), *Mexico in transition: Neoliberalism, the state and civil society* (pp. 72–88). Black Point, NS: Fernwood.

Malleson, Tom, & Wachsmuth, David (Eds.). (2011). *Whose streets: The Toronto G20 and the challenges of the summit protest*. Toronto: Between the Lines.

Maney, Gregory, Andrews, Kenneth, Kutz-Flamenbaum, Rachel, Rohlinger, Deanna, & Goodwin, Jeff. (2012). An introduction to strategies for change. In Gregory Maney, Rachel Kutz-Flamenbaum, Deanna Rohlinger, & Jeff Goodwin (Eds.), *Strategies for social change* (pp. xi–xxxviii). Minneapolis: University of Minnesota Press.

Marcos, Subcomandante. (1994/2002). Testimonies of the first day. In Tom Hayden (Ed.), *The Zapatista reader* (pp. 207–217). New York: Nation Books.

Marinelli, Alejandro, & Jaimovitch, Desirée. (2011, January 9). La peste del oro. *Viva* (pp. 42–47). Buenos Aires, Argentina.

Marotte, Bertrand. (2013, July 23). Guatemalan mine claims against HudBay can be tried in Canada, judge says. *Globe and Mail*. Retrieved from http://www.theglobeandmail.com/report-on-business/industry-news/energy-and-resources/guatemalan-mine-claims-against-hudbay-can-be-tried-in-canada-judge-says/article13360800/

Martínez Torres, María Elena. (2004). Survival strategies in neo-liberal markets: Peasant organizations and organic coffee in Chiapas. In Gerardo Otero (Ed.), *Mexico in transition: Neoliberalism, the state and civil society* (pp. 169–203). Black Point, NS: Fernwood.

McAdam, Doug. (1996). The framing function of movement tactics. In Doug McAdam, John McCarthy, & Mayer Zald (Eds.), *Comparative perspectives on social movements: Political opportunities, mobilizing structures, and cultural framings* (pp. 338–355). Cambridge: University of Cambridge Press.

McAdam, Doug, Tarrow, Sidney, & Tilly, Charles. (2001). *Dynamics of contention*. Cambridge: Cambridge University Press.

McBride, Stephen, & Shields, John. (1993). *Dismantling a nation: Canada and the new world order*. Halifax: Fernwood.

McCarthy, John, & Zald, Mayer. (1973). *The trend of social movements in America: Professionalization and resource mobilization*. Morristown, NJ: General Learning Press.

McCarthy, John, & Zald, Mayer. (1977). Resource mobilization and social movements: A partial theory. *American Journal of Sociology, 82*(6), 1212–1241.

McInturff, Kate. (2013, April). *Closing Canada's Gender Gap*. Ottawa: Canadian Centre for Policy Alternatives. Retrieved from http://www.policyalternatives.ca/sites/default/files/uploads/publications/National%20Office/2013/04/Closing_Canadas_Gender_Gap_0.pdf

McKenzie, Brad, & Morrissette, Vern. (2003). Social work practice with Canadians of Aboriginal background: Guidelines for respectful social work. In Alean Al Krenawi & John Graham (Eds.), *Multicultural social work in Canada* (pp. 251-282). Don Mills, ON: Oxford University Press.

McKnight, John, & Kretzmann, John. (2005). Mapping community capacity. In Meredith Minkler (Ed.), *Community organizing and community building for health* (2nd ed.) (pp. 158-172). New Brunswick, NJ: Rutgers University Press.

McNally, David. (2011). Social protest in the age of austerity: Prospects for mass resistance after the G20. In Tom Malleson & David Wachsmuth (Eds.), *Whose streets: The Toronto G20 and the challenges of the summit protest* (pp. 201-212). Toronto: Between the Lines.

McQuaig, Linda. (1995). *Shooting the hippo: Death by deficit and other Canadian myths*. Toronto: Viking.

Mendoza Rangel, Maria del Carmen. (2005). Social work in Mexico: Towards a different practice. In Iain Ferguson, Michael Lavalette, & Elizabeth Whitmore (Eds.), *Globalisation, global justice and social work* (pp. 11-22). London: Routledge.

Menocal, Alina Rocha, & Ruiz, Samuel. (1998). The politics of marginalization: Poverty and the rights of the Indigenous people in Mexico. *Journal of International Affairs, 52*(1), 85-100.

Mexico, Comisión Nacional de los Derechos Humanos [National Human Rights Commission]. (2013). *Diagnóstico sobre la situación de la trata de personas en México*. Retrieved from http://200.33.14.34:1033/archivos/pdfs/diagnosticoTrataPersonas.pdf

Mexico, Comisión Nacional de los Salarios Minimos [National Commission on Minimum Wages]. (2014). *Salario mínimo general promedio de los Estados Unidos Mexicanos 1964-2014*. Retrieved from http://www.conasami.gob.mx/pdf/salario_minimo/sal_min_gral_prom.pdf

Mexico, Comisión Nacional para el Desarrollo de los Pueblos Indígenas [National Commission for the Development of Indigenous Peoples] (CDI). (2010). *Informe sobre desarrollo humano de los pueblos indígenas en México*. Retrieved from http://planipolis.iiep.unesco.org/upload/Mexico/Mexico_HDR_2010.pdf

Mexico, Consejo Nacional de Evaluación de la Política de Desarrollo Social [National Council for Evaluation of Social Development Policy] (CONEVAL). (2012a). *Informe de pobreza en México 2010*. Retrieved from http://www.coneval.gob.mx/Informes/Coordinacion/INFORMES_Y_PUBLICACIONES_PDF/Informe_de_Pobreza_en_Mexico_2010.pdf

Mexico, Consejo Nacional de Evaluación de la Política de Desarrollo Social (CONEVAL). (2012b). *Pobreza y género en Mexico: Hacia un sistema de indicadores.* Retrieved from http://www.coneval.gob.mx/Informes/Coordinacion/INFORMES_Y_PUBLICACIONES_PDF/PobrezayGeneroenweb.pdf

Mexico, Consejo Nacional de Evaluación de la Política de Desarrollo Social (CONEVAL). (2013a). *Medición de la Pobreza.* Retrieved from http://www.coneval.gob.mx/Medicion/MP/Paginas/Lineas-de-bienestar-y-canasta-basica.aspx

Mexico, Consejo Nacional de Evaluación de la Política de Desarrollo Social (CONEVAL). (2013b). *Mendicíon de la pobreza: Resultados de pobreza en México—Anexo estadístico 2012.* Retrieved from http://www.coneval.gob.mx/Medicion/MP/Paginas/Anexo-estadístico -pobreza-2012.aspx

Mexico, Instituto Nacional de Estadística y Geografía [National Institute of Statistics and Geography] (INEGI). (2013). *Población.* Retrieved from http://www3.inegi.org.mx/ sistemas/temas/default.aspx?s=est&c=17484

Mexico, Instituto Nacional de las Mujeres [National Women's Institute] (INMUJERES). (2012). *Cuadernos de trabajo: Género y pobreza.* Retrieved from http://www.gob.mx/cms/ uploads/attachment/file/27485/ct32.pdf

Mexico, Secretaría de Economía—Coordinación General de Minería [Secretary of Economy—General Coordination of Mining]. (2012). *Proyectos mineros operados por compañías de capital extranjero.* Retrieved from http://www.economia.gob.mx/files/comunidad_ negocios/industria_comercio/proyectos_mineros_operados_comp_capital_ext_2012 .pdf

Meyer, Lois. (2010). Introduction. In Lois Meyer & Benjamín Maldonado Alvarado (Eds.), *New world of Indigenous resistance* (pp. 7–37). San Francisco: City Lights.

Mining Watch Canada. (2013). *Corruption, murder and Canadian mining in Mexico: The case of Blackfire Exploration and the Canadian Embassy.* Retrieved from http://miningwatch.ca/ sites/default/files/blackfire_embassy_report-web.pdf

Mining Watch Canada. (2014). *Catastrophic tailings spill at Mount Polley Mine.* Retrieved from http://miningwatch.ca/blog/2014/8/8/catastrophic-tailings-spill-mount-polley-mine

Mondros, Jacqueline, & Wilson, Scott. (1994). *Organizing for power and empowerment.* New York: Columbia University Press.

Moreau, Maurice. (1979). A structural approach to social services practice. *Canadian Journal of Social Work Education, 5*(1), 78–94.

Morris, Aldon. (2004). Reflections on social movement theory: Criticisms and proposals. In Jeff Goodwin & James Jasper (Eds.), *Rethinking social movements: Structure, meaning, and emotion* (pp. 233–246). Lanham, MD: Rowman & Littlefield.

Moyer, Bill. (2001). *Doing democracy: The MAP model for organizing social movements.* Gabriola Island, BC: New Society Publishers.

Mujeres para el Diálogo [Women for Dialogue]. (2011). *Quiénes somos.* Retrieved from https://mujeresparaeldialogo.wordpress.com/quienes-somos/

Mulay, Shree, & Siddiqui, Sadeqa. (2012). Feminist anti-violence activism in Montreal. In Scott Neigh (Ed.), *Gender & sexuality: Canadian history through the stories of activists* (pp. 97–121). Black Point, NS: Fernwood.

Mullaly, Bob. (1997). *Structural social work: Ideology, theory and practice.* Toronto: McClelland and Stewart.

Mullaly, Bob. (2007). *The new structural social work* (3rd ed.). Don Mills, ON: Oxford University Press.

Nation Talk. (2013, August 7). *Dene peoples seeking answers in the latest oil spill.* Retrieved from http://nationtalk.ca/story/dene-peoples-seeking-answers-in-the-latest-oil-spill

Native Women's Association of Canada (NWAC). (2007). *Aboriginal women and Bill C-31.* Retrieved from http://www.laa.gov.nl.ca/laa/naws/pdf/nwac-billc-31.pdf

Native Women's Association of Canada (NWAC). (2010). *What their stories tell us.* Retrieved from http://www.nwac.ca/wp-content/uploads/2015/05/2010_What_Their_Stories_Tell_Us_Research_Findings_SIS_Initiative.pdf

Native Women's Association of Canada (NWAC). (2014). *More than invisible, invisible to real action.* Retrieved from http://www.cwp-csp.ca/resources/sites/default/files/resources/ENG_NWAC_Official_response_to_SCVAIW.pdf

Nepstad, Sharon Erickson, & Bob, Clifford. (2006). When do leaders matter? Hypotheses on leadership dynamics in social movements. *Mobilization: An international journal, 11,* 1–22.

Nestor. (2009, December 3). *Mariano Abarca Roblero, REMA, Chicomuselo, Chiapas.* Retrieved from https://www.youtube.com/watch?v=6UUvYfZPKxQ

Nutini, Hugo, & Isaac, Barry. (2009). *Social stratification in central Mexico 1500–2000.* Austin: University of Texas Press.

Ontario, Attorney General. (2007). *The Ipperwash inquiry: Vol. 4 Executive summary—investigation and findings.* Retrieved from http://www.attorneygeneral.jus.gov.on.ca/inquiries/ipperwash/report/vol_4/pdf/E_Vol_4_Summary_1.pdf

Ontario Coalition against Poverty. (2013). *2013–2014 Ontario provincial budget breakdown by OCAP.* Retrieved from http://update.ocap.ca/node/1077

Ontario, Ministry of Community & Social Services. (2013). *Social assistance, pension, and tax credit rates.* Retrieved from http://www.durham.ca/departments/social/income_support/PensionRateJantoMar2013.pdf

Olesen, Thomas. (2011). Conclusion. In Thomas Olesen (Ed.), *Power and transnational activism* (pp. 252–261). London: Routledge.

Olson, Mancur. (1965). *The logic of collective action: Public goods and the theory of groups.* Cambridge, MA: Harvard University Press.

Organisation for Economic Co-operation & Development (OECD). (2000). *Public social expenditure 1980–1999.* Retrieved from www.oecd.org/dataoecd/43/14/2087083.xls

Organisation for Economic Co-operation & Development (OECD). (2008). *Growing unequal? Income distribution and poverty in OECD countries.* Paris: Author.

Organisation for Economic Co-operation & Development (OECD). (2011a). An overview of growing income inequalities in OECD countries. In OECD's *Divided we stand* (pp. 21–45). Retrieved from http://www.oecd-ilibrary.org/social-issues-migration-health/divided-we-stand/an-overview-of-growing-income-inequalities-in-oecd-countries_9789264119536-3-en

Organisation for Economic Co-operation & Development (OECD). (2011b). *Divided we stand— Country note: Canada.* Retrieved from http://www.oecd.org/social/soc/49177689.pdf

Organisation for Economic Co-operation & Development (OECD). (2011c). *Divided we stand— Country note: Mexico.* Retrieved from http://www.oecd.org/mexico/49177732.pdf

Organisation for Economic Co-operation & Development. (OECD). (2012). *Canada: Closing the gender gap.* Retrieved from http://www.oecd.org/canada/Closing%20The%20Gender%20Gap%20-%20Canada%20FINAL.pdf

Organisation for Economic Co-operation & Development (OECD). (2013a). *Gender equality.* Retrieved from http://www.keepeek.com/Digital-Asset-Management/oecd/economics/oecd-factbook-2013/introduction_factbook-2013-104-en.

Organisation for Economic Co-operation & Development (OECD). (2013b). *StatExtracts: Social protection: Social expenditure—aggregated data.* Retrieved from http://stats.oecd.org/Index.aspx?QueryId=26068

Organisation for Economic Co-operation & Development (OECD). (2013c). *StatExtracts: Social protection: Income distribution and poverty by country—inequality.* Retrieved from http://stats.oecd.org/Index.aspx?QueryId=26068

Organisation for Economic Co-operation & Development (OECD). (2013d). *StatExtracts: Labour force statistics by sex and age 2012.* Retrieved from http://stats.oecd.org/Index.aspx?QueryId=26068

Organisation for Economic Co-operation & Development (OECD). (2013e). *StatExtracts: Social Protection: Gender, institutions and development database 2009.* Retrieved from http://stats.oecd.org/Index.aspx?QueryId=26068

Organisation for Economic Co-operation & Development (OECD). (2013f). *How's life? Measuring well-being—Country snapshot: Mexico.* Retrieved from http://www.oecd.org/mexico/HsL-Country-Note-MEXICO.pdf

Otero, Gerardo. (2004). Mexico's double movement: Neoliberal globalism, the state and civil society. In Gerardo Otero (Ed.), *Mexico in transition: Neoliberalism, the state and civil society* (pp. 1–17). Black Point, NS: Fernwood.

Oxfam Canada. (2015). *Make trade fair.* Retrieved from http://oxfam.ca/our-work/campaigns/make-trade-fair

Oxfam International. (2014). *Working for the few: Political capture and economic inequality.* Retrieved from https://www.oxfam.org/sites/www.oxfam.org/files/bp-working-for-few-political-capture-economic-inequality-200114-en.pdf

Oxhorn, Philip. (1995). *Organizing civil society: The popular sectors and the struggle for democracy in Chile.* University Park: Pennsylvania State University Press.

Panet-Raymond, Jean, & Mayer, Robert. (1997). The history of community development in Quebec. In Brian Wharf & Michael Clague (Eds.), *Community organizing: Canadian experiences* (pp. 29–61). Toronto: Oxford University Press.

Paz, Octavio. (1985). *The labyrinth of solitude, the other Mexico, and other essays.* New York: Grove Press.

Peña Nieto, Enrique. (2012, November 21). Mexico's moment. *The economist: The world in 2013.* Retrieved from http://www.economist.com/news/21566314-enrique-pe%C3%B1a-nieto-mexicos-newly-elected-president-sets-out-his-priorities-mexicos-moment

Perkins, Patricia. (1996). Trade liberalization, the natural environment and cities. In Roger Keil, Gerda Wekerle, & David Bell (Eds.), *Local places in the age of the global city* (pp. 235–242). Montreal: Black Rose Books.

Petras, James, & Veltmeyer, Henry. (2001). *Globalization unmasked.* Halifax: Fernwood.

Pickard, Miguel. (2004, Avril). The Plan Puebla Panama revived: Looking back to see what's ahead. *Observatoire des Ameriques, 12,* 1–7. Retrieved from http://www.ieim.uqam.ca/IMG/pdf/Chro_0413_ppp-en.pdf

Pinard, Maurice. (2011). *Motivational dimensions in social movements and contentious collective action.* Montreal: McGill-Queen's University Press.

Piven, Frances Fox, & Cloward, Richard. (1977). *Poor people's movement: Why they succeed, how they fail.* New York: Pantheon Books.

Piza Lopez, Eugenia, & March, Candida. (1991). *Gender consideration in economic enterprises.* Oxford: Oxfam Gender & Development Unit.

Polaski, Sandra. (2003). Jobs, wages, and household income. In John Audley, Demetrios Papademetriou, Sandra Polaski, & Scott Vaughan (Eds.), *NAFTA's promise and reality.* Washington, DC: Carnegie Endowment for International Peace. Retrieved from http://carnegieendowment.org/files/nafta1.pdf

Porter, John. (1965). *The vertical mosaic: An analysis of social class and power in Canada.* Toronto: University of Toronto Press.

Postmedia News. (2012, December 14). *Senate passes Harper government's omnibus bill.* Canwest News Service.

Prevost, Gary, Vanden, Harry, & Olivia Campos, Carlos. (2012). Introduction. In Gary Prevost, Carlos Oliva Campos, & Harry Vanden, (Eds.), *Socialist movements and leftist governments in Latin America* (pp. 1–21). London: Zed Books.

Price, Kathy. (2012, Fall). Good news for Ines, Valentina and the struggle to protect Indigenous women in Mexico. *Candle* (Amnesty International), *11*(2), 1.

Proyecto Mesoamérica [Project Mesoamerica]. (2013). *Portal oficial de Proyecto Mesoamérica* (Project Mesoamerica). Retrieved from http://www.proyectomesoamerica.org/joomla/

Pugh, Richard, & Cheers, Brian. (2010). Indigenous peoples: Dispossession, colonisation and discrimination. In *Rural social work: An international perspective* (pp. 47–74). Bristol, UK: Policy Press.

Quarter, Jack, Mook, Laurie, & Armstrong, Ann. (2009). *Understanding the social economy: A Canadian perspective.* Toronto: University of Toronto Press.

Raging Grannies. (2009). *We're the women.* Retrieved from http://raginggrannies.net/were-the-women

Raphael, Dennis. (2011). *Poverty in Canada: Implications for health and quality of life* (2nd ed.). Toronto: CSPI.

Red Mexicana de Acción Frente al Libre Comercio [Mexican Network for Action against Free Trade] (RMALC). (2004). *Miente Fox en Centroamérica sobre el Plan Puebla Panamá.* Retrieved from http://www.rmal

Ricardo, David. (1817/1948). *The principles of political economy and taxation.* London: Dent.

Ricketts, Aidan. (2012). *The activists' handbook: A step-by-step guide to participatory democracy.* New York: Zed Books.

Rohter, Larry. (1989, April 16). *In Mexico, drug roots run deep.* Retrieved from http://www.nytimes.com/1989/04/16/world/in-mexico-drug-roots-run-deep.html?pagewanted=1

Rothman, Jack. (2001). Approaches to community intervention. In Jack Rothman, John Erlich, & John Tropman, (Eds.), *Strategies of community intervention: Macro practice* (6th ed.) (pp. 27–64). Itasca, IL: Peacock.

Roy, Arundhati. (2003). *Confronting empire.* A presentation at the World Social Forum in Porto Alegre, Brazil, January 27, 2003. In Eddie Yuen, Daniel Burton-Rose, & George Katsiaficas (Eds.), *Confronting capitalism: Dispatches from a global movement* (pp. 243–246). Brooklyn, NY: Soft Skull Press.

Roy, Carole. (2004). *The Raging Grannies: Wild hats, cheeky songs, and witty actions for a better world.* Montreal: Black Rose Books.

Saleebey, Dennis. (2001). Vulnerability and strength: Giving voice to the voiceless. *Midwest Bioethics Centre: Bioethics Forum, 17*(3–4), 31–38.

Schein, Edgar. (1999). *Process consultation: Building the helping relationship.* Reading, MA: Addison-Wesley Longman.

Schugurensky, Daniel. (2013). Democracy does not fall from the sky. In Ali Abdi & Paul Carr (Eds.), *Educating for democratic consciousness: Counter-hegemonic possibilities* (pp. ix–xii). New York: Peter Lang.

Shahani, Arjan. (2013, June 14). Human trafficking in Mexico. *Americas Quarterly.* Retrieved from http://www.americasquarterly.org/content/human-trafficking-mexico

Sher, Julian. (2013, May 5). *Canadian mining company got embassy help amid controversy in Mexico.* Retrieved from http://www.thestar.com/news/world/2013/05/05/canadian_mining_company_got_embassy_help_amid_controversy_in_mexico_advocacy_group.html

Shragge, Eric. (2003). Moving forward: New visions and hopes. In Eric Shragge, *Activism and social change: Lessons for community and local organizing* (pp. 151–161a). Peterborough, ON: Broadview.

Sicilia, Javier. (2013, April 9). *Las víctimas dos años después.* Retrieved from https://lastresyuncuarto.wordpress.com/2013/04/11/javier-sicilia-las-victimas-dos-anos-despues/

Silva, Juan. (2008). La globalización y el comercio justo. In Norma Giarracca & Gabriela Massuh (Eds.), *El trabajo por venir: Autogestión y emancipación social* (pp. 50–53). Buenos Aires: Antropofagia.

Smith, Adam. (1776/1978). *The wealth of nations.* New York: Dent.

Smith, Adrian, Stenning, Allison, & Willis, Katie. (2008). *Social justice and neoliberalism: Global perspectives.* London: Zed Books.

Smith, Andrea. (2007). The NGOization of the Palestine Liberation Movement: Interviews with Hatem Bazian, Noura Erekat, Atef Said, and Zeina Zaatari. In Incite! Women of Colour against Violence (Ed.), *The revolution will not be funded: Beyond the non-profit industrial complex* (pp. 165–182). Cambridge, MA: South End Press.

Snow, David, Rochford, E. Burke, Worden, Steven, & Benford, Robert. (1986). Frame alignment processes, micromobilization, and movement participation. *American Sociological Review, 51*(4), 464–481.

Snowden, David, & Boone, Mary. (2007). A leader's framework for decision making. *Harvard Business Review, 85*(11), 68–76.

Snyder, Linda. (2000). *Women's employment initiatives as a means of addressing poverty: A comparative study of Canadian and Chilean examples* (Dissertation). Wilfrid Laurier University, Waterloo, ON.

Snyder, Linda. (2004). Collective outcomes and social mobilization in Chilean and Canadian employment initiatives for women. *International Social Work, 47*(3), 321–335.

Snyder, Linda. (2006). Workfare: Ten years of pickin' on the poor. In Anne Westhues (Ed.), *Canadian social policy: Issues and perspectives* (4th ed.) (pp. 309–331). Waterloo: Wilfrid Laurier University Press.

Snyder, Linda. (2012). International development and its underlying ideologies. In Tuula Heinonen & Julie Drolet (Eds.), *International social development: Social work experiences and perspectives* (pp. 14–42). Black Point, NS: Fernwood.

Staggenborg, Suzanne. (2013). Organization and community in social movements. In Jacquelien van Stekelburg, Conny Roggeband, & Bert Klandermans (Eds.), *The future of social movement research: Dynamics, mechanisms, and processes* (pp. 125–144). Minneapolis: University of Minnesota Press.

Steigman, Martha, & Pictou, Sherry. (2010). How do you say *Netuklimk* in English? Using documentary video to capture Bear River First Nation's learning through action. In Aziz Choudry & Dip Kapoor (Eds.), *Learning from the ground up* (pp. 227–242). New York: Palgrave Macmillan.

Stevens, Geoffrey. (2012, December 3). Pushing trade at the expense of rights. *Waterloo Region Record*, A11.

Stolle-McAllister, John. (2005). *Mexican social movements and the transition to democracy.* Jefferson, NC: McFarland.

Stueck, Wendy. (2010, September 10). The political storm watch on Fish Lake. *Globe and Mail.* Retrieved from http://www.theglobeandmail.com/news/british-columbia/the-political-storm-watch-on-fish-lake/article1703514/

Stueck, Wendy, & Curry, Bill. (2010, September 2). Fight against mine could be a bloody affair. *Globe and Mail.* Retrieved from http://www.theglobeandmail.com/news/british-columbia/fight-against-mine-could-be-a-bloody-affair/article1694158/

Swank, Eric. (2006). Welfare reform and the power of protest: Quantitative test of Piven and Cloward's "turmoil-relief" hypothesis. In Keith Kilty & Elizabeth Segal (Eds.), *The promise of welfare reform: Political rhetoric and the reality of poverty in the twenty-first century* (pp. 287–300). New York: Haworth.

Tarrow, Sidney. (1998). *Power in movement: Social movements, collective action, and politics* (2nd ed.). Cambridge: Cambridge University Press.

Teeple, Gary. (1995). *Globalization and the decline of social reform.* Toronto: Garamond Press.

Terrazas, Aaron. (2010). *Mexican immigrants in the United States.* Retrieved from http://www.migrationpolicy.org/article/mexican-immigrants-united-states-0/

Tetreault, Darcy. (2013a). Fighting poverty in Mexico. In Henry Veltmeyer & Darcy Tetreault (Eds.), *Poverty and development in Latin America* (pp. 85–114). Sterling, VA: Kumarian.

Tetreault, Darcy. (2013b). Pathways out of rural poverty in Mexico. In Henry Veltmeyer & Darcy Tetreault (Eds.), *Poverty and development in Latin America* (pp. 191-211). Sterling, VA: Kumarian.

Tetreault, Darcy. (2013c). Agroecology and food sovereignty. In Henry Veltmeyer & Darcy Tetreault (Eds.), *Poverty and development in Latin America* (pp. 213-224). Sterling, VA: Kumarian.

Thobani, Sunera. (2007). *Exalted subjects: Studies in the making of race and nation in Canada.* Toronto: University of Toronto Press.

Thompson, Lisa, & Tapscott, Chris. (2010). Introduction: Mobilization and social movements in the south—The challenges of inclusive governance. In Lisa Thompson & Chris Tapscott (Eds.), *Citizenship and social movements: Perspectives from the global south* (pp. 1-32). London: Zed Books.

Tilly, Charles. (1978). *From mobilization to revolution.* Reading, MA: Addison-Wesley.

Tilly, Charles. (2002). *Stories, identities, and political change.* Lanham, MD: Rowman and Littlefield.

Tinker, Irene. (2000). Alleviating poverty: Investing in women's work. *Journal of the American Planning Association, 66*(3), 229-242.

Toye, Michael, & Chaland, Nicole. (2006). CED in Canada: Review of definitions and profile of practice. In Eric Shragge & Michael Toye (Eds.), *Community economic development: Building for social change* (pp. 21-41). Sydney: Cape Breton University Press.

Tremonti, Anna Maria. (2013, November 6). *A new battle plan for the war on drugs in Mexico.* Retrieved from http://www.cbc.ca/radio/thcurrent/nov-6-2013-1.2909152/a-new-battle -plan-for-the-war-on-drugs-in-mexico-1.2909153

Trigg, Mary. (2009). Introduction. In Mary Trigg (Ed.), *Leading the way: Young women's activism for social change* (pp. 1-18). New Brunswick, NJ: Rutgers University Press.

Tuckman, Jo. (2010, August 31). *Tenth of Mexico's federal police fired.* Retrieved from http://www .theguardian.com/world/2010/aug/31/tenth-federal-police-officers-fired-mexico -drug-wars?guni=Article:in%20body%20link

Tuckman, Jo. (2013, February 27). *Elba Esther Gordillo—Mexico's famed union boss—accused of embezzlement.* Retrieved from http://www.theguardian.com/world/2013/feb/27/elba -esther-gordillo-mexico-union-embezzlement

United Nations. (2013). *We can end poverty: Millennium Development Goals and beyond 2015.* Retrieved from http://www.un.org/millenniumgoals/poverty.shtml

United Nations Data. (2013a). *Country profile: Canada.* Retrieved from http://data.un.org/ CountryProfile.aspx?crName=Canada

United Nations Data. (2013b). *Country profile: Mexico.* Retrieved from http://data.un.org/ CountryProfile.aspx?crName=Mexico

United Nations Development Programme (UNDP). (1990–2014). *Global reports*. Retrieved from http://hdr.undp.org/en/global-reports

United Nations Development Programme (UNDP). (2013). *Human development report 2013*. Retrieved from http://hdr.undp.org/en/2013-report

United Nations Economic Commission for Latin America and the Caribbean (ECLAC). (2012). *Social panorama of Latin America: Briefing paper*. Retrieved from http://www.cepal .org/publicaciones/xml/4/48454/SocialPanorama2012DocI.pdf

United Nations Framework Convention on Climate Change. (2013). *The Kyoto Protocol*. Retrieved from http://unfccc.int/kyoto_protocol/background/items/2878.php

United Nations General Assembly. (2007). *UN Declaration on the Rights of Indigenous Peoples*. Retrieved from http://www.un.org/esa/socdev/unpfii/documents/DRIPS_en.pdf

United Nations Office of the High Commissioner for Human Rights (UN OHCHR). (2013a). *Basic facts about the UPR*. Retrieved from http://www.ohchr.org/EN/HRBodies/UPR/ Pages/BasicFacts.aspx

United Nations Office of the High Commissioner for Human Rights (UN OHCHR). (2013b). *Report of the Working Group on the Universal Periodic Review: Canada*. Retrieved from http://www.ohchr.org/EN/HRBodies/UPR/Pages/CASession16.aspx

United Nations Office of the High Commissioner for Human Rights (UN OHCHR). (2013c). *Report of the Working Group on the Universal Periodic Review: Canada addendum*. Retrieved from http://www.ohchr.org/EN/HRBodies/UPR/Pages/CASession16.aspx

United Nations Office of the High Commissioner for Human Rights (UN OHCHR). (2013d). *Report of the Working Group on the Universal Periodic Review: Mexico*. Retrieved from http:// www.ohchr.org/EN/HRBodies/UPR/Pages/MXSession17.aspx

United Nations Office of the High Commissioner for Human Rights (UN OHCHR). (2014). *Report of the Working Group on the Universal Periodic Review: Mexico addendum*. Retrieved from http://www.ohchr.org/EN/HRBodies/UPR/Pages/MXSession17.aspx

United Nations Permanent Forum on Indigenous Issues. (2013, February 14). *Study on the extractive industries in Mexico and the situation of Indigenous peoples in the territories in which those industries are located*. Retrieved from http://www.un.org/ga/search/view_doc .asp?symbol=E/C.19/2013/11

United Nations Women (UN Women). (2012). *Progress of the world's women: In pursuit of justice (Summary)*. Retrieved from http://www2.unwomen.org/~/media/headquarters/ attachments/sections/library/publications/2011/progressoftheworldswomen-2011-en .pdf?v=1&d=20150402T222835

Venne, Sharon H. (2013). NGOs, Indigenous people, and the United Nations. In Aziz Choudry & Dip Kapoor (Eds.), *NGOization: Complicity, contradictions, and prospects* (pp. 75–101). London: Zed Books.

Verástique, Bernardino. (2000). *Michoacán and Eden: Vasco de Quiroga and the evangelization of western Mexico*. Austin: University of Texas.

Vidal, John. (1999, December 5). Real battle for Seattle. *The Guardian*. Retrieved from http://www.theguardian.com/world/1999/dec/05/wto.globalisation

Villarreal, M. Angeles. (2012). *Mexico's free trade agreements*. Washington, DC: Congressional Research Service. Retrieved from http://www.fas.org/sgp/crs/row/R40784.pdf

Warren, Roland. (1975). Types of purposive social change. In Ralph Kramer & Harry Specht (Eds.), *Readings in community organization practice* (2nd ed.) (pp. 134-149). Englewood Cliffs, NJ: Prentice-Hall.

Watt, Peter, & Zepeda, Roberto. (2012). *Drug war Mexico: Politics, neoliberalism and violence in the new narcoeconomy*. London: Zed Books.

WEE Society. (n.d.). *Our history*. Retrieved from http://www.womenunlimitedns.ca/about-us

Wharf, Brian, & Clague, Michael (Eds.). (1997). *Community organizing: Canadian experiences*. Toronto: Oxford University Press.

Whittington, Lee, Brennan, Richard, & Delacourt, Susan. (2010, November 4). Jim Prentice resigns from Harper cabinet. *The Star*. Retrieved from http://www.thestar.com/news/canada/2010/11/04/jim_prentice_resigns_from_harper_cabinet.html

Wichterich, Christa. (2000). *The globalized woman: Reports from a future of inequality*. London: Zed Books.

Williams, Heather. (2001). Of free trade and debt bondage: Fighting banks and the state in Mexico. *Latin American Perspectives, 28*(4), 33-51.

Wilson, Maureen. (2009). Gender and development in Central America: Lessons from the field. In Gayle Gilchrist James, Richard Ramsay, & Glenn Drover (Eds.), *International social work: Canadian perspectives* (pp. 104-126). Toronto: Thompson Educational Publishing.

Wilson, Maureen, Calhoun, Avery, & Whitmore, Elizabeth. (2011). Contesting the neoliberal agenda: Lessons from Canadian activists. *Canadian Social Work Review, 28*(1), 25-48.

Wilson, Maureen, & Whitmore, Elizabeth. (2000). *Seeds of fire: Social development in an era of globalism*. Halifax: Fernwood.

Wise, Timothy, Salazar, Hilda, & Carlsen, Laura. (2003). *Confronting globalization: Economic integration and popular resistance in Mexico*. Bloomfield, CT: Kumarian Press.

World Bank. (2011a). *Migration and remittances factbook 2011*. Retrieved from http://site-resources.worldbank.org/INTPROSPECTS/Resources/334934-1199807908806/Mexico.pdf

World Bank. (2013a). *Mexico: Country at a glance*. Retrieved from http://www.worldbank.org/en/country/mexico

World Bank. (2013b). *Income share held by the highest 20%*. Retrieved from http://data.worldbank
.org/indicator/SI.DST.05TH.20/countries

World Bank. (2013c). *Income share held by the lowest 20%*. Retrieved from http://data.worldbank
.org/indicator/SI.DST.FRST.20

World Commission on Environment and Development. (1987). *Our common future, Ch. 2:
Towards sustainable development*. Oxford: Oxford University Press. Retrieved from http://
www.un-documents.net/ocf-02.htm

World Council of Churches. (2012, February 17). *Statement of the doctrine of discovery and its
enduring impact on Indigenous peoples*. Bossey, Switzerland: WCC Executive Committee.
Retrieved from http://www.oikoumene.org/en/resources/documents/executive-committee/
2012-02/statement-on-the-doctrine-of-discovery-and-its-enduring-impact-on
-indigenous-peoples

World Trade Organization. (2013). *Understanding the WTO: Settling disputes*. Retrieved from
https://www.wto.org/english/thewto_e/whatis_e/tif_e/disp1_e.htm

Wright, Ronald. (2005). *Stolen continents: 500 years of conquest and resistance in the Americas*.
Boston: Houghton Mifflin.

Xeni Gwet'in. (1989). Declaration of the Nemaiah Aboriginal Wilderness Preserve. Retrieved
from http://www.fonv.ca/nemaiahvalley/nenduwhjidguzitindeclaration/

Yalnizyan, Armine. (2013). *Study of income inequality in Canada—what can be done*. Retrieved from
http://www.policyalternatives.ca/sites/default/files/uploads/publications/National%
20Office/2013/05/Armine_Inequality_Presentation_HOC_Finance_Committee.pdf

Zapatista National Liberation Army [Ejercito Zapatista de Liberación Nacional] (EZLN).
(1994/2002). First declaration from the Lacandon jungle. In Tom Hayden (Ed.), *The
Zapatista reader* (pp. 217–220). New York: Thunder's Mouth Press.

Zoraida Vázquez, Josefina. (2004). De la independencia a la consolidación republicana. In
Pablo Escalante, Bernardo García, Luis Jáuregui, Josefina Zoraida, Elisa Speckman,
Javier Garciadiego, & Luis Aboites (Eds.), *Nueva historia mínima de México* (pp. 137–191).
Mexico City: El Colegio de México.

Zúñiga Zárate, Jose Guillermo, & Garza Treviño, Guillermina. (2007). Mexico. In Idit Weiss &
Penelope Welborne (Eds.), *Social work as a profession: A comparative cross-national perspective*
(pp. 105–118). Birmingham, UK: Venture Press.

Index

social development, 1, 138, 150, 180, 210, 232, 237

social justice work conceptualized by Finn & Jacobson, 183-84, 197, 238

social mobilization theory, 2-5, 137, 143, 175, 201, 227, 229-30, 231-46

social movement communities, 3, 17, 137, 148-49, 155, 160-62, 175, 178, 189, 194, 198, 209, 212-13, 218, 224, 230, 232-46; objectives of, 69, 155-56, 167, 173-74, 209-10, 227, 228-30, 234-36 (*see also* objectives, clarifying); principles of, 72, 97, 120, 148-53, 155-57, 167, 185, 188, 194, 201, 209-11, 218, 222, 228-30, 233, 238, 241

social movement theory. *See* political process approaches; resource mobilization theory; social constructionism; social mobilization theory; social movements: new; synthesis of social movement theory

social movements: building of, 2-5, 15-17, 28-30, 57-61, 157, 191, 198-99, 208-14, 219, 232; criminalization of (*see* social struggles: criminalization and repression of); definition of, 2-3; new, 5, 57, 232

social planning and social policy approach, 2, 235-36. *See also* strategies for change, campaign

social psychology, 1, 5, 232; Pinard's contribution to, 5, 145, 148, 153

social struggles: concerns of the, 150; criminalization and repression of, 67, 133, 148, 208, 216, 242, 245

social work, community organizing in. *See* community organizing

sociology. *See* social mobilization theory; social movement theory

solidarity, tradition of, 124, 144-45, 149-50

state-led developmentalism, 43-44, 52, 139. *See also* import substitution industrialization

strategies for change, 4, 8, 139, 145, 185, 188, 201-8; campaign, 201, 204-6; collaborative, 201-4; contest/protest, 201, 206-8 (*see also* blockades, demonstrations, vigils). *See also* community organizing methodology

strengthening the organization, 121, 165, 170, 185, 198, 208-14, 238, 240-41, 244-45

strengths-based practice, Dennis Saleebey's contribution on, 200, 237, 240

structural adjustment programs (SAPs), 12, 44, 52, 135

structural social work: dual focus of, 5, 233; Mullaly's perspective on, 5, 7, 233; root causes addressed in, 5. *See also* alternative development

structures of the organizations. *See* organizational functioning; organizational operations

support. *See* resources

synthesis of social movement theory, 4, 137, 232

TADECO (Taller de Desarrollo Comunitario) (Community Development Workshop) (Guerrero), 131-33, 143, 146, 148, 163, 168, 173, 174, 180, 181, 182, 188, 192, 194, 208, 214, 216, 220, 237, 240, 242, 244, 245

Taseko Mines Ltd., 105-10, 140, 144, 158, 170, 178, 221

taxation, decreased, 9, 12, 14, 24, 26, 28, 43, 52, 55, 56, 122

Tejalpa health and environmental well-being project (Morelos), 96-97, 146, 164, 166, 174, 196, 203, 226, 243

theology of liberation, 1, 5, 6, 46, 57, 82, 92, 97, 120-22, 125, 132, 146, 148-50, 153, 155, 157, 169-70, 174, 187-88, 210, 218, 225, 232, 233, 238, 242. *See also* Boff, Leonardo and Boff, Clodovis; Méndez Arceo, Sergio; Ruiz García, Samuel

theology of social ministry, 92, 120, 138

theories: summary of those at grand theory level (ideals), 232, 233-34; summary of those at objectives level (models, approaches), 234-36; summary of those at practice level (methods), 236-41. *See also* mobilization strategies, aspects of; organizers/leaders' roles

theory from movement actors' views of the problem and means of redress, 226-27, 233-34. *See also* community organizing; social mobilization; social movements

time: commitment required, 93-94, 97, 100-101, 109, 115, 118, 143, 146, 156, 158, 167, 168, 177, 187, 196, 207, 209, 210, 224, 226, 237; constraints, 92, 195, 220, 238, 245; flexibility, 168, 245

tortilla-making collective, 82-83, 155, 174, 202-3, 209

traditional values, 11, 121, 142, 218. *See also* patriarchy

training for managing the collective, 66, 77, 88, 121, 147, 169, 191, 192, 197, 209-12, 241

train-the-trainer approach, 74, 92, 191, 238

Tsilhqot'in Nation. *See* Chilcotin (Tsilhqot'in) Nation

Unión de Ejidos de la Selva (Federation of Land Collectives of the Jungle), Chiapas, 71-72, 74-76, 77, 159, 163, 165, 167, 169, 170, 222, 237

Unión Estatal de Artesanos de Michoacán (State Federation of Michoacán Artisans) (UNEAMICH), 85-88, 163, 165, 167, 172, 174, 182, 209

United Nations, Covenant on Economic, Social and Cultural Rights, 214

United Nations, decisions of: Beijing Platform for Action, 18, 33; Convention on the Elimination of all forms of Discrimination against Women (CEDAW), 18, 37; Declaration on the Rights of Indigenous Peoples (DRIP), 19, 37, 66; Kyoto Protocol, 13, 24; Millennium Development Goals (MDGs), 17-18. *See also* International Labour Organization (ILO)

United Nations, Office of the High Commissioner for Human Rights (UN OHCHR), Universal Periodic Review: of Canada, 36-37; of Mexico, 66-67

United Nations, World Commission on Environment and Development (1987), 13, 141

United Nations, world conference(s) on women, 18, 33, 63, 113, 147